The Proven Man

Clarity, Standards, and the Life You Intend to Live

Matthew Koeppen

The Proven Man Publishing

Published by The Proven Man Publishing
Clover, South Carolina 29710

First Edition
ISBN: 979-8-9958667-0-1
Library of Congress Control Number: 2026912585

Cover design and artwork by the author.

Disclaimer
The material presented in this book is intended for educational and informational purposes only. The concepts, frameworks, and perspectives discussed are based on observation, interpretation, and principles of personal development.

Nothing in this book should be interpreted as medical, psychological, or therapeutic advice. The relationship dynamics and behavioral patterns described are not clinical diagnoses and are not intended to diagnose or evaluate any individual.

If you have concerns regarding your mental health, emotional well-being, or relationships, seek guidance from a qualified mental health professional, licensed therapist, or medical provider.

The author makes no guarantees regarding individual outcomes and assumes no responsibility for decisions made based on the information presented. Readers are responsible for their own interpretation, judgment, and application.

For my sons—

and for those who choose clarity over confusion,

discipline over impulse,

and direction over drift.

CONTENTS

The Proven Man Awaits

A Framework for Clarity, Standards, and Intentional Living

The world demands something of you. It calls for action, decisions, and consistency. Yet many men move through life in reaction—driven by impulse, emotion, or the expectations of others. They hope for clarity. They wish for direction. But too often they find themselves lost in the noise of life, uncertain which path to take or what truly matters.

What if there were another way?

What if you could stop living in response to external forces and begin living with clarity and purpose? What if you could become the kind of man who stands firm in his values, makes decisions with confidence, and moves forward with integrity—no matter what the world places in front of him?

This book is your guide to becoming that man; the Proven Man.

The Proven Man is not a fantasy or a distant ideal.

A man is not proven by what he says, intends, or hopes will happen.

He is proven by how he decides, how he behaves under pressure, and what he consistently allows or rejects in his life.

Proof is not outcome-based. Outcomes can be influenced by timing, circumstance, and variables outside of your control.

Proof is decision-based.

Proof reveals itself in patterns:

-The standards you hold when it would be easier to lower them
-The restraint you show when emotion pushes for reaction
-The clarity you maintain when situations become uncertain
-The actions you take that align with your long-term direction

A man becomes proven when his decisions are no longer driven by impulse, insecurity, or external pressure—but by clarity and internal standard.

This is not a single moment. It is a pattern. And over time, that pattern becomes undeniable.

The Proven Man is the man who lives that pattern.

He is grounded in the real world and navigates it with clarity, discipline, and unshakable standards. He does not rely on luck, chance, or emotional momentum. Instead, he operates from awareness. His decisions are not dictated by fleeting feelings or outside pressure, but by a clear understanding of who he is, what he values, and where he is going.

Throughout this journey, you will learn the principles, mindsets, and practices that allow a man to build a life of strength, stability, and purpose. You will begin to recognize the patterns that shape your experiences and understand how to align your decisions with the life you want to create.

This is not a quick fix. It is not about surface-level change or temporary motivation. It is about lasting transformation, the kind that reshapes how you think, how you act, and how you move through the world.

Becoming the Proven Man does not happen overnight. It is a continuous process—a commitment to showing up with awareness, discipline, and intention each day. It requires the ability to see situations clearly, the strength to maintain your standards, and the patience to allow time to reveal the truth.

This book will help you build that foundation.

Strength is not the absence of warmth, joy, love, or connection—it is the stability that allows those things to deepen without chaos. A Proven Man does not detach from life; he learns to engage it with clarity, purpose, and grounded presence.

You will learn to recognize patterns in people, situations, and the environments you move within; detach from distractions that cloud your judgment; and evaluate connections and opportunities with clarity rather than emotion. Most importantly, you will learn how to make decisions that align with your values and your long-term direction.

The Proven Man is not defined by status or achievement alone.

He is defined by ownership of his life.

He understands that every decision matters. Every relationship influences direction. Every environment reinforces patterns. Every pattern either strengthens or weakens the life he is building.

He no longer drifts through life hoping things will work out. He shapes his path through awareness, discipline, and deliberate choice.

This journey is both empowering and demanding. It requires honesty, responsibility, and the willingness to examine your own patterns and take ownership of your decisions.

Everything in this book ultimately returns to three disciplines.

But it also brings something many men spend their lives searching for:

Clarity.

When you understand how to observe patterns, enforce standards, detach from what does not serve you, and allow time to reveal truth, life becomes simpler. Decisions become clearer. Direction becomes steady.

You stop reacting to life.

You begin shaping it.

The Proven Man is not someone separate from you. He is the man you become through the choices you make, the standards you uphold, and the clarity you develop along the way.

This book is the beginning of that transformation. Let's begin.

The Proven Man Framework

The Proven Man framework is built on three disciplines that shape how a man lives, sees, and chooses.

Identity: Become the man who leads his life with clarity and purpose.
Perception: Learn to recognize patterns and see reality without distortion.
Decision: Choose relationships and dynamics that align with the life you are building.

Every chapter that follows strengthens one of these abilities.

Becoming the Proven Man is not about reacting to life—it is about seeing clearly and choosing deliberately.

Together, these disciplines form the foundation of what will later become The Proven Man System: a structured way of practicing these principles in everyday life. The chapters ahead follow a deliberate progression.

First, you will learn to stabilize yourself.
Then you will learn to observe clearly.
Then you will learn to evaluate alignment.
Finally, you will learn how to enforce decisions that shape your direction.

The framework that follows reveals how these principles work together.

The Proven Man does not move in a straight line—he operates in a loop.

Who he is shapes how he sees.
How he sees determines what he chooses.
What he chooses creates the results he experiences.
And those results reinforce who he becomes.

Identity shapes perception.
Perception informs decision.
Decision creates alignment.
Alignment strengthens identity.

This cycle repeats—refining clarity, strengthening standards, and compounding direction over time. You are not completing a system; you are learning to operate within it.

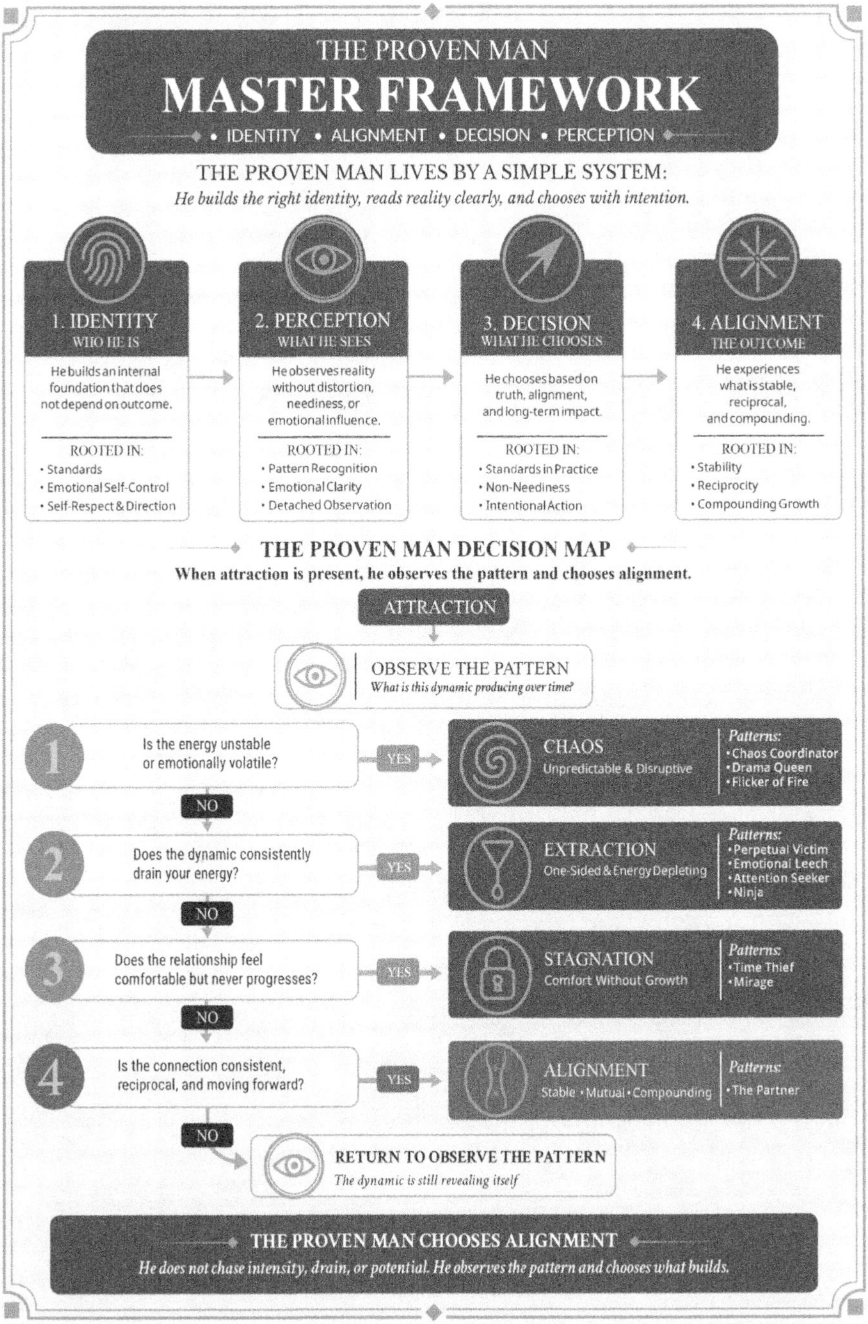
THE PROVEN MAN
MASTER FRAMEWORK
• IDENTITY • ALIGNMENT • DECISION • PERCEPTION
THE PROVEN MAN LIVES BY A SIMPLE SYSTEM:
He builds the right identity, reads reality clearly, and chooses with intention.
1. IDENTITY
WHO HE IS
He builds an internal foundation that does not depend on outcome.
ROOTED IN:
• Standards
• Emotional Self-Control
• Self-Respect & Direction
2. PERCEPTION
WHAT HE SEES
He observes reality without distortion, neediness, or emotional influence.
ROOTED IN:
• Pattern Recognition
• Emotional Clarity
• Detached Observation
3. DECISION
WHAT HE CHOOSES
He chooses based on truth, alignment, and long-term impact.
ROOTED IN:
• Standards in Practice
• Non-Neediness
• Intentional Action
4. ALIGNMENT
THE OUTCOME
He experiences what is stable, reciprocal, and compounding.
ROOTED IN:
• Stability
• Reciprocity
• Compounding Growth
THE PROVEN MAN DECISION MAP
When attraction is present, he observes the pattern and chooses alignment.
ATTRACTION
OBSERVE THE PATTERN
What is this dynamic producing over time?
1
Is the energy unstable or emotionally volatile?
YES
CHAOS
Unpredictable & Disruptive
Patterns:
•Chaos Coordinator
•Drama Queen
•Flicker of Fire
NO
2
Does the dynamic consistently drain your energy?
YES
EXTRACTION
One-Sided & Energy Depleting
Patterns:
•Perpetual Victim
•Emotional Leech
•Attention Seeker
•Ninja
NO
3
Does the relationship feel comfortable but never progresses?
YES
STAGNATION
Comfort Without Growth
Patterns:
•Time Thief
•Mirage
NO
4
Is the connection consistent, reciprocal, and moving forward?
YES
ALIGNMENT
Stable • Mutual • Compounding
Patterns:
• The Partner
NO
RETURN TO OBSERVE THE PATTERN
The dynamic is still revealing itself
THE PROVEN MAN CHOOSES ALIGNMENT
He does not chase intensity, drain, or potential. He observes the pattern and chooses what builds.

Chapter One

Emotional Self-Control

Staying Grounded Under Pressure

Emotional stability is tested in moments most men overlook. They believe control is lost during dramatic events—heated arguments, career crises, or obvious conflict.

But the reality is far more subtle.

Emotional self-control is tested quietly in the small fissures of everyday life: a delayed reply, a change in tone, a subtle pullback from someone you care about, or an unexpected shift in a professional or social interaction. Nothing overt. Nothing dramatic. Yet enough to trigger a reaction.

This is where the Proven Man is formed, not in chaos, but in the quiet pressure of real moments.

They are easy to overlook, yet they determine the direction of a man's character.

He does not drift through them.
He is revealed by his response.

Emotional self-control anchors him amid uncertainty. It allows him to act with clarity rather than compulsion, even when circumstances attempt to pull him off center. It is the discipline of navigating his internal world with awareness and intention.

For the Proven Man, emotional self-control becomes the foundation of everything that follows. It allows him to build intentional relationships, make decisions aligned with long-term goals, and move through life with a presence that is grounded, steady, and deliberate.

It is the difference between reacting to life and directing it.

Why emotional control matters

Emotional self-control is not simply "staying calm." It is mastery over the relationship between your mind, your body, and the energy you carry into the world.

Psychologically, human beings are wired to react first and analyze second. The amygdala, the brain's internal alarm system, fires when it perceives a threat, triggering the fight, flight, or freeze response. In relationships, these threats are rarely physical. Instead, they appear in subtle forms: a change in tone, a pause in communication, or a hint of disinterest.

Left unchecked, these signals trigger anxiety, insecurity, and impulsive behavior.

Physiologically, the body mirrors these reactions. The chest tightens, heart rate increases, and breathing becomes shallow. Energy surges through the body, preparing you to act—even when no real danger exists.

This tension feels like an internal storm, pushing you toward impulsive behavior that compromises clarity and integrity.

Every interaction carries a subtle exchange of emotional signals. You transmit and receive cues through tone, posture, attention, and presence.

A man who remains calm, centered, and stable communicates an energy others instinctively trust.

Emotional self-control is the mechanism through which the Proven Man stabilizes and directs this energy under pressure. Instead of allowing physiological impulses or emotional reactions to dictate his behavior, he converts those impulses into grounded presence.

Without emotional self-control, men drift. They react to subtle shifts, chase validation, and allow their internal state to dictate behavior. Decisions are made in turbulence, and perception becomes distorted by hope, fear, or projection.

With emotional self-control, those pressures no longer dictate his state.

The Proven Man remains anchored. His energy guides his decisions. His presence remains steady. And from that stability, clarity, alignment, and lasting influence begin to emerge.

I. Pressure Reveals Inner Stability

Life reveals your internal stability through moments of subtle pressure. Smooth interactions are easy, but stability is not proven in comfort; it is revealed when uncertainty enters the picture. Silence, minor shifts, and emotional distance act as mirrors, reflecting what truly exists inside you.

Psychologically, these disruptions activate latent insecurities, past patterns, and automatic responses.

Physiologically, the body reacts before you consciously recognize it. Heart rate quickens, cortisol rises, and attention narrows toward perceived threats. Your internal state is signaled before a word is spoken.

The Proven Man understands something critical:

Pressure does not create instability; it reveals what was already there.

Instead of reacting blindly, he observes these moments. He studies his internal responses and learns where he remains grounded and where old patterns attempt to take control. Each moment of pressure becomes information, revealing the difference between emotional habit and intentional discipline.

Real-life example
She makes an offhand comment that challenges your confidence. The reactive impulse is to defend yourself immediately rather than remain grounded.

The Proven Man does something different.

He pauses. He absorbs the moment without reacting. He allows the situation to reveal its meaning before he responds.

His response is deliberate, not reactive.

Energy cue
Reactivity appears as chest tension, racing thoughts, and restless energy.

Stability feels different: steady breathing, focused attention, and calm presence even when uncertainty is present.

II. Emotional Reactivity vs. Emotional Control

Feelings are automatic.
Responses are intentional.

In every moment of emotional intensity, the Proven Man faces a choice: react or respond.

Emotional reactivity is unconscious. It is the impulse to act without reflection, driven by emotion rather than intention. It happens quickly, in the blink of an eye.

Emotional control is deliberate. It exists in the space between stimulus and response, where you decide how to engage with what you feel instead of allowing it to dictate your behavior. Left unchecked, it leads to decisions that compromise clarity and control.

When something triggers you, the brain activates rapidly, pushing you toward immediate action. The urge to fix the situation or chase a desired outcome can become overwhelming. You may feel compelled to send an impulsive message, double-text, over-explain, or seek reassurance to quiet the discomfort.

Emotional control interrupts this chain reaction.

It creates space.

That space is where mastery lives.

Instead of reacting immediately, you observe the moment and decide whether action is necessary at all.

Reactivity shows up in behavior. You rush to act, over-correct, or seek reassurance to relieve the tension. Left unchecked, it leads to decisions that create regret.

Emotional control produces a different pattern.

Breathing steadies.
The body settles.
Clarity returns.

From that state, action becomes deliberate rather than urgent.

Energetically, reactivity carries turbulence. It radiates urgency and agitation into your interactions, disrupting the natural flow of connection.

Emotional control creates the opposite effect.

When you remain calm under pressure, your energy stabilizes. That stability becomes magnetic. Others instinctively trust the man who remains composed when situations become uncertain.

The key to emotional control is awareness—the ability to recognize the signals your body, mind, and energy send before they dictate your behavior.

With awareness comes choice.

The Proven Man does not suppress emotion, nor does he allow it to control him. He observes it, understands it, and chooses his response deliberately.

Emotional control is not avoidance.

It is readiness—the ability to engage with life fully while remaining grounded in clarity and intention.

That awareness becomes the foundation of every disciplined decision he makes.

III. Maintaining Stability Under Pressure

Stability is not something external. It does not come from the people around you, the circumstances you face, or the situations you encounter. The Proven Man operates from an internal anchor, a state of being that remains steady regardless of what unfolds around him.

The challenge is remaining grounded when pressure or emotional turbulence arise, whether from external events or internal insecurities. This is not about becoming unaffected by life. It is about choosing how to respond to life's natural ebbs and flows.

Maintaining stability requires awareness—the ability to observe your thoughts as they occur. Most men react impulsively because they never pause long enough to examine what they are thinking or feeling. They become swept up in the moment.

The Proven Man takes a different approach.

He steps back internally. He notices when his mind begins to race or when emotions start to intensify. Instead of attaching to those thoughts or feelings, he observes them, like clouds passing across the sky.

That moment of observation creates choice.
He responds intentionally rather than impulsively.
His actions align with his values instead of being driven by momentary emotion.

Physiologically, pressure activates the body's stress response. Adrenaline rises. Heart rate increases. Breathing becomes shallow. The body prepares for action.

Left unchecked, this cascade fuels impatience, anxiety, and reactive behavior.

The Proven Man resets himself.
The body settles.

Where there was urgency, there is now space for deliberate action.

Stability communicates trust. People instinctively recognize when someone is grounded, and they gravitate toward that steadiness.

When a man becomes rattled, his energy becomes erratic, creating an atmosphere of unpredictability. When he remains composed under pressure, the opposite occurs. Others relax. Conversations soften. Trust grows.

The Proven Man understands that emotional stability does more than serve him. It shapes the environment around him. His presence creates a ripple effect in the relationships and situations he enters.

True stability is not determined by circumstance.

The Proven Man does not allow external conditions to dictate his inner state. His stability comes from how he chooses to respond—not from how the world behaves.

By cultivating emotional stability, he becomes a quiet source of strength and presence. His ability to remain grounded under pressure allows him to navigate uncertainty with clarity, confidence, and composure.

In doing so, he creates an environment where others feel safe, respected, heard, and valued.

IV. Detachment From Outcome

One of the most profound practices the Proven Man develops is the art of detachment, not from people or experiences, but from the need for specific outcomes.

In a world that constantly pushes for immediate results, this idea can feel counterintuitive. We are taught to chase success, measure our worth by outcomes, and pursue visible results. Detachment operates at a deeper level. It is the ability to engage fully with life—to desire, to enjoy, and to connect—without allowing the outcome to determine your inner state.

Psychologically, attachment to outcomes often grows from fear: fear of rejection, fear of failure, or fear of losing control. When your emotional stability becomes dependent on a particular result, tension naturally follows. Urgency appears. Anxiety builds. Decisions begin to revolve around controlling the outcome rather than engaging with the moment itself.

The Proven Man understands that his worth is not tied to any single outcome. He participates fully in life, but he does so from a place of internal security and trust in the process.

Attachment to outcomes narrows your focus. The mind fixates on a single result, and everything else fades from view. Decisions become forced rather than natural.

When the mind becomes attached to a specific outcome, the body mirrors that internal pressure.

Detachment produces the opposite effect.

It is not indifference; it is freedom.

When you release the need for a particular result, the nervous system begins to settle. Breathing deepens, heart rate stabilizes, and physical tension eases. The mind regains its ability to observe rather than react.

Energetically, detachment creates a grounded presence. Instead of projecting need, urgency, or pressure, you communicate calm engagement. Your energy remains steady because it is no longer dependent on how a moment resolves.

When detachment is present, your actions begin to align with your true intentions rather than a need to manipulate the outcome.

The Proven Man moves through life with this clarity. Whether in relationships, career decisions, or personal growth, his focus is not on forcing events to unfold in a particular way. Instead, he remains rooted in his purpose and acts from inner stability.

These principles become clearer when observed in real situations.

Real-life examples

You invite someone to spend time together, and she says she will let you know. Hours pass. Many men begin to replay the interaction, wondering what they said wrong or whether they should reach out again.

The Proven Man does something different.

He continues with his day.

His sense of value does not depend on her response. Instead of reacting to a single moment, he observes patterns over time. By remaining calm and patient, he demonstrates emotional maturity and self-respect.

A similar dynamic appears in professional environments and long-term reputation building. You complete an important project and await feedback or approval. Many people become anxious during this waiting period, constantly checking their email or worrying about how their work will be judged.

The Proven Man remains steady.

He stays open to feedback, but he does not allow the outcome to determine his emotional state. His effort, discipline, and sense of worth exist independently of external validation.

Detachment also requires understanding that life rarely unfolds in a perfectly linear path. Effort does not always produce immediate results. There are seasons of waiting, periods of silence, and moments of uncertainty.

This is where true mastery appears.

The ability to move through uncertainty with patience, composure, and inner freedom separates the reactive man from the Proven Man.

The Proven Man understands that external circumstances do not govern his inner state. He is the steward of his internal world.

By releasing attachment to outcomes, he opens himself fully to the present moment. He engages in relationships, work, and personal growth not to force results, but to live with clarity and integrity.

From that alignment emerges something powerful.

Peace.

And from that peace, opportunities, connections, and meaningful outcomes begin to form naturally.

V. Real-Time Scenarios

Real-time scenarios bring emotional discipline into practice. They reveal how subtle pressures appear in everyday situations and where awareness is tested.

This is how emotional discipline appears in daily life.

In these moments, the situation is rarely dramatic. Pressure emerges from interpretation—the meaning assigned to a small event. By observing the moment rather than reacting to it, the Proven Man sees how emotional discipline operates in real time.

Scenario 1: No Reply

Reactivity: Anxiety-driven follow-up messages or attempts to force clarity.
Control: Continued presence and observation.

The emotional trigger is the feeling of being ignored or rejected. The impulse is to send multiple messages or seek reassurance.

The Proven Man does something different.

He pauses. He observes his internal response. He recognizes that the absence of a reply does not define his worth. He gives the moment space.

Clarity returns.

Patience and detachment guide his behavior.

Scenario 2: Cancelled Plans

Reactivity: Immediate rescheduling or frustration.
Control: Calm, intentional response.

Frustration or disappointment arises quickly. The impulse is to fill the gap or push for a new arrangement.

The Proven Man remains composed.

He acknowledges the shift without allowing it to disrupt his state. He maintains focus on his priorities.

Scenario 3: Energy Shifts

Reactivity: Adjusting your emotional state to match someone else's mood.
Control: Presence without compromise.

People shift emotionally, whether in conversation, collaboration, or social interaction. The impulse is to mirror that change.

The Proven Man maintains his internal stability.

He remains present without allowing another person's state to dictate his own. His steadiness creates space for expression without destabilizing his center.

Scenario 4: Tension Arises

Reactivity: Defensiveness, escalation, or withdrawal.
Control: Measured, deliberate response.

When tension appears, the impulse is to defend, attack, or retreat.

The Proven Man pauses.

He assesses the moment. He responds deliberately.

He does not escalate. He creates space for resolution.

These scenarios reveal a simple truth—emotional discipline, not intellect, determines influence and presence.

The Proven Man does not prove his strength through explanation or force.

He demonstrates it through composure, awareness, and consistency in the moments where most men react.

VI. Internal Anchors

Internal anchors allow the Proven Man to remain grounded when emotional turbulence arises.

They guide him through pressure without losing his center.

Whether mental, emotional, or physical, these anchors reset his internal state and create space for intentional response rather than impulsive reaction.

An anchor begins with awareness in action.
He recognizes what is happening internally in real time.

What am I feeling?
Why is it present?
Am I reacting or responding?

These questions create a pause where he chooses how to engage.

Anchors interrupt the stress response.

Breathing slows.
Tension releases.
The body settles.

Clarity returns.

The Proven Man does not rely on the moment to calm him.

He stabilizes himself.

That stability carries outward.

Presence becomes steady.
Reactivity fades.
Others feel it.

Even under pressure, he returns to center.

Emotional turbulence no longer dictates his behavior.

He observes it.
He stabilizes it.
He moves forward with intention.

And in doing so, he remains aligned with his values and direction.

VII. Emotional Strength as Attraction

True attraction is quieter than most men realize. In a world obsessed with instant gratification and dramatic gestures, real power lies in emotional self-control—the ability to remain grounded, centered, and present.

When the Proven Man maintains emotional composure, it becomes the foundation of a magnetic presence. He is not chasing attention; his energy draws others because it communicates stability, trust, and inner strength. His influence emerges not through force, but through the quiet authority of emotional discipline.

Emotional strength is mastery of one's internal state. It is rooted in self-worth that does not fluctuate with external circumstances. This stability becomes magnetic because it signals independence from validation.

When the Proven Man remains steady despite external turbulence, others are drawn to the reliability of his presence.

This confidence does not demand attention.

It is felt before it is seen.

Emotional strength appears in how he carries himself. Under pressure, his posture remains upright, his breathing slows, and his body stays relaxed. These signals communicate calm authority without a word spoken.

A grounded presence attracts the right people and experiences without the need to pursue approval or recognition.

Emotional strength resonates outward. The Proven Man carries a steady, composed presence that draws people in, not because he seeks attention, but because his stability creates a sense of safety and trust.

The storm may surround him.
He remains unshaken.

These anchors do not remove the storm.
They steady the man within it.

Others gravitate toward this steadiness because it communicates reliability, confidence, and emotional maturity.

In relationships, emotional strength cultivates trust and connection. By remaining grounded, the Proven Man creates an environment where others can express themselves without fear of judgment or manipulation.

He does not attempt to control others.

He maintains the stability that allows authentic connection to emerge.

When a man masters his own emotions, he no longer needs to manage the emotions of others. Instead, he creates the foundation from which meaningful relationships develop.

VIII. Discipline Within Emotional Self-Control

Emotional self-control is practical mastery, not suppression.

Many men confuse emotional control with becoming unemotional—as if feelings themselves are weakness. Emotional self-control is not about denying emotion. It is about responding with clarity, even when emotions run high.

It is not about detaching from your feelings. It is about choosing how to engage with them, knowing that your responses either strengthen or weaken your presence in any moment.

Emotional self-control develops through awareness—the ability to observe thoughts and emotions without becoming consumed by them. When anger or frustration arises, the Proven Man does not react immediately.

He notices the emotion.
He steps back.
He chooses his response.

That space changes everything. Intentional choice replaces impulsive reaction.

He does not ignore his feelings.
He refuses to be ruled by them.

As pressure builds, the body prepares for action. Emotional discipline interrupts the automatic response.

A pause. A breath.

The body settles.
Clarity returns.

Discipline is the ability to maintain your center regardless of external forces. The Proven Man does not absorb the chaos around him. He remains anchored in his internal state.

That stability communicates calm authority and shapes the environment around him. Others feel it.

The Proven Man understands that his emotional state is his responsibility. Stability does not come from controlling the world around him. It comes from mastering how he responds to it.

Through emotional self-control, he leads with clarity and integrity. He becomes an anchor for others—responding with composure and aligning his actions with long-term direction over short-term impulse.

Chapter Distillation

Emotional control is not about being unaffected.

It is about mastering how you respond to uncertainty, desire, and emotional shifts.

It lives in the pause before reaction—the space between stimulus and response, where awareness creates choice.

The Proven Man understands that he is not his emotions.

He is the one who chooses how to engage with them.

Like the stillness of a deep lake, storms may disturb the surface, but the depths remain clear and undisturbed. That depth is the foundation of the Proven Man: a calm that remains steady regardless of circumstance.

From that stability, perception sharpens. Emotional turbulence no longer clouds judgment. Patterns, behavior, and subtle shifts become visible. He responds with intention, not impulse.

Clarity replaces reaction.

From that clarity, disciplined decisions follow.

With emotional self-control as his anchor, the Proven Man becomes the steady presence within his own life and within the lives of others.

This influence does not come from force or control.

It comes from grounded stability.

Emotional self-control is where the Proven Man begins.

This is where proof begins.

Not in what a man claims—but in how he responds when emotion demands action.

When he holds his center under pressure, that is proof.
When he pauses instead of reacting, that is proof.
When he chooses clarity over impulse, that is proof.

Emotional self-control is the first visible shift.

It is where a man stops being driven—and begins directing.

From that point forward, every decision either strengthens or weakens that proof.

Before he can read reality clearly, before he can choose alignment, before he can shape the direction of his life, he must first stabilize himself.

Because when a man stabilizes his emotional state, he gains something far more powerful than control over a moment:

He gains command over the direction of his life.

The Proven Man Principle

Emotions inform.

Awareness pauses.

Discipline chooses.

Chapter Two

Reading Reality

Seeing Behavior Without Distortion

The first step in becoming the Proven Man is mastering emotional discipline. This foundation allows you to move through life with a steady presence rather than being controlled by impulsive reactions. But emotional discipline, while essential, is only the beginning. The next vital skill to develop is the ability to observe reality as it truly is, free from distortion.

Now that you have gained control over your impulses, you have created the space to see clearly. As emotional reactivity fades, perception sharpens. You no longer view reality through the lens of desire, hope, or assumption.

The Proven Man does not simply observe the world; he sees it with precision and awareness.

This is a subtle yet critical shift.

The problem is not lack of information. It is distorted perception. Instead of seeing things as they truly are, most men interpret reality through emotional filters that reshape their view. They do not respond to what is happening; they respond to their interpretation of it.

There are three primary emotional filters that distort perception: hope, projection, and ego. These filters are often subtle, but their effect is profound. They blur patterns, weaken judgment, and distort behavior. The truth of a situation is usually straightforward, but the lens through which it is viewed is not always clear.

When hope, projection, or ego take over, clarity disappears.

The Proven Man understands that clarity is not optional; it is foundational. The more grounded he becomes in emotional discipline, the more precise his perception becomes. He does not rush to interpret. He does not bend reality to match his preferences. He observes patiently and without distortion.

Removing those filters requires learning to see behavior as it truly is, not how you wish it to be, fear it might be, or hope it will become.

When you develop this ability, your decision-making sharpens. Your standards strengthen. Your alignment becomes undeniable. You stop reacting to isolated moments and begin recognizing patterns.

And from that place, you operate with certainty.

I. Why Clarity Breaks Down

When emotions are involved, perception begins to shift. Observing becomes more than simply taking in facts; it becomes interpretation. Interpretation is rarely neutral.

It is shaped by desires, fears, insecurities, and hopes. Your mind does not simply see the world; it reacts to it. And that reaction becomes the lens through which you view everything, whether it is a passing remark, a casual conversation, a moment of silence, or a subtle shift in a professional or social interaction.

The problem is not what happens. Life unfolds as it does, with no inherent judgment. But how it is interpreted is where clarity begins to break down. The Proven Man understands that truth, in its purest form, is often simple. It is the stories we tell ourselves, the interpretations we construct, that complicate it.

The mind skews reality in predictable ways.

You minimize what feels uncomfortable. When something does not align with your desires or expectations, you downplay that. "It's nothing," you tell yourself, even when something deeper suggests otherwise.

You amplify what feels promising. When something feels good, you make it bigger than it is, inflating potential and possibility to match your hopes.

You fill in the gaps with assumptions rather than waiting for the truth to unfold. The space between what is said or done and what remains unsaid creates room for interpretation. Emotional drive pushes you to fill that space, even when those conclusions are not rooted in reality.

This is where most men falter, not in the events themselves, but in their interpretations.

When you react impulsively to what is happening, you create a story that feels real, but it may not be true. The narratives you build about a person or situation may feel like clarity, but they are often projections of your own emotional state.

Real-life example

You notice that she occasionally initiates contact, but at other times becomes distant without explanation. Immediately your mind begins to race: "There must be a reason for this." "Maybe I'm reading it wrong." "I probably need to give it time." You convince yourself there must be an explanation for the inconsistency, and you begin filling in the gaps.

You tell yourself, "It will make sense soon," or "I just don't have the full picture yet."

But the truth may be simpler. Her behavior may reflect her own priorities or emotional state, not your worth and not an intentional game she is playing.

The stories you create are not her reality.
They are your reaction to uncertainty.

And once you begin to see this clearly, the signals become easier to recognize.

Energy cue

When perception is distorted, it often appears physically. The chest tightens. The mind races. Restlessness begins to build. Your energy becomes externally tethered to the situation as you wait for reassurance, validation, or confirmation.

When clarity appears, the experience shifts. Breathing slows. The body relaxes. The mind becomes open and receptive rather than reactive. The difference between distortion and clarity can be felt in posture, breath, and emotional state.

When clarity settles in, you are no longer hooked by external signals or fleeting emotional reactions.

You simply observe.

The Proven Man does not chase clarity. He does not fill in gaps or justify behavior that does not align. He observes patiently and allows truth to reveal itself over time.

The path to understanding is built on observation, not interpretation.

And as this discipline develops, you begin to see that clarity is not something you force.

It is something you allow to appear.

II. The Three Filters That Distort Perception

The truth, in its purest form, is often simple.

It does not hide.
It is often seen, then softened.

Yet emotions, desires, and unconscious biases can distort that simplicity. The Proven Man understands that to see reality clearly, he must first recognize the filters shaping his perception.

There are three primary filters that distort perception: hope, projection, and ego.

Hope

Hope is powerful. It drives progress and sustains belief. But when it becomes a filter, it distorts your perception of reality. Hope shifts attention away from what is happening and toward what could happen. It replaces observation with expectation. It convinces you that what you want to happen is already unfolding, or about to.

"It will even out."
"Things will fall into place."
"This isn't a big deal."

These thoughts feel reassuring, but they do not clarify what is happening. The Proven Man does not allow hope to override what is in front of him. He sees what is, without emotional interference.

Real-life example
She cancels plans twice in a week. Instead of recognizing the pattern, you assign a reason: "She's probably just busy." Over time, hope keeps you invested in something that does not align. The pattern was always there. Hope obscured it.

Energy cue
Hope-driven perception often feels tight, anxious, and outward-focused. Attention becomes anchored in what you want rather than what is. When clarity returns, the shift is immediate; you feel grounded, present, and connected to what is actually in front of you.

Projection

Projection is the assumption that others experience reality the way you do. It is the extension of your internal state onto someone else.

"If I feel connected, she must feel the same."
"We had a great date, so she must be just as interested."

Projection creates confusion. You interpret behavior through your own emotions rather than observing theirs. Expectation replaces observation. The Proven Man understands that his experience is his alone; it does not define another person's reality.

Real-life example
After a strong connection, you feel alignment and assume she does too. But her follow-through changes and her energy shifts. Confusion appears. The connection was real for you, but not necessarily for her.

Energy cue
Projection often feels heavy and uncertain. It creates tension as expectations are placed onto someone else. When projection dissolves, perception becomes lighter. Clarity replaces assumption, and observation replaces imposed meaning.

Ego

Ego is the need to protect identity. It feeds on validation, recognition, and the desire to feel chosen. When filtered through ego, perception becomes defensive. Reality is reshaped to preserve a narrative.

"She wouldn't do this to me."
"I'm different."
"I'm the one who understands her."

Ego resists contradiction. It rejects evidence that threatens identity and rationalizes behavior that does not align. The Proven Man does not protect a narrative; he observes reality, even when it is uncomfortable.

Real-life example
You set a boundary or express a preference, and it is dismissed or overlooked. Instead of acknowledging it, you tell yourself, "She didn't mean it," or "It's not a big deal." You protect the image of the connection rather than observe what happened.

Energy cue
Ego-driven perception often feels tight and defensive, as though you are holding onto something that may not be true. When ego releases, perception clears. Observation becomes neutral, and understanding follows.

Clarity emerges when these filters are recognized and released. Hope, projection, and ego are natural, but when they dominate perception, they distort truth. The Proven Man does not eliminate them; he sees them. And because he sees them, they no longer control him.

From that awareness, perception sharpens. And from that clarity, decisions align with what is true, not what is felt.

III. Words vs. Patterns

Words are immediate. They appear in the moment, shaped by emotion, circumstance, conversation, or the desire to create rapport. They can sound warm, reassuring, and promising. But they can also be inconsistent and disconnected from deeper truth.

The Proven Man understands that while words carry meaning, they do not tell the whole story.

Truth is rarely found in a passing compliment or a moment of enthusiasm. It is found in what repeats—patterns that emerge over time.

Real-life example

She compliments your humor, calling you funny or charming during your interactions. It feels good, reinforcing the belief that she must be interested.

But then, time and again, her follow-through drops. Plans are left open, and effort becomes inconsistent.

At first, you overlook it. But with each instance, the pattern becomes clearer.

Her words and her behavior are not aligned.

Compliments are easy. Showing up, investing time, and demonstrating consistency require intention. The truth of her interest is not found in the compliment—it is revealed in the pattern.

The Proven Man does not become attached to occasional praise or flattering words. He observes behavior across time.

Why patterns matter

Words, especially early in a connection, are often shaped by attraction, excitement, or the desire to create rapport. They may reflect how someone feels in the moment, but they do not always represent deeper commitment or consistent intention.

Words can be misinterpreted. They can be exaggerated. They can be influenced by emotion.

But patterns reveal something different.

Patterns show how someone behaves repeatedly across time. They reflect priorities, character, and the way a person engages with life, not just how they feel in a single moment.

The Proven Man understands that patterns reveal intention. He observes how someone behaves not only when things are easy, but when effort is required. How someone shows up during inconvenience, stress, or pressure reveals far more than words spoken during moments of excitement.

Energy cue
When attention is fixed on words, energy becomes elevated and unstable. Excitement rises, but it is not grounded. Attention chases reassurance.

When attention shifts to patterns, the body settles. Energy becomes steady and controlled. Clarity replaces fluctuation.

The Power of Patience and Time

Patterns require time to appear.
This is where most men falter.

It is tempting to hold onto encouraging words instead of observing whether behavior is repeated.

The Proven Man does not rush to judgment.

He is patient.

He allows time to reveal alignment.

He observes behavior repeatedly, knowing that patterns will show whether someone aligns with his standards, his values, and his direction.

IV. Consistency Is the Signal

In relationships and connections, it is easy to be pulled into moments of chemistry, attraction, or bursts of excitement.

These moments can feel powerful—but they can also mislead.

The true measure of intention is not found in isolated moments, but in consistency: how someone shows up again and again.

Consistency is the clearest signal of alignment.

Why consistency matters

The Proven Man understands that real connection is not built on high points of excitement or occasional gestures. It is built on repeated behavior, the small, consistent actions that reveal how someone actually lives and engages.

Alignment becomes visible in how someone shows up: how they communicate when things are not ideal, how they act without immediate reward, and how they behave when effort is required.

The Proven Man does not become distracted by chemistry or isolated moments of passion. He observes patterns that persist.

He understands that repeated action reveals intention.

Real-life example
She shows up reliably over time. Plans are followed through, and effort remains steady. But in group environments, her behavior becomes inconsistent. The way she engages changes depending on the setting. The pattern no longer remains stable. Consistency breaks.

Where consistency is absent, alignment is not secure.

Energy cue
Consistency feels grounding. The mind settles. Uncertainty fades.

When consistency is absent, energy becomes unsettled. Attention searches for meaning, and stability begins to slip.

V. Misalignment Is Rarely Hidden

In human connection, confusion often disguises itself as complexity. When things feel unclear, it is tempting to assume the situation is simply too complicated to understand.

But uncertainty is rarely complexity.

More often, it is misalignment.

The Proven Man understands that clarity is usually simple, even when it is uncomfortable. Confusion is not a puzzle to solve. It is often a signal that something is not aligned.

Misalignment appears as a gap between behavior and expectation. Actions no longer match what has been communicated, what is hoped for, or what the connection was believed to be.

This is not about missing details or analyzing every signal. It is about recognizing the disconnect between words and actions.

The signals are not hidden.

They repeat.

When behavior shifts frequently, one day there is engagement: interest, communication, effort. The next there is distance, silence, or withdrawal. This pattern of inconsistency reflects instability beneath the surface.

As the pattern continues, one week there is investment—plans, attention, presence. The next, it disappears. This push-pull dynamic creates confusion, but the signal is clear.

Consistency reflects alignment.
Inconsistency reveals misalignment.

When you are left questioning where you stand, clarity is already present. When alignment exists, position is rarely uncertain. Genuine connection does not require constant interpretation.

It is steady.
Transparent.
Clear.

If uncertainty persists, behavior is not supporting the words being spoken.

The Proven Man does not chase answers to complicated questions. He recognizes that clarity is simple, even when accepting it is not. Misalignment does not need to be decoded.

He sees it.

Real-life example
You express something important to you. The response is not direct or meaningfully discussed. It is deflected, minimized, or subtly resisted. At first, it is easy to overlook. You may tell yourself it was not intentional. But the pattern repeats.

When friction appears, alignment does not hold. The signal is not in agreement. It is in how resistance is handled.

Reflective question
Am I seeing the full pattern, or reacting to isolated moments?

This question shifts perspective. It moves attention away from emotional highs and toward the full pattern of behavior.

Patterns reveal truth.
Outliers do not.

If uncertainty persists, attention has been placed on moments instead of patterns.

Reality is usually simple. It is not always comfortable. The Proven Man sees clearly. He does not rationalize misalignment or remain in confusion. He acknowledges it, and he acts accordingly.

Through this discipline, his sense of self strengthens. Emotional control and clear perception guide him toward people and situations that align with his standards and direction.

VI. The Danger of Interpreting Too Early

One of the most common pitfalls men fall into is interpreting too early. In the rush of connection, excitement, and newness, it is easy to jump ahead of reality. You meet someone, feel an immediate spark, and your mind begins to build a picture of what it could become. You tell yourself, "This could be something special."

That reaction is natural.

But the Proven Man understands that early conclusions are unreliable.

The danger is not the feeling itself. It is the meaning assigned to it.

When you interpret too early, you confuse possibility with reality. Attraction, excitement, and chemistry can feel strong in the moment, but they are temporary experiences. Behavior—the only reliable signal—needs time to reveal itself.

Potential is not proof.

When emotions run high, it is easy to mistake what could be for what is. The Proven Man does not rush to define something based on an initial spark. He allows time to reveal the full picture.

After a few good interactions, it is easy to assume direction. A strong conversation or an enjoyable moment can feel like momentum. But those moments may simply be moments. What matters is what repeats: how both people continue to show up. The Proven Man is patient. He does not rush the narrative, because he understands that clarity develops through repeated behavior.

After a connection, it is easy to assume depth. Chemistry can feel immediate, and the interaction may seem meaningful. But depth is not established in early moments. Initial experiences often show highlights, the best parts of someone. Depth emerges through consistency, vulnerability, and shared experience. Until those elements appear, there is not enough evidence to draw deeper conclusions.

After initial interest, it is easy to assume continuation. Early enthusiasm can feel significant. But initial interest can remain just that, a moment of attention. What matters is whether it develops into consistent behavior, steady effort, and genuine follow-through.

The Proven Man remains grounded in the present. He does not project meaning forward.

Real-life example

You meet someone and feel an immediate spark—her energy, her humor, her presence. Within a few days, you begin adjusting your schedule to accommodate her, assuming something meaningful is unfolding. You want to believe this could be the beginning of something real.

A few weeks later, the pattern shifts. Her follow-through becomes inconsistent, and the initial excitement begins to fade. What once felt clear now creates frustration.

What felt like a strong connection was a moment, not a pattern.

This is the cost of interpreting too early.

The Proven Man waits for the full story to unfold. He understands that connection is not commitment, chemistry is not compatibility, and interest is not alignment.

The early phase is a beginning: the spark, not the flame.

Reflective question
Am I assigning meaning too quickly, or allowing time to reveal the truth?

Clarity comes from allowing things to develop rather than forcing conclusions. When the urge to define is removed, space is created for reality to appear. As behavior and patterns accumulate, it becomes easier to see what is real and what is not.

The Proven Man does not rush to conclusions because he understands that early stages are defined by potential, not proof. Only after time has passed and patterns have emerged can a clear judgment be made.

Until then, he remains patient, present, and grounded.

VII. Let Behavior Accumulate

Clarity rarely comes from isolated moments or single interactions—it comes from the accumulation of repeated behavior. The more you observe someone's actions, the clearer the picture becomes.

Moments of excitement, fleeting gestures, and isolated exchanges can feel meaningful. But they are only fragments. Truth reveals itself when you step back and allow the full pattern to emerge.

The Proven Man understands that clarity develops through time, consistency, and the unfolding of patterns. Rather than rushing to judgment, he allows behavior to accumulate, trusting that repetition reveals truth more reliably than any single interaction.

This process requires patience. It requires stepping back and observing from a place of calm.

First, allow actions to repeat.

You may witness positive behavior in isolated moments: kindness, enthusiasm, attention. But understanding comes from repetition. Are these actions consistent, or do they appear only occasionally? The Proven Man does not become attached to a single moment of kindness or a passing compliment. He observes whether that behavior continues.

Next, observe whether effort is consistent. Effort is not measured by occasional gestures or dramatic expressions of interest. Real effort appears in someone showing up even when circumstances are not perfect. The Proven Man observes whether someone continues to invest when things are ordinary, inconvenient, or difficult.

Finally, allow patterns to form. Understanding emerges through patterns that develop gradually. Patterns do not rely on promises or emotional intensity. They reveal how someone behaves.

Does she show up consistently?
Does she communicate when it is inconvenient?
Does she follow through even when there is nothing to gain?
Does effort remain when it is inconvenient or requires sacrifice?

These repeated behaviors reveal the truth more clearly than words ever could.

Patterns require time.

Real-life example
At first, the conversation feels engaging. You ask questions, and the exchange moves forward. Over time, a pattern begins to form. You continue to carry the conversation—asking, prompting, keeping it moving. The other person responds, but rarely initiates. Depth does not expand on its own.

At first, it is easy to overlook. But as the pattern repeats, the imbalance becomes clear. The signal is not in what is said—it is in what is not returned.

Instead of focusing on early moments, you step back and observe the pattern as it unfolds. What once felt engaging reveals itself as one-sided. The gap between words and actions becomes clear.

Clarity arrives without force.

Energy cue
When behavior is observed patiently, energy remains calm, centered, and grounded. Attention is not chasing meaning; it is allowing it to appear.

When interpretation happens too quickly, the mind begins to race, assembling incomplete information into a narrative. Energy tightens. Focus narrows. Stability begins to slip. The Proven Man understands that clarity requires time. Rushing to conclusions creates noise.

By allowing actions to repeat and patterns to form, truth becomes obvious, without explanation.

VIII. Separating Feeling from Fact

One of the most important skills for the Proven Man is the ability to separate feeling from fact. In a world driven by emotional highs and fleeting moments, it is easy to mistake how something feels for what is actually happening.

The Proven Man does not follow emotion blindly. He understands that feelings, while real, are not always reliable indicators of truth.

Attraction can feel strong.
A connection can feel meaningful.
A moment can feel undeniable.

But feeling is not proof.

Clarity begins when emotion is tested against behavior.

Are these feelings supported by consistent action?

The truth is not found in emotional intensity alone. It is found in what repeats: actions that align with what is expressed. Emotions shift. Behavior reveals.

Are actions aligned with words?

Words are easy in moments of emotion. Action carries weight. What matters is what follows: whether what is said is supported by what is done. When alignment is absent, it is not a small inconsistency. It is a signal.

Are you responding to isolated moments?

A single conversation, a moment of chemistry, or an unexpected gesture can feel significant. But intensity can mislead. Meaning is not found in the moment; it is found in the pattern that follows.

Real-life example

During a conversation, something more personal comes up. The exchange deepens. There is openness, reflection, and a sense of connection.

In the moment, it feels meaningful, like something real has formed.

But as time passes, there is no continuation. The depth does not return. The interaction resumes at the surface.

The feeling was real.

The pattern is not.

The Proven Man recognizes this distinction. Feelings are influenced by the moment and the possibility it creates. Facts are grounded in repeated behavior.

When emotion is not supported by consistent action, it distorts perception.

Clarity returns the moment attention shifts from how something feels to what it consistently does.

Energy cue

When feeling is mistaken for fact, excitement gives way to tension, uncertainty, and frustration. The emotional high gives way to instability as reality begins to emerge.

When feeling and fact are separated, the experience shifts. Energy becomes steady. Perception clears. Attention moves away from intensity and toward observation.

The Proven Man does not chase how something feels.
He observes what it does.
And through that observation, truth becomes clear.

IX. What Seeing Clearly Looks Like in Real Time

Clarity is quiet. It does not rush, justify, or chase explanations. The Proven Man understands that truth rarely needs to be forced. It simply reveals itself.

The reality of a situation is usually straightforward. It does not require overthinking or emotional narratives to make it easier to accept.

In real time, seeing clearly means observing what is happening without adding interpretation or assumption. It means seeing what is rather than what you wish it to be.

This is where the discipline you have been developing becomes visible.

What follows are examples of how clarity appears in real time.

Scenario 1: Inconsistent effort in communication or follow-through

Distorted: "There's probably something I'm not seeing."
Clear: "Her effort is inconsistent. That is the pattern."

At first it is easy to rationalize behavior that does not align with expectations. You might tell yourself she is busy or going through something. But these explanations often exist to make the situation feel more comfortable.

Clarity begins when you accept the pattern as it appears.

Her effort is inconsistent.

The Proven Man does not excuse behavior that misaligns with his values. He sees the pattern clearly and acknowledges it without distortion.

When you respond with clarity, the situation becomes straightforward. The pattern is visible, and there is no need to create a story to soften or justify it.

Scenario 2: Intensity without stability

Distorted: "This could be something real."
Clear: "It feels intense, but lacks consistency."

Emotional intensity can easily be mistaken for long-term potential. A strong connection in the moment may feel meaningful and promising.

But clarity is not carried away by intensity. It observes consistency instead.

The Proven Man recognizes that sustainable connections are built on reliability, steady effort, and mutual investment. Intensity without consistency is simply an emotional high—not a stable foundation.

Scenario 3: Uncertainty about where you stand

Distorted: "I just need to understand her better."
Clear: "If it were clear, I would not feel unsure."

When uncertainty appears, it is easy to believe the answer lies in more explanation or more time.

But clarity often reveals something simpler than that. Uncertainty itself can be a signal. If alignment were present, your position would be clear. Communication would be consistent. Behavior would support the connection.

The Proven Man does not chase clarity through endless interpretation. Instead, he observes and allows behavior to reveal what is actually happening.

Confusion is rarely a mystery waiting to be solved. It is often a signal that the situation lacks consistency.

When clarity is present, you do not need to search for answers.

They are already visible.

Energy cue
When you see clearly, there is no need for explanations or emotional justification. Your mind becomes quiet. Your attention becomes steady.

The energy feels calm, spacious, and grounded.

When perception is distorted, the experience feels different. Thoughts race. Emotions fluctuate. Attention becomes scattered as the mind tries to resolve uncertainty.

Clarity removes that mental noise. You no longer chase meaning. You simply observe without distortion.

X. The Discipline of Seeing What Is

Clear perception does not happen automatically. It requires discipline, the ability to resist the subtle urges that cloud judgment and distort reality. The Proven Man understands that clarity does not come from filling in gaps or forcing meaning too quickly. Truth reveals itself over time, but only when it is allowed to.

Discipline in seeing is the ability to remain steady. It means not rushing to conclusions, not allowing emotional reactions to shape understanding, and not creating stories to ease discomfort. Seeing clearly requires presence, observing without the need to explain, justify, or resolve everything immediately.

It is easy to explain things away when behavior does not align with expectation. Accepting reality can feel uncomfortable, and the mind often tries to soften that discomfort with interpretation.

If her behavior shifts at the last moment, the impulse is to assign a reason.

"Maybe I'm overthinking it."
"There's likely a reasonable explanation."

These explanations may ease discomfort, but they can also distort truth.

The Proven Man resists this impulse. He does not explain behavior.

He observes it.

The more you justify, the more you distort. When clarity is absent, the mind fills gaps with assumption. It attempts to complete the picture with a narrative shaped by hope, desire, or fear.

Consider a woman who flirts but remains inconsistent in effort. It is easy to conclude, "She's shy," or "She's playing hard to get." But these explanations often reflect internal need, not reality.

The Proven Man recognizes this pattern. Instead of constructing meaning, he observes behavior across time.

He watches the pattern.

Moments of chemistry, connection, or uncertainty can feel significant. But they do not define reality. Clarity comes from seeing the full picture, recognizing that isolated moments do not determine the truth of a connection.

The Proven Man does not draw conclusions from single experiences. He does not allow early excitement to shape understanding.

If several early interactions feel strong, it is easy to imagine direction. But when behavior later becomes inconsistent, clarity requires context.

A few strong moments do not outweigh repeated inconsistency.

The Proven Man does not allow emotional highs to distort what is repeatedly shown.

He waits.

And over time, the pattern becomes clear. Clarity requires patience. Truth reveals itself to the man who allows it.

Real-life example

You share something deeply meaningful about yourself. It is acknowledged in the moment. Later, it does not appear again. The detail is not referenced. It does not carry forward.

The impulse is to explain it away. "Maybe they forgot." "Maybe it wasn't important to them." But the behavior is simple. What is given attention tends to be remembered.

The Proven Man does not construct a narrative around it.

He observes the pattern, and over time, the signal becomes clear.

Energy cue
When you discipline yourself to see what is, your energy becomes lighter. There is no tension to maintain, no need to construct meaning or force outcomes.

Observation replaces interpretation.

The mind becomes clear.

When the urge to explain or justify is removed, perception sharpens. You stop chasing stories and begin recognizing reality as it is.

The Proven Man understands that clarity requires discipline and patience. He does not allow emotional turbulence to distort perception.

He waits for the pattern.

And from that clarity, he moves with precision: grounded, aware, and fully in control of himself.

XI. Practices for Reading Reality

Mastering clear perception requires discipline, the ability to remain grounded in reality despite emotional triggers, desire, or intensity. For the Proven Man, clarity is not occasional.

It is practiced.

Through discipline, the mind learns to observe with precision, track behavior across time, and resist the distortions created by emotional interpretation.

Self-regulation is essential. In moments of intensity, the instinct is to react. Excitement, frustration, or anxiety can pull attention away from what is actually happening.

The Proven Man begins with pause. He breathes. He centers himself. He allows the emotion to settle before responding. From that steadiness, his response reflects reality—not impulse.

Another discipline is tracking patterns rather than moments. Individual interactions can distort perception: a thoughtful message here, an engaging conversation there.

But truth does not appear in isolated moments.

It appears in patterns.

The Proven Man observes how behavior unfolds. He notices consistency and inconsistency, effort and neglect, presence and absence. As patterns develop, understanding becomes clear.

Hope must be held carefully. It can inspire, but it can also distort when it replaces observation. When emotionally invested, attention shifts toward what could be rather than what is.

The Proven Man returns to a simple question:

Is this real, or am I hoping it is?

This separation protects clarity.

Reflection becomes essential. When behavior conflicts with expectation, the instinct is to justify. But justification distorts perception.

The Proven Man reflects instead. He considers what has actually occurred and whether he is responding to reality, or to a narrative.

Reflection creates space.

Clarity follows.

Clear perception depends on asking the right questions:

What is consistent here?
Consistency reveals intention.

What is actually happening?
Observation reveals reality.

Am I seeing reality, or my projection?
Awareness restores clarity.

Real-life example
There is a strong sense of shared enthusiasm about the future. The connection feels aligned. Direction seems implied. But over time, her behavior does not support it. Follow-through is minimal. Plans remain undefined. Effort is inconsistent.

The pattern becomes visible. What felt aligned is not sustained. Behavior does not match expectation.

The Proven Man knows that clarity emerges when observation replaces interpretation.

Perception sharpens.
Decisions become precise.

This is what seeing clearly looks like in practice.

Chapter Distillation

The truth is rarely hidden. It is usually seen, and then softened. Many men remain in the wrong situations not because the truth is unavailable, but because they hesitate to confront it. They reinterpret what they see, soften inconsistencies, and convince themselves that things will change.

This is the subtle trap.

The truth is already present, but emotional investment makes it easy to ignore. The Proven Man does not lose clarity because reality is hidden. He loses it only when he chooses not to see what is already there.

Seeing clearly requires discipline. It requires the willingness to face uncomfortable truths without distortion, projection, or hope-driven interpretation.

Because the truth is often simple, whether it is comfortable or not.

It appears in repeated patterns.
It appears in consistent behavior.
It appears in the alignment or misalignment between words and actions.

The Proven Man does not search endlessly for answers hidden in complexity. He observes what is repeated. Over time, that discipline changes how he moves through the world. Where others react to impressions, he responds to patterns. Where others chase explanations, he recognizes reality.

Through that awareness, he protects the direction of the life he is building.

Clarity is not something you stumble upon. It is something you cultivate. It grows from the discipline of observing behavior honestly and refusing to allow emotion to distort what you see.

Because clarity does not end with observation.
It leads to discernment.
And discernment leads to choice.

Consistency confirms alignment.

This is where proof deepens.

Not in what a man believes—but in what he is able to see without distortion.

When he recognizes patterns instead of reacting to moments, that is proof.
When he sees misalignment without explaining it away, that is proof.
When he separates feeling from fact and lets reality stand, that is proof.

Clarity is no longer something he seeks.

It is something he embodies.

And from that point forward, what he sees begins to guide what he chooses.

The Proven Man Principle

Patterns reveal truth.

Truth creates clarity.

Clarity guides every decision.

Chapter Three

The Four Women Every Man Will Meet

Understanding Relationship Archetypes

Clarity in the moment is not enough when it comes to relationships.

The next step is understanding the archetypes of women you will encounter, and how each one can either support or divert you from the direction you have committed to in life.

Attraction, archetypes, and the discipline of choosing alignment define the next stage of the Proven Man's development.

In your journey, you will meet countless women. Some will captivate you, others will challenge you, and some will test the very core of your identity. But not every connection moves you toward the life you are building. Relationships are not defined by chemistry alone; they are defined by alignment with your deeper values, vision, and the legacy you intend to create. Recognizing which archetypes support your long-term mission, and which ones pull you away from it gives you the power to choose deliberately.

The initial pull between two people is instinctive and immediate, capturing your attention before you have time to evaluate it. Her presence, energy, and the qualities that make her captivating can feel magnetic. In those early moments, she may seem like exactly what you have been waiting for: effortless, exciting, and full of promise. The connection feels natural, intoxicating, and rare.

What feels powerful in the beginning can also be misleading.

Lasting relationships are not built on the emotional surge that accompanies first attraction. That surge is often driven by novelty and chemistry, forces that are intense but temporary. What you feel in those early moments is often a reaction to something new, not necessarily a reflection of genuine compatibility. As the excitement settles and the adrenaline fades, you begin to see who she actually is, and whether that reality aligns with the future you are building.

This is where many men lose clarity: they mistake short-term attraction for long-term alignment.

The Proven Man does not make that mistake. He understands that legacy is never built on momentary emotion.

Legacy is built on consistency.

It is created with someone who supports your mission, amplifies your energy, and grows alongside you over time.

Attraction may draw you in, but alignment is what allows something real to take root.

The Proven Man understands this distinction. He is not swayed by passing infatuations. He knows that while attraction may ignite the spark, it is consistency, shared values, and mutual growth that keep the fire alive.

Energy compounds over time, and the right partner aligns with your mission, strengthening the direction you are already moving.

The Proven Man does not make relationship decisions based on how something feels in the moment. He evaluates it based on where it leads, whether it contributes to the life he is building or quietly pulls him away from it.

By choosing alignment over impulse, he builds something stable, purposeful, and worthy of the legacy he intends to create.

I. Attraction vs. Reality: Why Men Misread Women

The pull between two people can be undeniable. Attraction often arrives quickly, capturing attention before deliberate evaluation has time to occur. In those early moments, everything can feel effortless. The energy is engaging, the interaction flows naturally, and the connection may seem unusually promising.

Early attraction can distort perception.

What feels powerful in the beginning is often driven by novelty and chemistry rather than genuine compatibility. The excitement of something new creates emotional momentum, making the connection appear deeper and more stable than it actually is.

As time passes and novelty begins to fade, patterns emerge. What once seemed effortless may begin to reveal inconsistencies. What initially felt natural may require increasing adjustments, compromises, or explanations.

This is where many men begin to lose clarity: they mistake the intensity of attraction for the presence of alignment.

When attraction feels strong, it is easy to assume it signals long-term compatibility. But attraction alone does not determine alignment. Not every woman who captures your attention is meant to build a future with you.

Some will entertain you for a time. Some will challenge your growth. Some will quietly drain your energy.

Only one, the rare one, will truly align with you and support the life you are building.

Legacy is never built on fleeting attraction. It is built on alignment, consistency, and shared direction over time. The Proven Man understands that lasting relationships are not formed in the intensity of the first spark, but through steady commitment to growth, shared values, and a vision both people actively build together.

II. The Four Core Archetypes

Before you can fully recognize these archetypes, it is important to understand the dynamics that shape each one. The four archetypes described here represent distinct ways women relate to attention, effort, and their potential for partnership. Some of these dynamics create friction and instability, while only one fosters alignment, growth, and mutual support.

The goal is not simply to avoid what drains your energy, but to recognize what truly strengthens and elevates you. The right partner does more than match your energy—she amplifies it. She strengthens your mission, supports your growth, and moves forward with you rather than pulling you off course.

The Proven Man understands this distinction. He does not evaluate relationships based on attraction or chemistry alone. He evaluates them by what they produce over time—whether they reinforce his direction or quietly erode it. He also considers who he will grow into over time, and who she may become as a partner many years from now.

When he sees the pattern clearly, his choice becomes simple.

Not every connection carries the same intention. Some seek attention. Some demand effort without contribution. Some quietly extract your energy.

Only one builds with you.

1. The Performer — Me, Me, All About Me!

The Performer craves the spotlight. She is magnetic, captivating, and effortlessly draws attention wherever she goes. When she enters a room, it is as if the world slows down to take notice.

She thrives on being seen, admired, and validated by others, especially in social settings. The energy she exudes pulls people in, creating an almost intoxicating sense of connection. But at its core, this connection is rooted in her desire for external validation, not in genuine partnership.

Psychologically, her sense of self-worth is deeply tied to how others perceive her. The compliments, admiration, and attention she receives fuel her ego, often more than the actual substance of the relationship. She may make you feel intensely desired in the moment, but that desire is often about the affirmation of her own worth rather than a true interest in building something lasting. She is adept at drawing you in and making you feel special, but there is a disconnect beneath the surface.

Energetically, the Performer reflects attention more than she offers it. You become the audience to her performance. Your energy is poured into her, yet it is seldom reciprocated in the same way. What you experience is an illusion of connection, one that leaves you momentarily exhilarated but ultimately drained. You are left holding the emotional space while she remains at the center of attention, never truly investing in you or your needs.

Attention is her currency, not connection.

Truth: The Performer is not seeking partnership.

She is sustaining the performance. She does not build with you; she seeks to shine alone, drawing energy from others to maintain her sense of significance.

How She Fits or Doesn't Fit With the Proven Man

For the Proven Man, the Performer is a challenging match. The Proven Man values depth, consistency, and alignment with his mission. He seeks relationships that empower both partners to grow, contribute, and build together. While the Performer may offer initial excitement, her need for constant validation and external attention creates a fundamental mismatch.

The Proven Man is grounded in his purpose. He does not have time to maintain someone else's emotional stage. He needs a partner who amplifies his energy, not someone who drains it by making everything about her performance.

In a relationship with the Performer, the Proven Man may feel a lack of emotional reciprocity. He will sense that the connection is superficial, built on the ebb and flow of her attention rather than mutual investment. Over time, the gap between attraction and alignment becomes evident. For the Proven Man, such a dynamic will not foster the growth and stability necessary for building a lasting legacy.

Real-life example
You go out together, and she captivates everyone in the room, drawing attention from every conversation around her. All eyes are on her, and conversations orbit around her presence. Yet when the night ends, she has not once asked about your day, your goals, or how you are feeling. You leave the night feeling energized, but there is a nagging emptiness because you were never truly seen for who you are. The connection felt electric, but you realize it was superficial, a one-sided exchange that lacked depth.

Energy cue
At first, you feel an intense rush of excitement, like a fire ignited by her presence. But soon a subtle tension builds. As you try to keep the interaction alive, you find yourself constantly adjusting, attempting to maintain the energy. This effort begins to chip away at your clarity, making you feel more like a supporting character than a true partner.

She captivates the moment, but she does not build the future.

Metaphor
She is like a meteor: brilliant, unforgettable, and dazzling in the moment. But just as quickly as she appears, she disappears, never grounded or rooted in anything substantial. The impact is striking but fleeting, leaving nothing behind but the memory of her light.

2. The Princess – I'm Worthy of Everything, But Giving Back? Meh.

The Princess is accustomed to receiving attention, comfort, and emotional prioritization without the expectation of equal effort. She sees herself as the prize to be won and believes life should be easy, provided by others. She expects to be taken care of, but when it comes to contributing to a shared future, she often steps back, leaving the responsibility on her partner.

Psychologically, the Princess tends to treat responsibility as optional rather than essential. She may admire your ambition, your accomplishments, and the life you are building, but she does not take ownership of her role in creating a shared vision. As a result, you often find yourself carrying the emotional and practical weight of the relationship while she enjoys the benefits without contributing equally.

Energetically, the Princess draws more energy than she gives. You become the provider, the one responsible for creating structure, stability, and momentum—while she resists the idea of mutual responsibility. Over time, the dynamic becomes imbalanced: you give while she receives, and neither of you feels truly fulfilled. A quiet tension develops as you begin to sense that you are investing more than the relationship is returning.

Truth: The Princess may admire your life, but she will not help you build it.

She may enjoy the rewards of your effort, but she lacks the drive or willingness to contribute to something lasting.

How She Fits or Doesn't Fit With the Proven Man

For the Proven Man, the Princess archetype is a poor match. He values balance, mutual growth, and the active pursuit of a shared vision. He does not build relationships where one person carries the weight while the other enjoys the results.

The Princess, with her expectation of being supported and prioritized without contributing in return, cannot align with the Proven Man's purpose-driven life. She may appreciate the life he creates, but she will not invest the energy required to build it alongside him.

In a relationship with the Princess, the Proven Man eventually finds himself carrying the majority of the emotional and practical load. Over time, this imbalance creates frustration and quiet resentment. His mission requires a partner who is equally committed to building something meaningful, and the Princess's resistance to responsibility makes that impossible.

Real-life example

You plan dinners, trips, and experiences that she enjoys. But when it comes time to organize, contribute, or take initiative, she steps back. When you ask for involvement, she may resist, or participate only reluctantly.

While you are working to create meaningful experiences, she is focused primarily on receiving them. Gradually, you begin to feel less like a partner and more like the person responsible for making everything happen.

Energy cue
A subtle heaviness settles into the relationship. You begin to feel as though you are carrying more than your share: emotionally, mentally, and practically. Over time, that imbalance creates frustration and fatigue, slowly eroding the connection.

Metaphor
She is like a porcelain figure: beautiful and delicate, but vulnerable under pressure. Her exterior appears flawless, but when real responsibility or adversity arrives, the structure beneath it proves far more fragile than it first appeared.

3. The Parasite – I Take Without Giving

The Parasite feeds on your energy without replenishing it. She often enters your life through vulnerability: hardship, trauma, or emotional need that draws out your empathy. At first, you may feel compelled to help, motivated by compassion and a genuine desire to support her. But over time, what begins as kindness gradually becomes an exhausting cycle. She does not fuel your mission; she drains it, leaving you emotionally depleted and disconnected from your direction.

Psychologically, the Parasite's needs gradually evolve into expectations. What begins as a request for support becomes an unspoken obligation. You find yourself constantly giving: listening, comforting, and stabilizing, while your own needs fade into the background. The more you provide, the more she takes, until the relationship becomes defined by a one-sided flow of energy.

Energetically, the dynamic shifts away from partnership and toward maintenance. The relationship becomes centered on managing her emotional state rather than building something together. Your time, attention, and emotional resources are continuously redirected toward keeping her stable. Instead of mutual growth, the connection becomes an ongoing extraction of energy. You may begin to feel as though you are carrying the entire relationship while receiving little in return.

In many cases, the dynamic begins to feed on shared negativity as well: conflict, stress, and emotional turbulence that keep the cycle of dependency alive.

Truth: This is not a partnership—it is extraction.

The Parasite does not offer growth, support, or shared direction. She takes what she needs and leaves you increasingly empty.

How She Fits or Doesn't Fit With the Proven Man

For the Proven Man, the Parasite archetype is one of the most destructive dynamics he can engage in. His life is built around purpose, direction, and the steady construction of a meaningful future. That requires energy, focus, and clarity.

The Parasite undermines all three.

Rather than amplifying his mission, she siphons energy away from it. Instead of building alongside him, she anchors his attention to her instability. Over time, this dynamic erodes his momentum and pulls him further from the legacy he is working to create.

In a relationship with the Parasite, the Proven Man finds himself constantly giving while receiving little in return. The emotional weight becomes overwhelming, and the lack of reciprocity begins to erode both his clarity and his sense of balance. Eventually, he recognizes that the relationship is not supporting his path, it is draining the resources required to move forward. With that clarity, he walks away.

Real-life example
She consistently leans on you for emotional support while neglecting your own needs and responsibilities. You give more and more of your attention and energy, hoping things will stabilize. But when you attempt to pull back or establish boundaries, she responds with guilt, pressure, or emotional escalation.

The relationship becomes unbalanced, and your emotional reserves begin to run dry.

Energy cue
A persistent emotional heaviness begins to follow your interactions. You feel subtle anxiety, fatigue, and a constant pull on your energy. The relationship revolves around stabilizing her rather than building something together. Gradually, you begin to sense that you are being used rather than genuinely valued.

Metaphor
She is like a vine wrapped around a tree. At first it appears harmless, almost natural. But over time, it tightens, slowly draining strength from the very structure that supports it. Eventually, the tree weakens beneath the weight of what it was never meant to sustain.

4. The Partner – Your Equal, Your Ally, Your Legacy Builder

The Partner embodies what the Proven Man is truly seeking. She is grounded, aligned, and intentional in how she lives and how she loves. Unlike women driven by external validation, fleeting excitement, or emotional drama, the Partner seeks something deeper: the opportunity to create meaningful impact both in her own life and in the life she builds with the man beside her.

She does not crave attention or admiration.
Her focus is contribution.

Her life is rooted in purpose, and she possesses a clear understanding of who she is and where she is going. She does not rely on external praise to define her value.

That inner confidence allows her to enter a relationship fully present, without the need for constant reassurance.

Psychologically, the Partner's sense of self-worth is secure and independent. She does not look to others to validate her identity. Because of this stability, she brings her full attention and presence into the relationship. While others may seek relationships to fill emotional gaps, the Partner arrives whole. She is emotionally grounded, resilient, and capable of navigating the inevitable challenges that come with life and partnership. Her value comes from her own growth and purpose, not from outside approval.

This psychological stability is essential for the Proven Man. His mission requires focus, clarity, and forward movement. He needs a partner who can stand beside him without requiring constant emotional maintenance. The Partner supports his vision without distracting from it. She strengthens his life rather than complicating it.

Energetically, the Partner is the most powerful match for the Proven Man. She does not compete with his direction; she complements it. She strengthens, supports, and amplifies his mission. This alignment is not accidental; it is built intentionally through shared values, mutual respect, and a commitment to growth. When the Proven Man walks beside the Partner, their combined energy multiplies because they are building toward the same horizon.

Her presence does not feel draining or distracting.
It feels expansive.

Instead of siphoning energy away from his mission, she contributes to it, creating a dynamic where both individuals grow stronger together. The Partner understands that legacy is never built alone; it is the result of two aligned individuals working toward a shared future.

Truth: The Partner expands your energy, strengthens your mission, and helps build your legacy.

Together you create something greater than either of you could achieve alone. This is where true partnership exists, not just in love, but in shared purpose.

How She Fits: Why It Works for The Proven Man

For the Proven Man, alignment is everything. His path is about building something that lasts, something that extends beyond the moment and continues long after it begins.

The Partner understands this vision and becomes an active participant in it. She does not simply observe the journey; she invests in it. She is committed to growth, contribution, and the steady evolution of the life you are building together.

The right partner does not merely join the journey; she accelerates it. Her clarity and self-awareness allow her to bring her strongest self into the relationship, enabling the Proven Man to operate at his highest level. With her beside him, uncertainty fades. Direction sharpens. Momentum increases.

A partnership like this elevates both people. She does not need to be carried emotionally or constantly reassured. Instead, she stands as an equal: sometimes the pillar when you need support, sometimes the spark that reignites momentum when progress slows. The Proven Man meets her with the same steadiness, offering strength when she needs grounding and momentum when her path demands more.

With this kind of partnership, you are not simply existing together; you are thriving together. She challenges you when growth is required, celebrates your victories with genuine pride, and helps keep both of you grounded in your shared purpose. Over time, the relationship deepens into something resilient and enduring, built on trust, respect, and alignment.

Real-life example
You are pursuing your goals, but you never feel alone in the pursuit. Your partner does more than encourage you—she actively contributes to the process. She offers her strengths, her perspective, and her energy in ways that move both of you forward.

She knows when to step back and allow you to lead, and she knows when to step forward and take initiative herself. Together you create an environment where growth, creativity, and momentum can flourish.

Energy cue
The energy in this dynamic is calm, steady, and focused. There is no constant need to prove, reassure, or stabilize the relationship. It feels grounded and natural. Both of you move as a unit, supporting one another while growing in the same direction.

Metaphor
She is like a deeply rooted tree: stable, enduring, and life-giving. Her roots intertwine with yours, creating a foundation strong enough to support growth through every season. Together your roots nourish one another's strength and development, allowing you to rise upward and outward and expand your canopy together through consistency, wisdom, and shared effort over time.

III. The Forces Behind Attraction

At first glance, the archetypes you encounter may seem completely different from one another. The Performer draws attention and excitement. The Princess invites admiration and caretaking. The Parasite pulls on empathy and responsibility. And the Partner brings stability and shared direction.

Beneath these differences, each archetype appeals to a deeper psychological force that drives attraction.

The Performer stimulates your desire for validation. Her energy, attention, and charisma make you feel chosen, admired, and elevated. The dynamic feeds the ego, which is why it can feel so powerful in the beginning.

The Princess activates your instinct to protect and provide. She appears valuable, desirable, and worthy of effort. Being the man who can care for her or win her attention can feel like proof of your strength and status.

The Parasite engages your empathy. Her vulnerability, hardship, or emotional need can trigger the instinct to help, stabilize, and rescue. At first this may feel meaningful, even noble, but over time it can quietly shift into obligation.

The Partner is different.

She does not pull you through ego, rescue, or validation. Instead, she connects through alignment. Her presence reinforces your direction rather than distracting from it. The attraction feels calmer, but the impact is far more powerful because it compounds rather than drains.

This is why the early stages of attraction can be misleading. What initially feels compelling is not always what ultimately proves sustainable. Excitement, admiration, and emotional intensity can create powerful connections, but they do not necessarily build anything lasting.

The Proven Man understands that attraction often reveals what pulls at him instinctively, while alignment reveals what will actually strengthen his life.

And the difference between the two determines everything that follows.

IV. From Archetypes to Patterns

Understanding archetypes gives you a way to recognize the kinds of women you may encounter. But archetypes alone do not determine the outcome of a relationship.

What ultimately shapes the dynamic is the pattern that forms between two people over time.

An archetype describes a tendency. A pattern reveals the reality.

Someone who appears confident may still create instability. Someone who seems supportive early on may struggle with consistency later. And someone who appears calm and grounded may ultimately prove to be the most aligned partner you could have chosen.

This is why the Proven Man does not make decisions based solely on first impressions or initial attraction. He allows behavior to repeat. He watches how effort, communication, and emotional stability hold up over time.

Archetypes reveal tendencies.
Patterns reveal truth.

And learning to recognize those patterns in real time is what allows the Proven Man to choose alignment instead of distraction.

The next step is understanding how those patterns appear in the real world, and how to recognize them before they cost you time, energy, or direction.

V. The Alignment Question

Every archetype you have encountered teaches you something—not about women, but about what you are willing to accept in your life.

Every dynamic you participate in reflects your standards, whether you realize it or not.

What you tolerate, what you justify, and what you allow to continue all shape both your relationships and the man you become. Over time, those choices either reinforce your clarity or slowly blur the direction you are trying to follow.

The real shift happens when you stop asking, "Do I like her?" and start asking a different question:

"Does this align with the life I am building?"

That question changes everything.

It cuts through the emotional highs, the intensity, and the excitement of the moment. Instead of focusing on how something feels right now, it forces you to evaluate what is actually happening over time.

The Proven Man operates from this perspective.

He understands that liking someone is easy, but true alignment is rare. A meaningful relationship requires more than moments of connection; it requires consistency, shared values, and direction that strengthens both people over time.

Because of this, the Proven Man does not make decisions based on temporary emotion. He evaluates relationships based on what they contribute to the life he is building.

At this stage, the Proven Man now evaluates relationships through a different lens, one grounded in clarity rather than emotion.

The Proven Man Filter

The Proven Man evaluates relationships through a clear internal filter that protects his direction.

Instead of reacting to attraction or emotional intensity, he asks three questions:

1. *What archetype is present?*
2. *What pattern is forming over time?*
3. *Does this align with the life I am building?*

Attraction may appear instantly.

But alignment reveals itself through behavior.

This filter prevents emotional momentum from turning into premature investment. Rather than reacting to the moment, the Proven Man observes what the interaction consistently produces.

Through this process, decisions become clearer, not because he forces them, but because patterns reveal what belongs.

Understanding archetypes gives him the language to recognize dynamics.

Recognizing patterns over time gives him the clarity to choose wisely.

Chapter Distillation

Clarity begins with recognition, but it matures through discipline.

The Proven Man does not treat archetypes as abstract ideas. He learns to see them as patterns that reveal themselves through behavior over time.

Attraction may capture attention quickly.

But patterns determine direction.

Because of this, he does not rush to conclusions or allow emotional intensity to dictate his choices. He observes what repeats. He pays attention to consistency. And he allows time to reveal what a connection truly produces.

Where others become caught in the moment, he watches the pattern that forms beneath it.

This discipline changes everything.

Instead of reacting to attraction, he evaluates alignment. Instead of chasing intensity, he recognizes stability. Instead of hoping things will improve, he observes what is consistently demonstrated.

Through that awareness, the Proven Man protects the direction of his life.

Because once you learn to see patterns clearly, relationships stop feeling unpredictable.

They become readable.

Archetypes introduce the pattern.
Time reveals it.
Alignment determines the decision.

The Proven Man does not react to attraction alone. He observes what repeats, watches what stabilizes, and chooses only what aligns with the direction he is building.

Because patterns—not moments—determine where relationships lead.

This is where proof becomes visible.

Not in what a man says he wants—but in what he chooses when clarity is present.

When he walks away from what does not align, that is proof.
When he resists the pull of attraction that leads him off course, that is proof.
When he chooses consistency, alignment, and shared direction over momentary intensity, that is proof.

Clarity has already shown him what is real.

Now his decisions reveal who he is.

And from that point forward, what he chooses determines the life he builds.

The Proven Man Principle

Recognition creates clarity.

Patterns reveal truth.

Alignment determines the path.

Chapter Four

Attraction in Motion

How Patterns Reveal Themselves in Reality

By this point, you have already seen how different archetypes and dynamics appear in relationships.

Recognition alone is not enough.

The Proven Man must learn to observe patterns as they unfold and respond with discipline. Archetypes introduce the dynamic, but the patterns that emerge over time reveal where a relationship is truly going.

The four archetypes represent the core motivational drivers behind relationship behavior. The subvariants in this chapter show how those motivations most commonly appear in real relationships.

Because clarity is not just about what you see.
It is about what you choose.

I. Recognizing Patterns in Real Time

Navigating relationships is not about identifying dysfunction immediately. More often, it is about recognizing the subtle patterns that quietly blend into what we assume is "normal."

In the beginning, everything feels fresh, exciting, and full of possibility. Attraction is strong, chemistry flows easily, and the novelty of the connection keeps the experience engaging. But as time passes, the underlying dynamics begin to reveal themselves. What first feels effortless either becomes stable, or gradually unravels into something draining.

The real challenge is recognizing the shift as excitement fades and deeper patterns begin to surface.

These patterns often appear harmless at first, especially when they are wrapped in familiarity, emotional intensity, or strong attraction. But over time they begin to influence the direction of the relationship. What initially seems promising can slowly evolve into something that pulls you away from your clarity, your focus, and the life you are trying to build.

A relationship may feel right in the moment, yet still move in the wrong direction over time.

For the Proven Man, the ability to recognize these patterns early becomes essential. The difference between a relationship that strengthens you and one that drains you is rarely obvious in the beginning; it is revealed through repeated behavior.

Learning to see those patterns as they emerge allows you to make decisions from clarity rather than emotion.

Once you learn to recognize them, you begin to see the patterns everywhere: in relationships, environments, and the dynamics unfolding around you.

II. Relationship Subvariants

These subvariants represent some of the most common relationship dynamics you will encounter in the real world. While the archetypes introduced earlier describe broad tendencies, these combinations show how those tendencies often appear in practice.

1. The Chaos Coordinator (Performer + Drama)
Pattern: High highs, low lows.

Initial appeal
She is magnetic, dramatic, and electric, bringing excitement wherever she goes. You are drawn in by her intensity and the adrenaline that follows her presence. In the beginning, the thrill feels undeniable. She lights up the room, and the energy around her is intoxicating.

What happens over time

As time passes, the excitement fades and the instability begins to surface. One moment everything feels incredible; the next, you find yourself in the middle of conflict you never anticipated. What once felt thrilling slowly turns into an emotional rollercoaster where stability becomes increasingly difficult to maintain. Small problems begin consuming disproportionate amounts of emotional energy. Instead of building something steady, you realize you are constantly managing reactions, moods, and escalating drama.

Why it drains you

Chaos can feel exciting at first, but it becomes exhausting over time. The emotional highs keep you engaged, but the unpredictability that follows gradually erodes your focus. The Proven Man cannot stay aligned with his mission when he is repeatedly pulled into emotional turbulence. What begins as excitement slowly becomes a cycle of instability that disrupts clarity and momentum.

Energy cue

A rush of excitement followed by subtle anxiety, like walking on eggshells or trying to manage a storm. Even when things seem calm, the tension never fully disappears.

How The Proven Man Responds

The Proven Man understands that volatility disguised as passion is still volatility. He does not get seduced by emotional highs, nor does he waste energy trying to stabilize chaos. Instead, he observes the pattern clearly. When instability becomes consistent, he steps back rather than stepping deeper into it. He protects his focus and removes himself from dynamics that pull him away from his purpose.

The takeaway

With the Chaos Coordinator, your energy is constantly diverted away from what matters. What begins as excitement eventually becomes instability. The Proven Man recognizes the pattern early and chooses stability, clarity, and alignment over emotional chaos.

Instability is not passion. It is misalignment.

2. The Perpetual Victim (Parasite Variant)

Pattern: Bonds through struggle.

Initial appeal

At first, you are drawn to her vulnerability. You want to help, to be the strong, supportive partner she can rely on. She leans on you for emotional support, and you willingly provide it. Offering stability during a difficult moment can feel meaningful, even honorable.

What happens over time

Over time, she becomes accustomed to leaning on you. What began as occasional support gradually turns into an unspoken expectation. The lines blur between being present for her and becoming responsible for her emotional well-being. When you attempt to set boundaries or step back, you are met with guilt, resistance, or subtle pressure to resume the role you have been playing.

Why it drains you

The relationship begins to revolve around solving problems rather than building something together. You become her emotional support system, while your own needs quietly move into the background. Reciprocity fades, replaced by a cycle of giving that rarely feels replenished.

Energy cue

You begin to feel emotionally drained. A quiet fatigue sets in, and you start questioning whether your support is truly appreciated—or simply expected.

How The Proven Man Responds

The Proven Man understands that empathy does not require self-abandonment. He does not confuse helping with carrying another person's emotional burden. While he is capable of offering support, he does not assume responsibility for another person's emotional stability. He recognizes when compassion turns into dependency and establishes firm boundaries without guilt. If the dynamic remains one-sided, he disengages because he understands that a relationship must be built on mutual strength, not sustained through imbalance.

The takeaway

In the Perpetual Victim dynamic, you find yourself giving without receiving. Over time, the imbalance quietly depletes you, leaving you feeling unfulfilled and unappreciated. The Proven Man recognizes the pattern and chooses mutual growth and strength over being trapped in a cycle of dependency.

Support that only flows in one direction is not partnership—it is dependence. Compassion does not require self-abandonment.

3. The Attention Seeker (Pure Performer)
Pattern: Validation is her currency.

Initial appeal
She is captivating, and you feel fortunate to be with her. Attention seems to follow her naturally, and standing beside her can make you feel singled out and valued. The chemistry feels magnetic, and the connection carries an exciting sense of energy and admiration.

What happens over time
As the relationship develops, you begin to notice that her primary motivation is external validation. While she may make you feel valued in certain moments, her deeper need is to be admired and affirmed by everyone around her. Gradually, your role shifts from partner to supporter of her image. Instead of building something together, you find yourself sustaining the attention and admiration she depends on.

Why it drains you
The relationship never deepens beyond the surface. Your energy becomes directed toward sustaining her sense of worth rather than contributing to shared growth. Over time, the connection begins to feel like a performance, focused more on maintaining appearances than creating genuine partnership.

Energy cue
At first, the attention feels energizing. But eventually you realize you are spending your energy keeping the spotlight alive. What began as mutual excitement slowly turns into the effort required to sustain her constant need for validation.

How The Proven Man Responds
The Proven Man is not driven by the need to be chosen, he is grounded in his own value. He does not compete for attention or attempt to secure admiration. When he recognizes that a woman is seeking constant external validation, he simply observes the pattern. If the relationship lacks depth, reciprocity, or alignment,

he steps back and disengages. His focus remains on building something real, not maintaining someone else's image.

The takeaway
The Attention Seeker may feel exciting at first, but the connection rarely moves beyond surface attraction. Over time you realize the relationship revolves around sustaining her need for validation rather than growing together. The Proven Man recognizes this dynamic early and chooses depth, reciprocity, and genuine connection over the illusion of admiration. \

Validation is not the same as connection.

4. The Ninja (Covert Control)
Pattern: Subtle manipulation.

Initial appeal
She is charming, intelligent, and perceptive, making you feel as though you have found someone who truly understands you. The connection feels deep early on, and you may believe you have found someone who genuinely "gets" you.

What happens over time
Gradually, you begin to sense that something is not quite right. She rarely demands control directly, but situations seem to bend quietly in her favor. Conversations leave you questioning your own decisions. You may find yourself feeling guilty, responsible, or unsure of where you stand, even when you cannot clearly identify why. Over time, her influence grows beneath the surface, creating doubt where clarity once existed and exploiting vulnerability when resistance is low.

Why it drains you
The Ninja's manipulation is subtle but powerful. It slowly erodes your confidence and autonomy, causing you to second-guess yourself and your instincts. The constant uncertainty drains your mental and emotional energy, leaving you unsettled and off balance.

Energy cue
After interactions, you often feel confused, defensive, or emotionally drained, as though something has shifted against you without your full awareness. You may start questioning your own judgment even when you cannot clearly explain what happened.

How The Proven Man Responds

The Proven Man trusts his internal clarity over subtle influence. When something feels off, he does not ignore the signal or rationalize it away. Instead, he observes the pattern behind the interaction, not just the words being spoken. He refuses to let guilt, pressure, or manipulation override his sense of direction. Rather than trying to decode or fix the dynamic, he steps back, regains his center, and evaluates the situation with clarity. If the pattern continues, he disengages. He chooses autonomy, truth, and stability over emotional entanglement.

The takeaway

The Ninja creates quiet instability by introducing doubt and subtle control into the relationship. The Proven Man recognizes manipulation early and protects his clarity, choosing autonomy and honesty over the slow erosion of his confidence.

Control that hides in subtlety is still control.

5. The Drama Queen (Chaos Amplified)

Pattern: Escalation.

Initial appeal

She is intense, passionate, and emotionally powerful. The attraction feels like fireworks: electric, urgent, and impossible to ignore. The connection carries a sense of intensity that can make the relationship feel exciting and deeply emotional from the very beginning.

What happens over time

Over time that same intensity begins to shift. What once felt like passion gradually turns into a cycle of conflict. Small disagreements escalate quickly, and calm conversations are replaced by emotional reactions. The excitement that once felt thrilling begins to feel overwhelming. Instead of building stability together, you find yourself constantly reacting to emotional upheaval.

What once felt like passion reveals itself as instability.

Why it drains you

The Drama Queen thrives on escalation. Conflict becomes the emotional fuel that sustains the relationship. Energy that should be invested in growth, stability, and shared direction is instead spent managing emotional crises. Over time this reactive cycle leaves you exhausted and distracted from your own purpose.

Energy cue
You begin to feel constantly on edge. Even normal conversations carry the tension that they could suddenly turn into arguments. The relationship feels unpredictable, as though emotional eruptions are always just beneath the surface.

How The Proven Man Responds
The Proven Man does not engage in emotional chaos. He remains grounded, composed, and in control of his responses. He refuses to match intensity with intensity or participate in reactive cycles. When he recognizes a consistent pattern of escalation, he steps back rather than stepping into the conflict. He understands that relationships built on instability cannot support his mission or long-term vision. Instead of trying to calm the storm, he removes himself from it, choosing peace, clarity, and stability over emotional turbulence.

The takeaway
In the Drama Queen dynamic, your energy becomes focused on managing emotional fires instead of building a future. The Proven Man recognizes escalation early and chooses stability, clarity, and consistency over a relationship defined by constant conflict.

Emotional intensity is not emotional stability.

6. The Flicker of Fire (Hot–Cold)
Pattern: Intensity followed by withdrawal.

Initial appeal
She draws you in with intensity, passion, and the powerful connection you feel when she is fully engaged. The spark feels undeniable. When she is present, the connection is electric. The emotional highs feel exciting and rare, creating the sense that something special is unfolding.

What happens over time
Just as the relationship begins to deepen, she pulls away, emotionally, physically, or both. You are left wondering what changed, questioning yourself, and trying to recreate the connection you felt before. But as soon as the connection begins to rebuild, the cycle repeats: closeness followed by distance. The relationship becomes a repeating pattern of intense engagement and sudden withdrawal.

Why it drains you

The push–pull dynamic creates an exhausting cycle of anticipation and withdrawal. You are never quite sure where you stand, which makes it difficult to build trust or stability. The unpredictability keeps you chasing the emotional high you felt at the beginning, but the high never lasts. Instead of building something steady, you find yourself caught in a cycle of anticipation and disappointment.

Energy cue

You feel energized during the highs but confused and depleted during the lows. The emotional swings leave you feeling as though you are running in circles, constantly trying to regain a connection that keeps slipping away.

How The Proven Man Responds

The Proven Man does not chase inconsistency. He refuses to try to earn stability from someone who cannot provide it. When he recognizes a pattern of intensity followed by withdrawal, he sees it for what it is—misalignment. Instead of leaning in harder, he leans back and observes the pattern clearly. He values consistency over emotional spikes and chooses stability over unpredictability. If the cycle continues, he disengages because he builds his life on what is steady, not what flickers.

The takeaway

The Flicker of Fire keeps you chasing emotional highs without allowing the relationship to become stable or real. The Proven Man recognizes the pattern early and chooses consistency, clarity, and emotional security over the pursuit of fleeting intensity.

Consistency reveals truth. Intensity hides it.

7. The Emotional Leech (Parasite in Full Form)

Pattern: Constant emotional output required, with little return.

Initial appeal

She presents herself as someone who needs nurturing, patience, and care. You feel compelled to support her, to be the steady presence she can rely on. Stepping into that role can feel meaningful, even admirable. Being someone's emotional anchor can create the sense that you are playing an important part in her life.

What happens over time

As the relationship continues, you begin to notice that her needs never truly subside. Every challenge, frustration, or emotional struggle flows toward you. You are constantly listening, reassuring, and stabilizing. But when you need support yourself, it rarely arrives in the same way. Gradually the imbalance becomes clear: you are the source of emotional support, but she is not a source of emotional strength.

Why it drains you

The relationship becomes a one-way exchange. Your emotional energy is continuously drawn out, while very little is returned. Over time this creates exhaustion, not just emotionally, but mentally as well. Instead of feeling supported, you begin to feel depleted.

Energy cue

A persistent emotional fatigue. You begin to feel as though you are responsible for maintaining the relationship's emotional stability while your own needs remain unmet.

Over time, the pattern becomes clear: the relationship survives on your energy alone.

How The Proven Man Responds

The Proven Man does not confuse responsibility with overextension. He gives from strength, not obligation. When he recognizes a pattern of constant emotional extraction without reciprocity, he establishes clear boundaries. He refuses to become someone else's emotional supply at the expense of his own well-being. If the imbalance continues, he disengages—because he understands that healthy relationships are mutually reinforcing, not one-sided.

The takeaway

The Emotional Leech survives through dependency, drawing energy without replenishing it. The Proven Man recognizes emotional extraction early and chooses balanced reciprocity, strength, and mutual support over quiet depletion.

Support must move both directions.

8. The Mirage (False Alignment)

Pattern: Appears aligned until tested.

Initial appeal

She feels like everything you have been looking for. She shares your values, supports your goals, and seems to understand your vision. Conversations flow effortlessly, and alignment feels natural. You begin to believe you have found something real, something rare. The connection feels deep and easy, almost as if it were meant to be.

What happens over time

The alignment begins to fracture when pressure is introduced. When the relationship requires effort, sacrifice, or consistency, her behavior begins to shift. She may still say the right things, but her actions no longer match her words. Support becomes conditional. Consistency fades. What once felt aligned now feels uncertain, and the cracks in the foundation become harder to ignore.

Why it drains you

The Mirage is difficult to detect because the connection feels genuine in the beginning. You invest based on perceived alignment, only to discover that it does not hold under pressure. The confusion comes from the absence of obvious dysfunction. Instead, you are dealing with inconsistency disguised as compatibility. This creates uncertainty and leaves you trying to reconcile what you believed with what you are now observing.

Energy cue

At first you feel grounded and confident in the connection. Over time, subtle doubt begins to surface. Something feels slightly off, but it is difficult to identify exactly why. The words still sound right, but the behavior no longer fully supports them. This growing gap creates quiet internal tension.

How The Proven Man Responds

The Proven Man does not define alignment by words or early chemistry; he defines it by consistency under pressure. He understands that time reveals the true nature of a relationship. When actions and words diverge, he trusts behavior over intention. He does not cling to potential or the idea of what something could become. If alignment falters, he adjusts accordingly. His focus remains on demonstrated consistency, not perceived compatibility.

The takeaway

The Mirage may appear aligned at first, but time exposes the difference between words and reality. What feels right initially must be proven through consistent behavior and mutual effort. The Proven Man recognizes the illusion when it appears and chooses proven alignment over temporary compatibility.

Words promise. Patterns prove.

9. The Time Thief (Comfort Without Direction)

Pattern: Easy connection, no progression.

Initial appeal

She is easy to be around. There is no drama, no chaos, no tension. Time together feels comfortable, natural, and low-pressure. You enjoy her company, and being with her feels effortless, like a breath of fresh air in a busy world. The connection is calm and stable, appearing to be the kind of relationship many people hope for: peaceful and uncomplicated.

What happens over time

The connection remains exactly where it started. There is no deeper alignment, no shared direction, and no meaningful growth. Weeks turn into months, and months turn into years, yet the relationship never evolves. You are not building anything; you are simply passing time. What once felt comfortable slowly reveals itself as stagnation.

Why it drains you

The Time Thief does not drain you through chaos or conflict. Instead, she quietly consumes your most valuable resource: time. The relationship lacks tension, but it also lacks momentum. You are not being challenged, supported, or pushed toward your greater purpose. Over time you begin to realize that while nothing feels wrong, nothing is moving forward.

Energy cue

You feel relaxed and comfortable, yet subtly stagnant. There is no urgency, no momentum, and no sense of direction. The absence of forward movement begins to feel heavier as time passes.

How The Proven Man Responds
The Proven Man understands that comfort without direction carries a hidden cost. He does not measure a relationship solely by how easy it feels, but by where it leads. If there is no growth, no alignment, and no shared vision, he will not remain simply for the sake of convenience. Time is his most valuable resource, and he protects it accordingly. He chooses relationships that contribute to his purpose, not ones that quietly delay it.

The takeaway
The Time Thief does not create chaos; she prevents progress. She offers ease and stability while quietly keeping you in place. The Proven Man recognizes stagnation for what it is and chooses purpose, alignment, and forward movement over passive complacency.

Comfort without direction is stagnation.

III. The Proven Man Filters—He Doesn't Chase

Once you have seen these patterns clearly, the next discipline is knowing how to respond to them. Recognition alone is not enough. The Proven Man must learn to filter what he sees in real time—before attraction, emotion, or habit distort his judgment.

Most men move through relationships reactively. They feel something and immediately follow it. They experience chemistry and assume meaning. They encounter intensity and interpret it as depth.

The Proven Man does the opposite.

He observes first. He allows patterns to form. He lets behavior reveal itself over time. He is not in a rush to label something as meaningful, because anything real will prove itself, and anything that cannot sustain consistency does not deserve interpretation.

Instead of chasing clarity, he allows it to emerge through repetition, patterns, and time. This is discipline, not emotional suppression, but controlled observation.

He does not ignore attraction, but he does not submit to it. He does not deny emotion, but he does not allow it to dictate direction. He experiences love fully, but evaluates it objectively.

Where most men ask,
"How do I keep this?"

The Proven Man asks,
"What is this showing me over time?"

That distinction changes everything.

Because chasing pulls you out of position, while filtering keeps you grounded in your direction.

When you chase, you invest before evidence. You fill in gaps, create narratives, and attach to potential.

When you filter, you slow down. You watch. You allow actions to repeat. You allow patterns—not moments—to define reality.

This is where most men lose control, not because they lack intelligence, but because they lack patience. They try to decide too early. They try to define too quickly. They try to secure something that has not yet proven it can exist.

The Proven Man does not force clarity; he creates the conditions for it.

He understands that time is not the enemy; it is the filter.
Patterns are not obstacles; they are the signal.
And inconsistency is not confusion; it is information.

So he stays grounded. He stays present. And he allows reality to separate itself from illusion, without interference.

Because he knows:

What is aligned will remain.
What is inconsistent will reveal itself.
And what reveals itself clearly requires no explanation.

IV. How Patterns Combine

Most relationship patterns do not appear in isolation. They often combine, creating outcomes that are either highly destructive or highly supportive. When two misaligned patterns reinforce each other, the result is instability, confusion, or long-term stagnation. But when alignment meets discipline, the result can produce powerful growth.

Understanding how these patterns combine allows the Proven Man to see relationships more clearly. Some combinations amplify dysfunction. Others amplify alignment.

Because of this, it is not enough to identify individual patterns. The deeper skill is recognizing how those patterns interact and reinforce one another over time.

The examples that follow are representative, not exhaustive. Pattern combinations vary widely in real situations, but these illustrate the most common and instructive dynamics.

The Relationship Crossover Pattern Dynamics illustrate how combinations of behavior either strengthen alignment or reinforce instability over time.

Relationship crossover patterns create either instability or alignment depending on the combination. Awareness of these dynamics allows the Proven Man to recognize what strengthens his direction, and what quietly pulls him away from it.

RELATIONSHIP CROSSOVER

PATTERN DYNAMICS

How patterns combine to create either or alignment.

DESTABILIZING COMBINATIONS	ALIGNMENT COMBINATIONS
Patterns rooted in extraction produce instability and chaos.	Patterns rooted in alignment produce stable, repeatable outcomes.
PERFORMER + PRINCESS High validation+ low contribution creates an ego trap with no growth.	**PARTNER + PROVEN MAN** Alignment and shared direction reinforces stability consistently over time.
PERFORMER + PARASITE Attention-seeking combined with dependency drains energy quickly.	**PARTNER+ SOCIAL BALANCE** Social energy exists, but stability leads the dynamic.
PRINCESS + PARASITE Entitlement combined with dependency means you carry everything.	**PARTNER + SELF-AWARENESS** Growth is present, but requires consistent correction.
PERFORMER + NINJA Validation combined with covert control creates concealed instability.	**PARTNER + SHADOW WORK** Imperfections are addressed without destabilizing the dynamic.
MIRAGE + TIME THIEF Illusion of potential combined with stagnation creates long-term confusion.	**PARTNER + SHARED MISSION** A unified direction reduces friction and accelerates progress.
PARASITE + TIME THIEF Energy drain combined with lack of direction erodes progress over time.	**PARTNER + STABILITY** Consistency removes volatility and builds trust.
PERFORMER + TIME THIEF Excitement without progression leads to years of distraction	**PARTNER + RECIPROCITY** Mutual investment reinforces and sustains stability.

Relationshig crossover patterns create either instabllity or alignment depending on the combination. Awareness of these dynamics is the key to choosing what elevates you.

V. The Reinforcement Effect

Every time a Man tolerates misalignment, he reinforces it. Every time he remains in a dynamic that drains him, he normalizes it. Every time he ignores inconsistency, justifies behavior, or clings to potential, he trains himself to accept less than what he truly wants.

This is how men drift, not through one catastrophic mistake, but through a series of small allowances.

One overlooked red flag.
One justified inconsistency.
One extended benefit of the doubt.

Each decision feels minor in isolation. Easy to explain away. Easy to rationalize.

But over time, those small allowances compound. They reshape your standards, weaken your discipline, and quietly redefine what you are willing to accept.

Eventually you are no longer choosing your path—you are reacting to it.

Your decisions begin to reflect what you have already tolerated.
Your expectations lower without you realizing it.
What once felt wrong begins to feel familiar.
And what becomes familiar soon becomes acceptable.

The Proven Man breaks this cycle.

He understands that discipline is not defined only by what he does, but by what he refuses.

He refuses to normalize inconsistency.
He refuses to justify behavior that contradicts alignment.
He refuses to remain in dynamics that require him to abandon his standards in order to maintain connection.

Because the Proven Man understands a simple truth:

Every standard he upholds strengthens his direction.
And every standard he compromises slowly erodes it.

VI. The Cost of Misalignment

The wrong relationship rarely looks destructive in the beginning.

It looks exciting.
It looks promising.
It feels like something that could become meaningful.

Early on there is enough chemistry, enough connection, and enough potential to keep you engaged. Nothing seems clearly wrong—which is exactly why it is easy to stay.

But over time, a man begins to pay the cost.

His focus fragments as more of his attention is pulled into managing the dynamic.

His energy drains, not all at once, but gradually, through repeated moments of inconsistency and imbalance.

His emotional state begins to fluctuate with the highs and lows of the connection.

And his progress slows, as energy that should be directed toward his mission is redirected into something that is not building with him.

This rarely happens through one dramatic event.

It happens through subtle misalignment.

Small compromises.
Repeated adjustments.
A slow drift away from clarity.

Without realizing it, a man begins adjusting instead of advancing.

Reacting instead of building.
Maintaining instead of growing.

His role shifts quietly, from someone moving with purpose to someone managing instability.

And the most dangerous part is that it feels normal while it is happening.

The gradual nature of the shift makes it difficult to recognize in real time.

What would have once stood out as misalignment now blends into the background.

He adapts to it.
He works around it.
He accepts it.

The pattern was there all along.

Until eventually the Proven Man sees the truth:

He has been investing time, focus, and energy into something that was never aligned to begin with.

And time is the one resource he cannot recover.

Misalignment always collects its cost.

VII. The Reward of Alignment

The Proven Man understands that choosing alignment is an investment in his future. It requires patience and discipline in the short term, but it compounds in ways that shape the course of his life and legacy.

The right choice is never about a temporary win or a fleeting connection. It is about building a foundation strong enough to support growth, purpose, and shared direction over time.

While the wrong choice often appears exciting in the beginning—filled with chemistry, intensity, or novelty; the right choice reveals its strength gradually. It is steady. It is consistent. And with time, it deepens.

Alignment strengthens the Proven Man's energy instead of scattering it. It reinforces his direction instead of distracting from it. What begins as stability becomes momentum.

Momentum is not created by intensity.
It is created through consistency.

At first, choosing alignment can feel like sacrifice, especially when the pull of immediate excitement is strong. But what the Proven Man leaves behind is not something valuable. He leaves behind the noise of inconsistency, emotional volatility, and wasted focus.

And what he gains is far greater:

Clarity.
Stability.
Mutual support.

The true reward of alignment is freedom.

Freedom to build without constant disruption.
Freedom to focus without emotional turbulence.
Freedom to invest energy into something that multiplies rather than drains.

A relationship built on alignment becomes an amplifier. Both partners contribute. Both partners grow. Both partners strengthen the direction they are moving together.

Instead of managing instability, the Proven Man moves forward with purpose. His attention is no longer consumed by uncertainty. His energy is directed toward building a life that compounds over time.

With the right partner beside him, the relationship does not merely feel good; it strengthens everything he is creating. This is the standard he builds toward.

Every moment spent in alignment reinforces the path toward his legacy.

And over time, what once required discipline becomes something more powerful:

Momentum.

The right choice no longer feels like sacrifice.

It feels like clarity.
It feels like strength.
It feels like building the life he was meant to lead.

VIII. The Standard Is Not Attraction—It's Alignment

The Proven Man does not evaluate relationships based on how they feel in the moment. He evaluates them based on what they consistently produce over time: reciprocity, stability, and direction.

He understands that feelings can be immediate, powerful, and convincing. But emotion alone is not a reliable indicator of long-term alignment.

Instead of getting pulled into emotional intensity, the Proven Man steps back and observes what is actually being demonstrated.

Does the behavior remain consistent, or does it fluctuate?
Is the effort mutual, or one-sided?
Is the connection stable, or does it rely on emotional highs to sustain itself?
And most importantly, is there a clear direction, or does the relationship remain undefined?

These questions anchor him in reality.

He asks himself:

Does this dynamic strengthen me, or distract me?
Does it create clarity, or confusion?
Does it move me forward, or keep me in place?

By focusing on what the relationship consistently produces, he sees beyond momentary emotion into its true direction.

Because the Proven Man understands something most men overlook:

Not everything that feels good is good for him, and not everything that feels intense is real.

IX. The Pattern Principle

Every misaligned dynamic shares one core trait: Inconsistency.

It may appear in different forms, through inconsistent effort, emotional stability, support, or direction. But the underlying pattern remains the same.

At first, inconsistency is easy to overlook. It is often spaced out, softened by moments of intensity, or disguised by temporary alignment. One good interaction can blur three unclear ones. One strong moment can make you question what you have already observed.

Over time, the pattern becomes undeniable.

Inconsistency is not randomness; it is a signal. It reveals a lack of grounding, a lack of clarity, and a lack of true alignment. No matter how strong the emotional highs may feel, they cannot compensate for what is missing between them.

Because over time, inconsistency always leads to one thing:

Instability.

And instability is where everything begins to break down.

You cannot build momentum when the foundation keeps shifting.
You cannot create trust when behavior is unpredictable.
You cannot move forward when direction keeps changing.

The Proven Man understands this at a fundamental level.

He does not get distracted by moments; he studies patterns.
He does not anchor himself to potential; he anchors himself to consistency.

Because the Proven Man knows:

You cannot build a legacy on unstable ground.
Consistency is the only foundation that holds.

X. Alignment Dynamics

Misaligned dynamics always reveal themselves through inconsistency.

The aligned partner is different.

She is not defined by intensity, excitement, or even initial chemistry. She is defined by consistency, alignment, and contribution over time.

Where others fluctuate, she stabilizes.
Where others consume, she contributes.
Where others distract, she aligns.

Her presence is not built on emotional spikes or fleeting moments. It is built on steady, reliable behavior over time. You are not left guessing where you stand or pulled between extremes. What you see is what continues.

She does not pull you off your path.
She walks it with you.

With her, effort is mutual. There is no imbalance where one carries while the other coasts. Both invest. Both show up. Both contribute.

Direction is shared. You are not moving in parallel or in conflict, you are building toward the same outcome.

Growth is continuous. The relationship does not stall or regress; it evolves as you both do.

Most importantly, energy is multiplied, not drained. What you give is not lost; it is reinforced, returned, and expanded.

This is what makes her rare, not because she is perfect or without flaws,
but because she is aligned and consistent.

The Proven Man recognizes this difference quickly.

He does not overlook her because she feels calm instead of intense.
He does not mistake stability for lack of chemistry or chase volatility while ignoring alignment.

What lasts does not announce itself loudly. It reveals itself through consistency, presence, and the absence of confusion.

Because the Proven Man has the discipline to see clearly, he does not pass her by.

He chooses her—every single day.

XI. The Standard of Alignment

The Proven Man no longer evaluates women based on how they make him feel in the moment. He evaluates based on what endures.

He understands that feelings can be immediate, intense, and convincing, but they are not always reliable indicators of what is sustainable or real.

So he watches patterns over time, not isolated moments. He pays attention to consistency under pressure, not just behavior when things are easy. And above all, he measures alignment with his mission because anything that conflicts with his direction will eventually cost him more than it gives.

His standard is simple.

He does not chase intensity.
He does not tolerate instability.
He does not settle for comfort without direction.

His standard is not based on emotion; it is based on outcome. He chooses based on what builds.

Because he understands a truth most men learn too late:

The woman you choose will either multiply your life—or divide your focus.
Every relationship either strengthens your direction or slowly erodes it.

There is no neutral.

XII. The Proven Man Decision Map

Once you understand the patterns that appear in relationships, you begin to recognize them quickly.

The Proven Man does not evaluate connections based on isolated moments or emotional intensity.

Instead, he observes what a relationship consistently produces.

This simplifies what often feels complicated by revealing the direction a relationship is consistently moving toward. Over time, the pattern becomes difficult to ignore.

With enough time, every relationship dynamic reveals its direction. Most misaligned relationships eventually move toward chaos, extraction, or stagnation.

Only one outcome consistently builds something lasting:

Alignment.

These four outcomes form the underlying structure of how the Proven Man evaluates relationships.

XIII. The Alignment Question

Every relationship dynamic you encounter reveals something, not about women, but about what you are willing to accept in your life.

Each dynamic you engage in reflects your standards, whether you recognize it or not. What you tolerate, what you justify, and what you allow to persist shape both your relationships and your identity. Over time, these choices either reinforce your clarity, or quietly blur the path you are walking.

By now, the question has already been established:
"Does this align with the life I'm building?"

The difference is no longer whether you ask it, but whether you act on the answer.

Most men hesitate at this point.

They recognize misalignment, but delay the decision.
They justify what they see.
They wait for change instead of responding to what is already clear.

The Proven Man does not.

He understands that clarity without action is meaningless. When something does not align, he does not negotiate with it. He does not reinterpret it. He does not allow time to blur what has already been revealed.

He acts.

Not from impulse, but from structure.
Not from emotion, but from standards.

Because alignment is not defined by what you recognize, it is defined by what you accept or refuse to accept.

And in the end, the relationships you choose do more than shape your experiences.

They shape the life you build.

XIV. Seeing the Pattern Clearly

Behavior rarely appears as a single, isolated trait. Over time, patterns combine, repeat, and reinforce one another, forming recognizable dynamics that shape the direction of a relationship.

What feels complex in the moment becomes clear when viewed through pattern recognition.

The structures outlined here are not labels. They are recurring behavioral combinations that reveal how instability forms, how energy is directed, and where a dynamic leads.

The Proven Man does not attempt to interpret every moment. He steps back and observes the pattern as it forms.

When the pattern is clear, direction is no longer uncertain.

Viewed together, these recurring dynamics form a clearer map of where relationships ultimately lead.

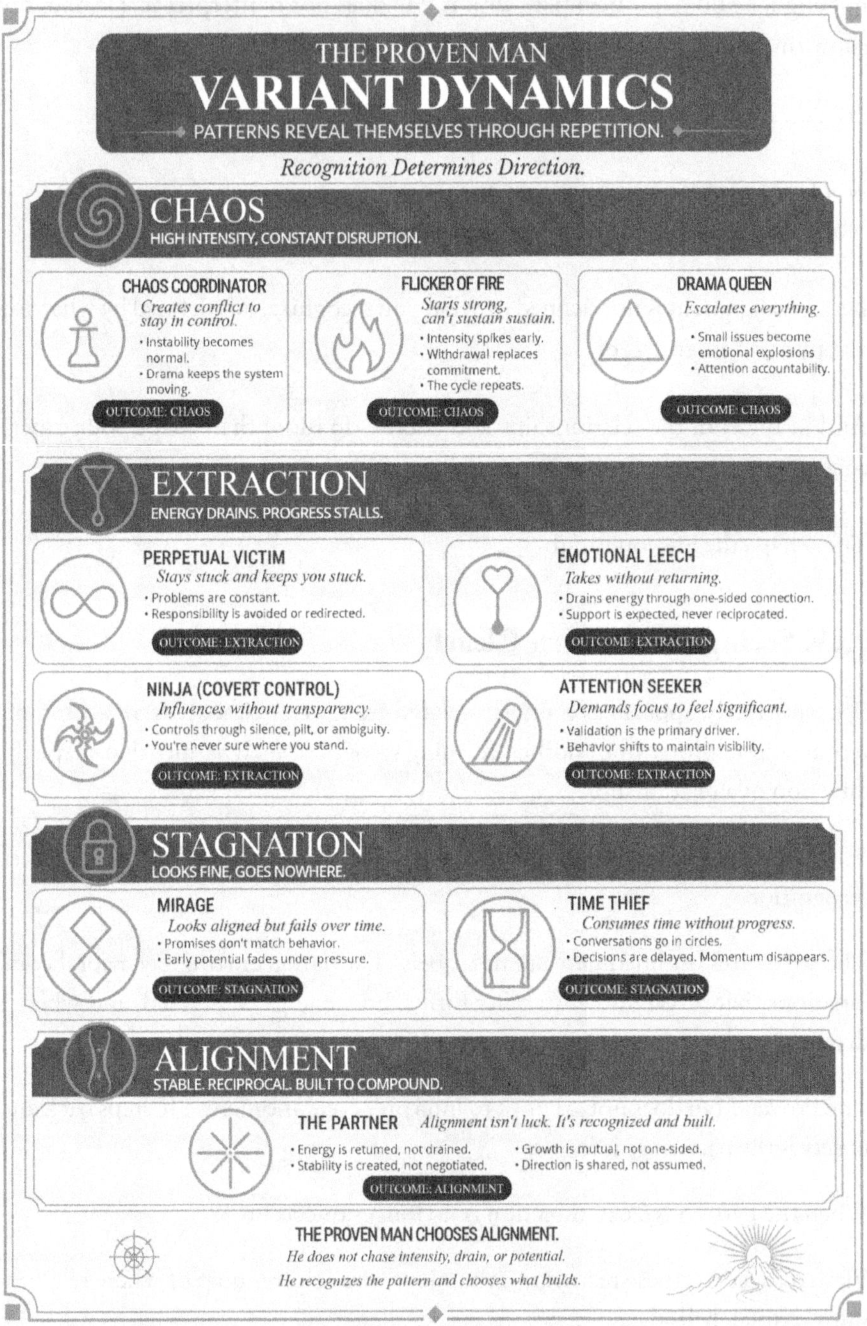
THE PROVEN MAN
VARIANT DYNAMICS
PATTERNS REVEAL THEMSELVES THROUGH REPETITION.
Recognition Determines Direction.
CHAOS
HIGH INTENSITY, CONSTANT DISRUPTION.
CHAOS COORDINATOR
Creates conflict to stay in control.
• Instability becomes normal.
• Drama keeps the system moving.
OUTCOME: CHAOS
FLICKER OF FIRE
Starts strong, can't sustain sustain.
• Intensity spikes early.
• Withdrawal replaces commitment.
• The cycle repeats.
OUTCOME: CHAOS
DRAMA QUEEN
Escalates everything.
• Small issues become emotional explosions
• Attention accountability.
OUTCOME: CHAOS
EXTRACTION
ENERGY DRAINS. PROGRESS STALLS.
PERPETUAL VICTIM
Stays stuck and keeps you stuck.
• Problems are constant.
• Responsibility is avoided or redirected.
OUTCOME: EXTRACTION
EMOTIONAL LEECH
Takes without returning.
• Drains energy through one-sided connection.
• Support is expected, never reciprocated.
OUTCOME: EXTRACTION
NINJA (COVERT CONTROL)
Influences without transparency.
• Controls through silence, pilt, or ambiguity.
• You're never sure where you stand.
OUTCOME: EXTRACTION
ATTENTION SEEKER
Demands focus to feel significant.
• Validation is the primary driver.
• Behavior shifts to maintain visibility.
OUTCOME: EXTRACTION
STAGNATION
LOOKS FINE, GOES NOWHERE.
MIRAGE
Looks aligned but fails over time.
• Promises don't match behavior.
• Early potential fades under pressure.
OUTCOME: STAGNATION
TIME THIEF
Consumes time without progress.
• Conversations go in circles.
• Decisions are delayed. Momentum disappears.
OUTCOME: STAGNATION
ALIGNMENT
STABLE. RECIPROCAL. BUILT TO COMPOUND.
THE PARTNER
Alignment isn't luck. It's recognized and built.
• Energy is returned, not drained.
• Stability is created, not negotiated.
• Growth is mutual, not one-sided.
• Direction is shared, not assumed.
OUTCOME: ALIGNMENT
THE PROVEN MAN CHOOSES ALIGNMENT.
He does not chase intensity, drain, or potential.
He recognizes the pattern and chooses what builds.

Chapter Distillation

Clarity is not created by attraction.

It is created through observation.

The Proven Man understands that relationships reveal themselves through patterns, not promises. A moment of chemistry may capture attention, but only consistent behavior reveals whether something is truly aligned.

Because of this, he does not rush to conclusions or allow emotional intensity to determine his decisions. He observes what repeats. He watches how someone shows up over time. And he measures every dynamic against the direction of the life he is building.

Where others chase feelings, he recognizes patterns.
Where others react to moments, he evaluates outcomes.

Through this discipline, relationships become easier to understand.

Patterns reveal what attraction often hides.

When a man learns to see these patterns clearly, attraction no longer controls his decisions.

Clarity does.

And from that clarity, the Proven Man chooses only what strengthens the life he is building.

This is where proof becomes discipline.

Not in what a man prefers—but in what he consistently allows or refuses.

When he enforces his standards without hesitation, that is proof.
When he removes himself from patterns that erode his direction, that is proof.
When he chooses long-term alignment over short-term comfort, that is proof.

Clarity has already revealed what is real.

Now his standards determine what stays.

What he consistently enforces becomes the structure of his life.

Attraction captures attention.
Patterns reveal direction.

Over time, every relationship dynamic moves toward one of four outcomes:

Chaos
Extraction
Stagnation
Alignment

The Proven Man does not chase emotional intensity. He observes what the connection consistently produces.

Because the relationships a man chooses do more than shape his experiences.

They shape his direction, his energy, and the life he builds.

The Proven Man Principle

Alignment compounds.

Everything else drains.

Chapter Five

Standards

What You Accept Defines Your Life

In the previous chapters, you learned how to recognize patterns—to see beyond surface-level attraction and observe what behavior actually reveals over time. Recognition alone, however, does not change outcomes in relationships, environments, or the dynamics a man allows to continue in. Awareness without action leaves a man in the same cycles, only with clearer vision.

This is where standards become non-negotiable.

Standards convert awareness into decision. They form the internal structure that determines what you allow to continue, and what you end. Without them, you may recognize misalignment and still remain in it. You may see inconsistency yet continue to rationalize it. You may understand the pattern but still lack the discipline to disengage from it.

The Proven Man does not operate that way.

He understands a simple principle:

Patterns establish.
Standards decide.

Standards close the gap between observation and action. They eliminate hesitation, remove emotional negotiation, and protect him from investing in what he already knows is wrong.

Without standards, clarity becomes useless. A man can see everything and still choose nothing.

Standards must be enforced.

Standards are not simply principles to understand. They are behaviors practiced until they become instinct.

This discipline later becomes one of the core pillars of what I call **The Proven Man System**.

The Proven Man moves differently. He does not drift through experiences hoping things will eventually align. He moves with intention. He responds with clarity rather than impulse. Instead of waiting indefinitely for situations to prove themselves, he evaluates them against what he already understands to be true.

When something does not meet that standard, he does not argue with it, attempt to fix it, or reinterpret it.

He removes himself from it.

This is not rigidity; it is self-respect.

Standards are often misunderstood as control, as rules meant to shape another person's behavior. In reality, they serve a different purpose. Standards do not govern other people. They govern the man who holds them. They define how he engages, what he tolerates, and where he invests his time and energy.

They are not loud.
They are not performative.
They are demonstrated through action.

The Proven Man does not need to explain his standards or justify his boundaries. His behavior communicates them clearly. What he continues, and what he walks away from defines how others engage with him.

Because of this, his presence carries weight.

His decisions are not driven by momentary attraction, emotional highs, or temporary connection. He does not confuse chemistry with compatibility, or intensity with alignment. Every interaction passes through a single lens:

What does this build?

Because he understands something most men overlook:

Attraction creates urgency.
Emotion creates attachment.
Standards create stability.

Without standards, a man moves toward what feels good in the moment. With standards, he moves toward what is actually good for him over time.

That distinction changes everything.

Standards protect his time by eliminating distractions early. They protect his energy by preventing over-investment in unstable dynamics. They protect his direction by ensuring that what he engages with actually supports where he is going.

They simplify decision-making and remove unnecessary complexity. As a result, he moves through relationships without confusion, second-guessing, or emotional overextension.

The Proven Man does not chase clarity through experience. He does not require repeated lessons to confirm what he already sees.

He creates clarity through standards.

Once those standards are defined, decisions become simple.

He understands that his resources are limited: his focus, his time, and his energy. Because of this, he treats them with precision. He does not give them away based on potential, emotion, or temporary connection.

He invests them where alignment exists.

Nothing else qualifies.

This changes how he moves, and how others respond. He no longer seeks validation or overextends to maintain connection. He no longer tolerates what he already knows does not align.

He evaluates and decides.

Because of that, he does not chase.

He attracts—not through effort, but through clarity.

People feel his standards without him needing to state them. They either rise to meet them or fall away naturally. He does not attempt to control either outcome.

Alignment requires nothing forced.

Anything forced is already misaligned.

The Proven Man does not try to make things work.

He chooses what already does.

And that is what separates him, not only in relationships, but in everything he builds.

I. Why Standards Matter

Standards are not suggestions.
They are structure, and they are enforced.

They are the boundaries that anchor the Proven Man's behavior, especially in moments when emotion, attraction, or external pressure attempt to pull him off course. Without these internal guardrails, even clear thinking is compromised. Emotional discipline weakens, non-neediness becomes situational, and decisions begin to drift toward what feels good in the moment rather than what remains right over time.

Awareness alone is not enough to protect him. He may recognize misalignment and still tolerate it. He may see inconsistency and continue to engage with it.

Standards eliminate that gap.

They act as a filter, ensuring that what he sees is matched by what he does. They prevent over-investment in relationships, situations, or dynamics that do not align with his vision, and they keep him grounded when emotion attempts to override judgment.

Emotion is not the problem.
Lack of structure is.

Standards provide that structure. They separate reacting to circumstances from responding with clarity. Without them, a man becomes reactive, adjusting to behavior, chasing stability, and negotiating with situations that should never have been accepted in the first place.

With them, decision-making becomes simpler.

Doubt, overanalysis, and emotional attachment no longer dominate the process.

Decisions become clear.

The Proven Man does not guess his way through interactions or rely on time to confirm what he already sees. He moves with an internal map, one that applies across every area of his life. Whether in relationships, friendships, or his purpose, his standards remain consistent. They define how he engages, what he invests in, and what he walks away from.

One of the most immediate ways standards shape his life is by preventing over-investment.

Without standards, it is easy to give too much: time, attention, and energy invested in something that has not earned it. This usually happens gradually. A small inconsistency is ignored. A lack of reciprocity is rationalized. Effort becomes one-sided, yet instead of pulling back, a man leans in further, attempting to correct, stabilize, or prove value.

The Proven Man does not fall into that pattern.

He recognizes when something drains rather than builds and when effort is not matched. Instead of compensating for imbalance, he disengages early, before his energy becomes entangled in something unproductive.

He does not chase alignment.

He invests where alignment already exists.

This is not detachment.

It is precision.

His awareness of patterns, combined with his standards, allows him to protect his time and energy without hesitation. When direction is already clear, he does not require extended proof. He trusts what behavior reveals, and he acts accordingly.

Standards also create clarity in decision-making. Most confusion does not come from complexity; it comes from a lack of internal criteria. When a man does not know what he stands for, every situation requires analysis. Every interaction feels uncertain. Instincts are questioned. Decisions are second-guessed. Over time, that hesitation produces emotional fatigue.

The Proven Man does not operate in that state.

His standards function as an internal compass. They remove ambiguity and eliminate the need for constant evaluation.

When he encounters a situation, he does not ask how he feels in the moment.

He asks a simpler question:

Does this align?

If the answer is no, the decision is already made.

There is no overthinking.
No emotional negotiation.
No internal conflict.

Just clarity.

That clarity allows him to move forward with confidence, not because outcomes are guaranteed, but because his standards are certain.

And that certainty changes how he is perceived.

Standards do not only protect the Proven Man; they shape how others experience him.

He does not announce boundaries or attempt to convince others of his worth. The way he moves makes his standards visible. What he accepts, and what he does not shapes how others engage with him.

People recognize this quickly. They see that his time is not easily accessed, that his attention is not casually held, and that his presence is not given without alignment.

Two outcomes follow.

People rise to meet that standard, or they fall away.

He does not manage either outcome.

He allows it.

Because both serve him.

A simple example illustrates this.

Imagine interacting with someone who makes a subtle criticism disguised as humor during conversation. In that moment, you see how tension is introduced, how it is handled, and what is revealed beneath the surface. Without standards, it is easy to rationalize the behavior. You might assume it was harmless, unintentional, or simply part of her personality. You overlook it, remain agreeable, and continue the interaction without addressing what was actually expressed.

The question becomes whether that moment stands alone, or reflects a pattern.

The Proven Man does not ignore the possibility that it reflects a pattern. He recognizes what is being expressed and evaluates it accordingly. Rather than accommodating the behavior, he adjusts his investment. He remains grounded, observes consistency over time, and, if it reveals a pattern that fails to align with his standards, he disengages.

Not emotionally.
Not reactively.
Decisively.

There is no need for confrontation, frustration, or extended explanation.

His response is simple.

He no longer participates in what does not meet his standard.

That decision communicates everything.

Standards shape more than behavior.
They shape internal state.

When the Proven Man is aligned with his standards, his energy remains stable. There is no tension between what he sees, and what he does. His decisions feel clean. His focus stays intact. He experiences clarity: groundedness, and control over where his energy is directed.

There is no internal conflict.

Only alignment.

When standards are compromised, the shift is immediate. Energy tightens, decisions become reactive, and a subtle imbalance emerges, as if something is off even when it cannot yet be fully explained. A man feels himself adjusting, compensating, or overextending in ways that do not feel natural.

That feeling is not random.

It is misalignment.

The Proven Man does not ignore it. He treats it as information. It signals the need to recalibrate; return to the standard and make the decision he already understands is necessary.

Because in the end, standards are not only about what a man accepts.

They determine the quality of everything he experiences.

And the Proven Man ensures that quality is never left to chance.

II. What Standards Really Are

Standards are not arbitrary rules or surface-level preferences. They are the internal criteria by which the Proven Man evaluates every interaction, every relationship, and every investment of his time and energy. They are rooted in something deeper than attraction or convenience: his values, his discipline, and the vision he holds for his life.

Without standards, even the most self-aware man becomes vulnerable to drift. He may recognize patterns, but recognition alone does not prevent misalignment or protect him from emotional pull, inconsistency, or distraction.

Standards convert awareness into structure.

They ensure that clarity leads to action.

For the Proven Man, standards are not flexible depending on mood or circumstance. They are stable, defined, and lived. They form the foundation that allows him to move through life with certainty, knowing what aligns, what does not, and what requires no further negotiation.

They are not something he explains.

They are something he embodies.

Because of this, interactions become simpler, not necessarily easy, but clear. He is no longer evaluating situations from scratch. Instead, he measures them against a standard that already exists.

The Core Elements of Standards

At their core, standards are not about perfection in others. They are about consistency, alignment, and reality over time. The Proven Man understands that anyone can show up well in isolated moments. What matters is how someone shows up repeatedly across situations, especially when it is inconvenient or uncomfortable.

Behavioral Consistency

The Proven Man does not get distracted by isolated moments of attention, affection, or effort. He understands that a single moment proves nothing. Anyone can perform temporarily, and anyone can show up well when it benefits them.

What matters is what consistently repeats.

He watches how someone behaves over time, how they treat him, how they treat others, and how they show up when there is no immediate reward for doing so.

He asks whether their behavior remains stable, whether it holds under pressure, and whether it remains aligned in both public and private.

Because he understands a simple truth:

Consistency is not a trait.
It is a pattern.

Patterns do not lie.

Where others become attached to moments, he stays grounded in repetition. He does not build expectations on exceptions; he builds understanding on what is sustained.

Energy Alignment

The Proven Man treats his energy as a finite and valuable resource. Because of this, he does not ignore how interactions affect him, he studies it.

Not intellectually.
Experientially.

He pays attention to what happens after an interaction, not only during it. Does he feel clear, focused, and grounded—or drained, distracted, and mentally scattered?

Energy is not abstract.

It is measurable through experience.

Alignment is not only about shared interests or surface compatibility. It is about whether the dynamic strengthens him, or slowly depletes him over time.

If someone consistently pulls him into emotional instability, confusion, or unnecessary processing, he does not rationalize it or try to force it to work. He recognizes the pattern as misalignment.

No matter how compelling something feels in the moment, if it consistently drains him, it is working against his direction rather than supporting it.

Emotional Availability

The Proven Man does not chase surface-level connection. He requires depth, not in intensity, but in presence, stability, and mutual engagement.

He understands that real connection is not built through occasional vulnerability or emotional spikes. It develops through consistent openness, mutual effort, and the ability to remain present when interactions become real.

He pays attention to how someone responds when conversations require honesty, when tension arises, or when emotional depth is necessary.

Do they lean in or pull back?
Do they communicate or avoid?
Do they engage or disappear?

The Proven Man also understands that people process difficult conversations differently. Some respond immediately, while others need time to reflect before returning with clarity. He respects that difference. What matters is not the speed of the response, but the willingness to return to the conversation with honesty and engagement.

Without emotional availability, connection becomes fragmented. It turns into cycles of closeness and distance, engagement and withdrawal, clarity and confusion.

Over time, that instability erodes trust.

The Proven Man does not try to pull depth from someone who cannot sustain it. He recognizes the limitation and adjusts his investment accordingly.

Shared Values

Attraction can create momentum.
Shared values create direction.

The Proven Man does not evaluate alignment based solely on chemistry, excitement, or short-term compatibility. He looks deeper at how someone thinks, how they prioritize, and how they approach life over time.

Do they value growth?
Do they respect discipline?
Do they take responsibility for their actions?
Do they move with intention or react to circumstances?

Without shared values, even strong attraction eventually creates friction. The conflict may not appear immediately, but it emerges over time through decisions, priorities, and the way life is approached once novelty fades.

The Proven Man does not wait for that friction to fully develop. He observes the direction early and decides accordingly.

He does not attempt to force alignment where it does not exist.

The Internal Filter: Questions That Create Clarity

The Proven Man does not rely on guesswork. He uses direct questions to cut through emotional noise and maintain clarity in real time, not to overanalyze, but to remain aligned.

One question anchors long-term awareness:

Would I feel proud integrating this person into my life?

This question shifts focus away from temporary feelings and toward integration into his environment, his values, and his future. If the answer feels uncertain, that uncertainty becomes information.

Misalignment rarely feels obvious at first.

But it almost always feels uncertain.

Another question keeps him anchored in direction:

Does this behavior align with what I'm building?

This prevents him from getting pulled into short-term emotional experiences that do not support his long-term vision. It allows him to evaluate behavior not by how it feels in the moment, but by what it produces over time.

Anything that consistently pulls him away from his path, no matter how engaging, is a liability.

The Purpose of Standards

For the Proven Man, standards are not restrictions.

They are refinement.

They simplify decisions, eliminate confusion, and remove the need for constant emotional negotiation. They allow him to move through life with precision, engaging fully where there is alignment and disengaging cleanly where there is not.

He does not argue with reality.

He recognizes it.

He does not chase potential.

He responds to patterns.

Because in the end, standards are not about controlling outcomes.

They are about controlling direction.

And direction, repeated over time, becomes the life a man lives.

III. External vs. Internal Standards

External standards are everywhere. They come from culture, social expectations, peer groups, family dynamics, and the constant noise of comparison. They attempt to define how you should behave, what you should tolerate, and what success, attraction, or validation is supposed to look like. On the surface, they can feel useful, like guidance or social calibration.

In reality, however, they are unstable.

They shift depending on who you are around, what environment you are in, and what pressures are being applied in the moment.

When a man operates from external standards, he becomes reactive by default. His behavior adjusts to maintain approval, and his decisions become influenced by perception rather than alignment. Over time this creates a subtle dependency in which his sense of direction is no longer self-defined but externally reinforced.

He begins measuring himself through feedback instead of truth.

And the result is inevitable:

Disconnection from his own identity.

External standards are not only distracting; they are destabilizing. They pull attention outward and create pressure to conform, accommodate, and be liked rather than aligned. When this happens, compromise becomes easier, not because it makes sense, but because it feels socially acceptable in the moment.

This is how men drift.

Not through dramatic mistakes, but through small, repeated decisions made to maintain comfort instead of clarity.

The Proven Man recognizes this pattern early, and rejects it.

Internal standards operate differently.

They are not shaped by the environment; they determine how a man moves through it. They are built deliberately through self-awareness, experience, values, and long-term vision.

They are not reactive.

They are anchored.

Because of this, internal standards create stability under pressure. When situations become emotionally charged, uncertain, or tempting, the Proven Man does not need to figure out what to do in the moment.

He already knows.

His standards have already defined the boundary. The decision is not emotional.

It is structural.

This is what separates clarity from confusion.

A man grounded in internal standards does not negotiate with pressure. He does not bend to urgency or override long-term alignment for short-term reward. His decisions remain consistent because they are not recalculated in real time.

They are expressions of identity, not reactions to circumstance.

This is where self-respect becomes visible.

Internal standards eliminate the need for validation because they replace it with certainty. The Proven Man does not look outward to confirm his value.

He expresses it through his choices.

He does not seek approval.

He filters for alignment.

That shift changes everything. His energy stabilizes, his focus sharpens, and his interactions become intentional rather than exploratory.

The difference is not subtle.

It is foundational.

When pressure appears, the contrast becomes clear.

External standards ask: How will this be perceived?
Internal standards ask: Is this aligned?

That single distinction determines direction.

Over time, someone begins requesting more of your time—interrupting your schedule, expecting immediate responses, and gradually shifting the balance of attention within the relationship.

If you are operating from external standards, the pull is immediate. You may feel pressure to accommodate, avoid tension, or maintain approval. You adjust your behavior, rationalize the pattern, and compromise—not because it aligns, but because resistance feels more difficult in the moment.

The Proven Man interprets the situation differently.

He does not see pressure.

He sees information.

The pattern becomes clear: a disregard for boundaries and a misalignment in respect for time and structure. Instead of reacting emotionally, he responds through his standard. He does not become defensive or over-explain his reasoning. He simply reinforces the boundary through action, maintaining his schedule, communicating clearly, and refusing to reorganize his life around inconsistency.

There is no friction in this decision.

Because it was never a negotiation.

This is the power of internal standards. They remove ambiguity and allow the Proven Man to move through interactions with calm authority, not because he is rigid, but because he is clear.

He is not attempting to control outcomes.

He is controlling alignment.

That distinction creates a different kind of presence, one that does not seek validation, yet naturally commands respect.

Because in the end, the real question is not what the world expects of you.

It is whether you are grounded enough to move independently of it.

IV. Standards in Real Interactions

Standards are rarely tested in obvious or dramatic moments. They are tested quietly and consistently through small interactions that most men overlook: a delayed response, a canceled plan, a dismissive tone, or a shift in effort. Individually these moments may seem insignificant, but together they form patterns. Within those patterns, the truth of the dynamic becomes visible.

The Proven Man understands this. He does not wait for situations to become extreme before paying attention. Every interaction provides feedback. Every behavior offers information. Moments that challenge his boundaries are not invitations for emotional reaction but opportunities to reinforce his standards with clarity.

He does not interpret these moments personally.

He interprets them structurally.

Because what is being tested is not simply his patience.

It is his self-respect.

When faced with inconsistent attention, most men feel the urge to compensate. They lean in harder, give more, and adjust their behavior in an attempt to restore balance. Their focus gradually shifts away from their own direction and toward her responses.

The Proven Man does the opposite. He notices when effort is not sustained, and adjusts his investment accordingly. He does not chase what fluctuates and does not invest where effort is unstable. Instead, he steps back, not out of frustration, but out of clarity. His attention remains directed toward his own life, his own momentum, and his own standards.

He understands something many men overlook.

Attention that must be chased is not alignment.

It is imbalance.

When confronted with disrespect or boundary violations, the distinction becomes even clearer. Without standards, a man begins negotiating with behavior that should never be negotiated. He rationalizes it, adjusts to it, and tolerates it—creating internal conflict because part of him recognizes that he is compromising himself simply to maintain the interaction.

The Proven Man does not operate this way. He does not escalate emotionally or attempt to control the situation. Instead, he becomes clear. He asserts his boundary calmly, without tension, explanation, or the need for validation. If the behavior continues, he disengages.

No drama.

No negotiation.

No loss of composure.

Because he understands a simple truth.

Respect is not something you convince someone to give.

It is something you require through your standards.

Misaligned intentions create a quieter but equally important test. Without standards, it is easy to become pulled into potential, into chemistry, into possibility, into what something could become rather than what it is. A man may overlook inconsistencies or ignore misalignment simply to preserve the connection.

The Proven Man evaluates the situation differently. He does not prioritize how something feels in the moment. He evaluates what it builds over time. He asks whether the direction aligns, not only the experience. When it does not, he does not attempt to force the situation into place.

He lets it go.

Without hesitation.

Because misalignment does not resolve through time.

It compounds.

Energy Cue

Alignment with standards produces a recognizable internal state. When a man's actions match his standards, his energy remains steady and grounded. His thinking is clear, his focus remains intact, and there is no urgency to control outcomes because his decisions are anchored in something stable—his own standards.

When those standards are compromised, the shift becomes immediate. Energy tightens. Thoughts become reactive. Focus fragments as he attempts to stabilize a situation that cannot be stabilized. It feels like constantly adjusting to maintain balance within a dynamic that lacks stability.

The Proven Man recognizes this signal immediately.

He does not ignore it.
He corrects course.

Because your energy will often reveal misalignment before your mind is willing to acknowledge it.

V. How Standards Reinforce Emotional Self-Control

Standards are not only about who you allow into your life.

They are about how you govern yourself within it.

The Proven Man understands that emotional self-control is not achieved through suppression. It is achieved through structure, and that structure comes from standards. Without standards, decisions become emotional, interactions become reactive, and outcomes begin to feel uncertain.

With standards, the dynamic changes.

Decision-making becomes clearer. Responses become intentional. Emotions lose their ability to dictate behavior because the framework guiding action is already established.

Standards Reduce Internal Conflict

One of the greatest sources of emotional instability is indecision. When a man lacks clear standards, he negotiates with himself constantly. He questions his instincts, overrides his judgment, and remains in situations longer than he should—trying to rationalize what he already senses is misaligned.

This creates friction.

The Proven Man eliminates that friction at its source. His standards determine direction before his emotions become involved. When something misaligns, there is no internal debate, no second-guessing, and no rationalization.

The decision is already made and he simply executes it. This is what creates calm—not the absence of challenge, but of confusion.

Standards Allow Selective Investment

Time, focus, and energy are finite resources. Most men spend them reactively, investing based on attraction, emotion, or temporary engagement. They often give too much too early, and frequently to the wrong dynamics.

The Proven Man invests differently. He observes first, evaluates patterns, and aligns before he commits. His standards function as a filter that directs his energy toward what is consistent, reciprocal, and aligned with his vision.

This is not distance—it is discernment.

Because of that precision, he avoids the emotional depletion that comes from over-investment in unstable dynamics.

Standards Strengthen Non-Neediness

Non-neediness is not a technique.

It is a byproduct of clarity.

When a man lacks standards, he seeks validation externally. He chases attention, adjusts himself to maintain connection, and allows his stability to depend on how others respond to him.

When his standards are clear, that dependency disappears. He no longer needs approval because he already has direction. He does not chase connection because he engages only where alignment exists. He does not fear loss because he does not attach to what fails to meet his standards.

This creates a different presence entirely: grounded, composed, and unshaken.

Paradoxically, this stability often increases his attractiveness. Not because he is attempting to create that effect, but because he is no longer operating from need.

Consider a dynamic where the interaction is smooth, engaging, and seemingly aligned, but small moments begin to reveal a lack of consideration. Plans are agreed to, but not prioritized. Commitments are acknowledged, but not consistently honored. What is said and what is demonstrated begin to diverge.

Most men overlook these signals. The overall experience feels positive, so the inconsistencies are minimized or explained away. They focus on how the interaction feels rather than what it consistently shows.

The Proven Man responds differently.

He steps back and observes the pattern clearly. He does not rely on isolated moments of connection. Instead, he evaluates whether behavior consistently reflects what is being communicated.

If it does not, he acts, not impulsively, not emotionally, but decisively.

He may reduce his investment, establish a boundary, or disengage entirely. Whatever action he takes, it comes from clarity rather than reaction.

Energy Cue

Alignment with standards produces a distinct internal state. When a man's actions match his standards, his energy feels calm, controlled, and certain. There is no urgency to act, no pressure to respond, and no fear of losing something that was never stable to begin with.

Compromise produces the opposite effect. It creates urgency, uncertainty, and reactivity. A man feels as though he is trying to stabilize something that cannot hold.

The Proven Man pays attention to this distinction.

Because emotional self-control is not about forcing yourself to feel less. It is about structuring your life so you do not have to fight yourself.

VI. Discipline Within Standards

Standards alone are not enough. They are principles, but without discipline they remain theoretical. The Proven Man understands that standards only have power when they are upheld consistently, especially in the moments when it would be easier to compromise.

Those are the moments that matter most.

Discipline is what turns clarity into action. It allows him to hold his ground when attraction is high, when emotions are involved, or when external pressure is present. Without discipline, even strong standards can erode under the weight of convenience, desire, or temporary comfort. With discipline, they become stable and reliable.

The Proven Man does not rely on how he feels in the moment to guide his behavior.

He relies on what he has already decided is aligned.

Maintaining that alignment requires deliberate engagement with himself. Self-awareness forms the foundation. He pays attention to his internal state, not casually, but intentionally. He notices when something feels off, when his energy shifts, or when he feels the impulse to act in a way that contradicts his standards.

Instead of ignoring that signal, he addresses it directly. He asks himself a simple question:

Is this aligned—or am I about to compromise?

That question interrupts reactive behavior and brings him back to intention.

From there, he observes. He does not rush to conclusions or attach labels too quickly. He allows behavior to reveal itself over time, watching patterns rather than promises. He notices how someone responds under pressure, how they handle inconsistency, and how they show up when it is inconvenient.

Behavior reveals itself through repetition.

Not isolated moments.

Because he understands this, he gives himself the space to see clearly before deciding where to invest.

When it comes time to act, he is decisive. The Proven Man does not stall in uncertainty or hide behind overthinking. He evaluates honestly:

Does this align with what I am building—or not?

If it does, he engages fully. If it does not, he steps back without hesitation. There is no need for dramatics or explanations beyond what is necessary. His decisions remain clean because they are rooted in clarity rather than emotion.

Above all, he is consistent.

Consistency is where discipline becomes visible. It is easy to maintain standards when there is no pressure. It is easy to speak about alignment in theory. Discipline reveals itself when a situation becomes tempting, unclear, or emotionally charged, and he still holds the line.

He does not bend based on who he is dealing with.

He does not adjust his standards to maintain connection.

He does not negotiate with misalignment.

Because he understands something many men learn too late.

Every time you compromise your standards, you weaken your identity.

Every time you uphold them, you reinforce it.

Over time, he begins to notice a pattern. When situations are easy, the interaction feels aligned, communication is smooth, and connection is natural. But when priorities conflict or inconvenience arises, the dynamic shifts. Commitments are deprioritized, boundaries are tested, and what was once consistent begins to adjust under pressure.

Without discipline, this is where many men become pulled into the dynamic. They focus on how things feel when they are easy, overlooking what is revealed when they are not. They justify the behavior, assume the earlier version of the interaction is the "real" one, and continue investing based on moments rather than patterns.

The Proven Man approaches the situation differently.

He steps back and observes the pattern for what it is, not what it appears to be under ideal conditions.

He recognizes that alignment is not revealed when everything is convenient, but when it is not. Instead of focusing on isolated moments, he evaluates how consistency holds under pressure.

When it becomes clear that alignment does not sustain itself, he adjusts his behavior accordingly.

He may reduce his investment.
He may disengage entirely.

Not out of frustration—
But out of alignment.

His actions are not reactive.

They are corrective.

That distinction changes everything.

Energy Cue

When discipline is present, his energy reflects it. He feels steady, grounded, and clear because his actions remain consistent with his standards. There is no internal negotiation and no second-guessing about what he already knows is misaligned.

When discipline weakens, the shift becomes immediate. His energy tightens and his thinking becomes reactive. He finds himself trying to justify behavior that does not sit right or attempting to rationalize what is already clear.

That tension is not confusion.

It is misalignment.

The Proven Man listens to that signal. He understands that discipline is not simply about self-control; it is about maintaining alignment through action.

He does not uphold his standards occasionally.

He upholds them consistently.

Because standards define the path.

And discipline is what keeps him on it.

VII. The Power of Standards

Standards are not barriers.
They are direction.

They do not exist to limit life, restrict options, or create distance between you and others. They exist to direct you, to anchor you, and to ensure that the time, energy, and attention you invest actually lead somewhere meaningful.

The Proven Man understands this clearly. He does not view standards as something that takes away freedom. He recognizes them as the very structure that protects it. Without standards, every interaction becomes negotiable, every emotion becomes persuasive, and every moment has the potential to pull him off course.

Standards eliminate that drift.

They function as the internal compass by which he navigates relationships, decisions, and personal growth. Because that compass is internal, it does not shift with circumstance, attraction, or external pressure.

It remains steady.
And that steadiness is the power of his standards.

When standards are clear, an important shift occurs.

Non-neediness becomes natural.

The Proven Man no longer feels compelled to chase validation, approval, or attention—not because he forces himself to detach, but because his value is no longer dependent on outcomes. His self-worth is anchored internally rather than externally.

He is not trying to win people over.
He is evaluating alignment.

That shift changes everything. He enters interactions from a position of strength rather than lack. He is not seeking to be chosen.

He is choosing.

Because of this, his presence carries a different weight. It is grounded, certain, and unforced.

He does not need to prove value.
He lives it.

Standards also strengthen emotional control—not by suppressing emotion, but by giving it structure. The Proven Man still experiences attraction, interest, disappointment, and frustration. Emotion remains present, but it does not dictate his behavior.

It informs him.
It does not lead him.

Because his standards are already in place, they act as an anchor in moments when most people lose balance. Whether he experiences praise or rejection, excitement or uncertainty, he remains centered—not detached, but disciplined.

He responds instead of reacts.

That distinction allows him to move through situations with clarity rather than volatility.

Standards also sharpen his ability to distinguish between alignment and attention.

Many men confuse the two. They chase what feels good in the moment—validation, excitement, recognition—without asking what it actually builds over time.

The Proven Man filters everything through a different lens.

He asks a simple question:

Does this align with what I am building?

If the answer is no, the feeling does not matter.

Because attention is easy to obtain.
Alignment is rare.

And only one of them builds something real, so he stops chasing what is temporary, and chooses what is sustainable.

VIII. Standards Under Pressure

The Proven Man uses his standards as a framework for how he lives, not only for how he dates, interacts, or responds. They shape his decisions, protect his energy, and define his direction. Every choice he makes either reinforces his identity or weakens it, and he is intentional about which one he is strengthening.

When standards are clear, several things become undeniable. Choices become cleaner. Energy becomes steadier. Presence becomes stronger. A man no longer moves through life reacting to whatever happens around him; he moves through it aligned with what matters.

That distinction is what makes the difference.

Not effort.
Not intensity.
Not perception.

Alignment.

Once standards are established, the next challenge is no longer defining them; it is maintaining them. The real test is not clarity in isolation but clarity under pressure. Desire will test you. Attraction will test you. Emotion will test you. In those moments, what you do matters more than what you know.

This is where non-neediness begins to take form, not as detachment or indifference, but as freedom. It is the freedom that comes from no longer needing a specific outcome, from no longer seeking validation, and from refusing to compromise yourself simply to maintain connection.

The Proven Man does not suppress what he feels.

He refuses to let it override what he knows.

That balance—between emotional presence and disciplined action—is what separates reactive men from grounded men. It allows him to remain centered regardless of circumstance, because he is not anchored to the moment.

He is anchored to himself.

With that foundation established, the next step becomes clear:

Understanding non-neediness—not merely as a concept, but as a way of operating. Because this is where discipline becomes identity.

Chapter Distillation

Standards are not restrictions.
They are structure.

They create the internal boundary that protects a man from being shaped by attraction, emotion, or external pressure. Without them, decisions drift with circumstance. With them, direction becomes stable.

Standards determine direction.

They protect energy.

Without them, attraction, emotion, and external pressure shape a man's decisions. With them, every interaction becomes easier to evaluate.

The Proven Man does not rely on motivation or momentary clarity to guide his actions. His standards already define what belongs in his life and what does not.

Because of this, he does not negotiate with misalignment.

He observes it.
He recognizes it.
And when necessary, he releases it.

The Proven Man does not measure relationships by how they feel in the moment.

He measures them by whether they align with the life he is building.

Standards simplify decisions.

This is where proof compounds.

Not in a single decision—but in what holds.

When his standards remain consistent, that is proof.
When alignment strengthens instead of fading, that is proof.
When what he builds continues to reinforce his direction, that is proof.

Time does not create clarity.
It reveals it.

And over time, what remains aligned becomes undeniable.

Standards shape the life a man ultimately builds.

Because attention is temporary. Alignment is structural.

And only one of them builds something lasting.

The Proven Man Principle

Standards protect alignment.

Alignment protects direction.

Chapter Six

Non-Neediness

The Power of Releasing the Outcome

Non-neediness is the ability to engage fully without becoming attached to the outcome. It is the freedom to interact from a position of certainty rather than pressure, where actions are guided by self-respect instead of the need for validation.

Over time, you begin to notice a pattern in how priority is expressed. When it is convenient, the interaction is present, engaged, and responsive. But when something else demands attention, the dynamic shifts. Plans are adjusted, communication slows, and your place becomes secondary.

Without discipline, this is often where the situation is misread. A man focuses on moments of attention, assuming they reflect overall importance. They rationalize the inconsistency, believing the connection is stronger than what is consistently demonstrated.

The Proven Man approaches the situation differently.

He does not evaluate priority based on isolated moments. He observes how time and energy are consistently allocated. He understands that priority is not expressed through words or intention, but through consistent action.

When it becomes clear where he stands, he responds accordingly.

He may reduce his investment.
He may disengage entirely.

Not out of reaction—
but out of clarity.

Because priority is not claimed.
It is demonstrated.

Most men misunderstand neediness. They assume that as long as they are not chasing, begging, or acting desperate, they remain in control. In reality, neediness is rarely loud. It operates internally, appearing as subtle dependence on someone's response, approval, or continued interest.

The Proven Man recognizes this distinction. His power comes from the fact that he does not require the interaction for validation. He is already anchored. Because of this, he does not attempt to force outcomes.

He allows outcomes to unfold.

At its core, non-neediness is not detachment from people.

It is detachment from dependency.

The Proven Man can engage deeply, but he is never emotionally reliant. He connects by choice rather than by need, and that difference changes the quality of every interaction.

That is what gives him presence.

And that presence allows him to maintain control, without force.

I. Understanding True Neediness

Neediness is not desire.
It is dependence.

It appears the moment a man's emotional state becomes tied to someone else's behavior: their response, their attention, or the outcome of the interaction. The shift is subtle, but it changes his position. Instead of remaining grounded, he becomes reactive.

The Proven Man does not allow this shift.

His emotional center is self-contained. Whether an interaction progresses smoothly or becomes uncertain, he remains steady. He does not chase clarity or seek reassurance.

He notices.

In another moment, the dynamic may shift.

You maintain a standard, something simple, but clear. You do not overextend, accommodate unnecessarily, or shift your position to preserve the interaction.

The response changes.

There is either respect for the boundary, subtle resistance to it, or a quiet withdrawal from the interaction altogether.

Without discipline, this is often where adjustment begins. They soften their position, reintroduce flexibility, or attempt to reengage in order to restore the dynamic.

The Proven Man does not.

He observes the response for what it is. He understands that how someone reacts to his standards reveals their alignment with them. He does not interpret resistance as something to manage or overcome.

He recognizes it as information.

From there, he responds accordingly.
He may maintain the interaction.
He may reduce his investment.
He may disengage entirely.

Not out of reaction—but out of alignment.

Because standards do not require agreement.
They reveal it.

Non-neediness creates space. It allows a man to remain present, grounded, and unaffected by uncertainty.

This is not indifference.
It is self-control.

The Proven Man engages fully, but he does not attach himself to what happens next. His presence remains calm, his energy steady, and his decisions aligned with his standards rather than the emotional pressure of the moment.

That is where his stability comes from.

Understanding the idea is only the beginning.

The real challenge is recognizing how neediness appears in subtle ways, often when it is least obvious.

II. Subtle Signals of Neediness

Neediness is rarely obvious. It does not appear as dramatic behavior or overt desperation. Instead, it emerges through small, almost invisible shifts in how a man thinks, responds, and carries himself. Left unchecked, these shifts gradually pull him away from a grounded position.

The Proven Man is aware of this dynamic. He understands that neediness is not defined only by what is said, but by what is felt internally. It lives beneath the surface in quiet dependence on someone else's response, attention, or approval.

These signals appear in small, often unnoticed shifts.

A man may begin replying faster than usual, not from intention, but from urgency. The response is no longer natural; it becomes driven by the need to maintain momentum or hold attention.

He may start overthinking his next message. Instead of speaking directly, he begins calculating, predicting reactions, adjusting wording, and attempting to shape the outcome. Expression gives way to control.

Sometimes the shift appears in how he presents himself. He adjusts his tone, humor, or opinions to match what he believes the other person wants. In doing so, he moves away from authenticity and toward approval.

It can also appear as over-explaining. A man adds unnecessary detail to justify his actions or intentions, not for clarity, but for reassurance.

In other cases, he begins managing the interaction itself, anticipating responses, planning ahead, and mentally staying several steps in front of the moment. His attention leaves his own life and becomes fixed on the interaction.

Individually, these behaviors appear minor. Taken together, however, they form a pattern. That pattern gradually reinforces internal dependence, tying a man's emotional state to what someone else does next.

The Proven Man recognizes this early. He does not wait until the behavior becomes obvious or exaggerated. He notices the internal shift, the moment his focus moves from grounded presence toward controlling the outcome.

And he corrects it.

He does not force himself to appear less interested. He does not play games or create artificial distance.

He returns to himself.

This shift is often easiest to recognize in the moment it happens.

You're in the middle of an interaction and catch yourself adjusting, shifting your tone, choosing words more carefully, trying to keep the other person engaged.

The Proven Man notices the shift.

Not the interaction itself—
but the intention behind it.

He recognizes the moment his attention moves toward the outcome. Instead of continuing down that path, he resets his position, returning to clarity, authenticity, and presence.

Because he understands a simple principle.

The moment you shape yourself for the outcome, you lose your position.

Non-neediness is not maintained through effort.
It is maintained through awareness.

And the more aware a man becomes, the less space there is for neediness to take hold.

III. The Core Cause

At the heart of neediness is a single belief:
The outcome matters more than your grounded position.

The moment this belief takes hold, everything shifts. Focus moves away from standards, clarity, and self-respect, and toward the result. A man begins measuring his value by what happens next rather than by who he is within the moment.

This is where the shift begins.

The mind quietly moves away from presence and begins calculating outcomes. Attention drifts toward what the other person might think, how the interaction might unfold, or what must be done to keep momentum moving forward.

Once making it work becomes the objective, internal leverage is reduced.

This is the turning point.

Clarity is replaced with urgency.
Self-respect is replaced with negotiation.
Presence is replaced with control.

Even if nothing is said directly, the shift is felt.

The Proven Man operates differently. He does not assign his worth to outcomes. Instead, he remains anchored in his identity, his standards, and his direction, regardless of what unfolds externally.

He does not treat the moment as something that needs to be secured.

He treats it as something to observe.

Because he understands a simple truth.

If it aligns, it will continue.
If it does not, forcing it only delays the truth.

His position does not change based on the situation. His worth is not tied to attention, approval, or continuation. He remains steady, clear in who he is regardless of what happens next.

Because of that stability, he can engage fully without needing the outcome to define him.

IV. Why Neediness Breaks Attraction

Attraction is rooted in perception. It is influenced not only by what a man says or does, but by how he carries himself under uncertainty. The way he feels internally, whether steady or unsettled, shapes the dynamic of the interaction.

Neediness alters that internal state. It introduces subtle signals of dependence, scarcity, often expressed through urgency, and instability that are sensed before a word is analyzed.

The Proven Man understands this. He knows attraction is not built through effort but revealed through presence. Presence, however, collapses the moment he becomes attached to the outcome.

Dependence

When a man relies on someone else's attention or approval to feel grounded, he communicates dependence. It appears through subtle shifts in energy and behavior.

His emotional state begins to follow the other person's responses. Clarity becomes conditional. Confidence becomes reactive.

The result is imbalance.

In conversation, this may appear as subtle checking, watching for reactions, adjusting tone in response to shifts, or seeking confirmation that the interaction is still "on track."

Dependence carries expectation. It silently asks the other person to stabilize him, and that pressure is often felt immediately.

The Proven Man does not place that weight on anyone. His emotional state is self-sustained. He does not require reassurance to remain steady, and because of this, his presence feels light, grounded, and unforced.

That quality naturally draws people in.

Scarcity

Neediness often emerges from scarcity: the belief that a particular moment, person, or opportunity must be held onto.

That belief introduces urgency. A man begins managing the interaction, attempting to preserve it. He becomes careful instead of clear, and the tension created by that shift is often noticeable.

Scarcity repels because it signals fear of loss.

This can appear in small ways, holding onto a moment too tightly, trying to extend an interaction that has naturally concluded, or prioritizing the continuation of the connection over clarity about what it actually is.

The Proven Man operates from a different perspective. He understands that alignment is not rare; it reveals itself as the pattern develops. Because of this, he does not cling to a single outcome or depend on a specific interaction.

If alignment exists, the connection continues.
If it does not, he allows it to pass.

This absence of urgency creates an energy that feels calm, confident, and naturally attractive.

Instability

At the core of neediness lies instability. When a man's emotional state depends on external validation, he cannot remain steady when uncertainty appears. Instead of observing the situation, he begins reacting to it.

That reaction communicates something clearly:

His foundation is external.

The Proven Man operates from a different foundation.

He remains anchored internally. His state does not fluctuate based on response, timing, or outcome. When uncertainty arises, he does not rush to resolve it or search for immediate reassurance.

He is already stable.

That stability creates something uncommon.

Safety without pressure.

People respond to it because it feels grounded, calm, and real.

This pressure is often revealed in small moments.

A man mentions a trip he would like to take someday. The response is minimal.

That silence creates internal tension. He begins filling the space, adding explanations, justifying why the place matters, or softening his enthusiasm in an attempt to keep the conversation moving forward.

What began as a simple statement gradually turns into explanation, reassurance, or adjustment.

But what is being communicated in that moment is not simply enthusiasm.

It is pressure.

The Proven Man responds differently. He notices the pause, but he does not rush to fill it. He allows the moment to exist without attempting to control it.

He remains steady.

There is no need to clarify, no urge to rescue the moment, and no need to secure agreement.

His position remains the same whether the response comes immediately or after reflection.

That steadiness communicates confidence more clearly than words ever could.

The Energy Shift

Neediness is not primarily about behavior.

It is about pressure.

Even when unspoken, it is felt through subtle signals such as urgency to respond, heightened sensitivity to changes in behavior, or the desire to control the direction of the interaction.

Each of these signals gradually weakens attraction.

The Proven Man protects his internal state. He does not react to uncertainty; he allows it. He does not chase clarity; he takes in what is happening. He does not attempt to force connection; he creates the space for it to form naturally.

Because of this, his presence feels calm, grounded, and unattached.

Within that space, genuine attraction can develop.

Neediness does not simply weaken attraction.
It disrupts it.

Attraction thrives in stability, independence, and self-assured presence. The Proven Man does not seek attention or approval to feel secure.

He remains grounded in his own worth.

From that position, connection can form without pressure, without force, and without dependency.

V. Wanting vs. Needing

The difference between wanting and needing is subtle, but it defines everything.

The Proven Man understands that desire is natural. He can want someone. He can enjoy connection, feel attraction, and engage fully in the moment. There is no suppression in him and no distance from the experience itself.

He allows himself to feel.

But he is never dependent on the outcome.

That is the line.

When he is wanting, he engages freely. His presence remains grounded, his actions unpressured, and his emotional state stable regardless of what unfolds. He is present because he chooses to be, not because he needs something from the interaction.

There is no urgency behind his behavior and no attempt to secure a result. He allows the connection to develop at its natural pace.

Wanting feels expansive. It creates space for both people to exist without pressure or expectation, keeping his attention grounded in the present rather than projecting forward.

Needing begins when the outcome shifts from being preferred to being required.

At that point, desire tightens into attachment. Attention moves away from the present and toward anticipation. A man begins adjusting his behavior, subtly guiding the interaction toward a specific result.

What once felt natural becomes calculated, and in that shift, he loses his grounding.

Needing carries a different internal state. It feels tight, reactive, and controlled. Emotional stability begins to rise and fall with the other person's responses. What may appear externally as strong interest often reflects something else entirely: attachment disguised as intensity.

At its core, needing is an attempt to control reality in order to stabilize one's emotional state.

But the more control a man attempts to impose, the less stable he becomes.

The distinction ultimately comes down to a simple contrast.

Attachment focuses on what happens next.
Presence remains grounded in what is happening now.

The Proven Man remains present. He does not measure the success of an interaction by its outcome but by whether his behavior remains aligned with who he is. He does not chase a result.

He watches without interference.

Wanting creates space.
Needing creates pressure.

He chooses to remain in that position, engaged, open, and fully present without becoming dependent on what happens next.

Because the moment presence is replaced by attachment, the interaction stops revealing truth and begins reflecting pressure instead.

VI. Dependency on Outcome

The more a man depends on a specific outcome, the less control he has over his behavior.

When an emotional state becomes tied to a result, actions are no longer guided by clarity; they are driven by fear. Fear of losing the connection, fear of missing an opportunity, or fear of not being enough. In that state, a man is no longer grounded.

He is reacting.

The Proven Man understands this dynamic clearly. He does not attempt to control outcomes because he recognizes that the need for control is rooted in insecurity, not strength. Instead, he remains anchored in what is his to control: his actions, his standards, and his direction.

He observes rather than interferes.

This distinction becomes most visible in moments of uncertainty. When communication shifts or behavior becomes inconsistent, the impulse to regain control can arise quickly. There is a pull to fix the situation, adjust behavior, or restore certainty.

Most people follow that impulse.

The Proven Man does not.

He pauses and notices the reaction without immediately acting on it. Rather than trying to correct the situation, he steps back and evaluates it. He asks whether what he is experiencing aligns with his standards instead of trying to force the situation into alignment.

This is where his power remains intact.

Dependency on outcome is, at its core, attachment, the belief that emotional stability depends on what happens next. It creates internal pressure, clouds judgment, and pulls attention away from clarity and into reactivity.

Detachment, however, is not indifference.

It is stability.

The Proven Man does not disengage from life or connection. He simply refuses to allow any outcome to determine his internal state. Uncertainty is a natural part of interaction, and he remains steady within it.

Reactive energy feels rushed, anxious, and outcome-focused. That state constantly attempts to close the gap between what is happening and what is wanted.

Grounded energy operates differently. It is calm, observant, and self-contained. It does not rush to resolve uncertainty; it allows truth to reveal itself over the course of interactions.

That is where clarity emerges.

When the Proven Man is not dependent on the outcome, he becomes more present, more precise, and more aligned in his actions. He is no longer trying to secure something. He evaluates what is actually present.

From that position, he regains full control of himself.

And that control does not come from forcing outcomes.
It comes from remaining anchored in who he is.

VII. From Chasing to Selecting

Non-neediness restores clarity.
It shifts the focus from chasing to selecting.

The Proven Man does not move through interactions hoping to be chosen. He moves through them deciding what is worthy of his time, attention, and energy. This is the fundamental shift: from chasing to selecting.

Most people approach interactions from a place of uncertainty, asking themselves, *Do they like me?* That question alone places their sense of value outside of themselves. It creates a subtle dependence on external validation and gradually shifts behavior toward seeking approval.

The Proven Man replaces that question entirely.

He asks a different one:

Do I like what I'm seeing?

That shift changes everything.

It returns attention to where it belongs, his standards, his values, and his long-term direction. Instead of negotiating for interest or attempting to maintain attention, he lets the interactions unfold over time and evaluates it with clarity.

He looks for consistency rather than intensity.
He looks for alignment rather than potential.
He looks for patterns rather than moments.

Because he understands a simple principle: attraction without consistency creates instability, and interest without alignment becomes distraction.

This is where many people lose themselves. They react to flashes of attention, overlook inconsistency, and invest in what they hope something will become rather than what it actually is.

The Proven Man plans his life forward, but he does not project outcomes onto an interaction.

He reads what is present.

If something is inconsistent, he notices. If something feels misaligned, he acknowledges it. He does not ignore signals in order to preserve the interaction, and he does not adjust himself to force something that does not naturally align.

He simply chooses.

Chasing is reactive. It is driven by urgency, uncertainty, and the need for validation. It attempts to secure attention and hold onto it.

Selecting is different.

It is grounded, deliberate, and self-directed. It does not attempt to convince.

It evaluates.

That distinction is felt immediately. When a man selects rather than chases, he is no longer operating from fear of loss. He is operating from clarity of standards. His energy becomes focused and intentional rather than scattered or dependent.

Because of this, he does not over-invest. He does not force connections. He does not remain where alignment is missing.

He moves forward without hesitation.

Because his energy is not something he gives away freely.

It is something he invests—carefully, intentionally, and only where it is returned.

Selection requires patience.
Without it, clarity is easily replaced by urgency.

VIII. Patience in Practice

Non-neediness is sustained through patience.

Without patience, interactions collapse back into urgency, control, and subtle dependence on outcomes.

The Proven Man understands that clarity does not come from forcing movement. It comes from allowing time to reveal what is true. He does not rush interactions, decisions, or emotional conclusions. Instead, he remains steady enough to allow situations to unfold without interference.

This is not passivity.

It is discipline.

In this context, patience is the ability to hold one's position without reacting to uncertainty. It is the decision to remain grounded when there is no immediate answer, no defined direction, and no guaranteed outcome.

Most people struggle with this stage.

Uncertainty creates pressure, and that pressure often leads to action, labeling the interaction, escalating it prematurely, or seeking reassurance to regain a sense of control.

The Proven Man does not follow that impulse.

He stays with the process.

He does not rush to define what something is. Instead, he allows patterns to emerge before drawing conclusions. Where others seek immediate clarity, he recognizes that premature definition often distorts reality.

What is real does not need to be forced into form.

It reveals itself with time.

He also avoids forcingg progression. There is no need to accelerate connection, push for intensity, or create momentum where it does not naturally exist. He engages fully in the interaction, yet he allows the pace to remain organic.

If something grows, it grows.
If it stalls, he notices without reacting.

He does not interfere to manufacture an outcome.

Because forcing progression is still a form of neediness.

Instead, he watches behavior, not isolated moments, words, or temporary emotion, but patterns. He allows time to reveal consistency or inconsistency. Time becomes a filter, and he trusts that process.

This is where patience becomes internal strength for the Proven Man.

While others react to short-term fluctuations, he remains anchored. He does not chase clarity.

He allows clarity to arrive.

The distinction is subtle but decisive. Urgency narrows attention, speeds decisions, and creates tension around what might be lost.

Patience creates space. It expands awareness, slows reaction, and keeps attention grounded in what is actually unfolding.

That shift is felt.

When a man operates with patience, his energy feels calm, observant, and self-contained. There is no pressure behind his actions and no attempt to force resolution. He remains present while remaining unattached to timing.

Because of that, he sees more clearly.

Consider a situation where interest exists but consistency does not. The instinct for most people is to define the interaction—to ask where things stand, push for clarity, or attempt to stabilize uncertainty.

Often, however, that action is driven by discomfort rather than alignment.

The Proven Man takes a different approach.

He does not chase answers or rush definition. Instead, he continues forward, focused on his own direction while observing what unfolds. If consistency develops, he recognizes it. If inconsistency remains, he sees that clearly as well.

Either way, he does not force the truth.

It reveals itself.

This is why patience is not weakness.

It is control without force.

Patience requires the ability to tolerate uncertainty without collapsing into reaction. It requires trust in one's standards, direction, and willingness to walk away when alignment is absent.

As it becomes clear, that patience produces something most people rarely access:

Clarity without confusion.
Connection without pressure.
Decisions made from certainty rather than fear.

The Proven Man does not rush what matters.

He allows truth to prove itself.

IX. Real-Time Examples

The shift does not happen in theory. It happens in small moments—in pauses, reactions, and internal impulses that most people never question. These moments reveal the difference between neediness and grounded presence.

The Proven Man recognizes them as they occur.
Not afterward.
In the moment.

Attention vs Intent

There is consistent communication. Engagement is present. The interaction feels active, messages are exchanged, interest appears mutual, and attention is given freely.

But nothing moves forward.

Plans remain undefined. Direction is unclear. The interaction continues, but it does not develop.

Subtle tension begins to form. The activity feels like progress, so it is treated as such. Time and attention are invested under the assumption that movement is occurring.

More quietly, attention begins to follow the interaction, checking for responses, anticipating engagement, and maintaining momentum that does not exist.

The Proven Man does not confuse activity with direction.

He observes whether the interaction develops over time. He does not assign meaning to attention alone, and he does not invest further in something that remains undefined through repetition.

Because attention can simulate alignment.

But only direction confirms it.

Reaction to Your Standards

You maintain a standard—something simple, but clear. You do not overextend, accommodate unnecessarily, or shift your position to preserve the interaction.

The response changes.

There is either respect for the boundary, subtle resistance to it, or a quiet withdrawal from the interaction altogether.

This moment creates pressure. The instinct is to adjust, to soften the position, reintroduce flexibility, or restore the previous dynamic.

The Proven Man does not do this.

He notices the impulse to preserve the interaction.

And he holds his position.

He understands that how someone responds to his standards reveals their alignment with them. He does not interpret resistance as something to manage or overcome.

He recognizes it as information.

From there, he responds accordingly.

Not out of reaction—
but out of alignment.

Attraction Intensity

Strong initial attraction creates momentum. The interaction feels natural, engaging, and effortless. Energy is high, and the connection appears immediate.

In that moment, the shift does not happen externally.

It happens internally.

Attention begins to move forward, past what is happening now and toward what the interaction could become. The mind starts to project, imagining progression, anticipating outcomes, and assigning value to what has not yet been established.

From there, the impulse appears.

To define it.
To secure it.
To ensure it continues.

Most people follow that impulse.

They invest quickly, escalate early, and attempt to turn potential into something established.

The Proven Man does not.

He recognizes the shift away from the present moment.

And he returns to it.

He allows attraction to exist without attaching it to a future outcome. He does not assign meaning to intensity alone, and he does not move to secure something that has not yet proven itself through time.

Because attraction is not the signal.

Consistency is.

And until that consistency exists, there is nothing to secure.

Priority Placement

There are moments when the interaction feels strong—engaged, attentive, and present. Time is given, conversation flows, and interest appears clear.

But over time, a pattern begins to form.

Engagement appears when it is convenient. It is displaced when something else takes priority. Plans shift. Attention moves.

The stronger moments begin to carry more weight. They are used to define the interaction, while inconsistency is minimized or explained away.

The Proven Man does not do this.

He observes how time and energy are consistently allocated.

He does not measure importance by isolated moments of attention, but by where he is consistently placed.

Because priority is not expressed occasionally.
It reveals itself over time.

Silence After Momentum

The interaction has been consistent. Engagement is present. Conversation flows easily, and momentum builds naturally over time.

Then it stops.

There is no clear signal of disinterest. No conflict. No visible shift, only silence where engagement once existed.

This moment creates internal pressure. Attention tightens. The mind begins searching for explanation, replaying what was said, anticipating what might come next.

The impulse appears quickly.

To reach out.
To re-engage.
To restore momentum before it is lost.

The Proven Man does not react impulsively to that feeling.

He notices the reaction, not the silence itself, but the need to resolve it immediately.

He does not rush to restore momentum simply to relieve discomfort.

Because the urge to restore momentum is not driven by clarity.
It is driven by discomfort.

From that position, he remains steady.

He does not force continuation.
He observes first—then responds when clarity emerges.

Across these situations, the pattern remains the same.
Neediness reacts.
Grounded presence observes.

Neediness tries to control the outcome.
Grounded presence allows the outcome to reveal itself.

This is the dividing line.

The more a man searches outward for signals, what she thinks, how she responds, or where the interaction is going, the more unstable he becomes. His actions begin to follow external cues, and his sense of self-control weakens.

The Proven Man moves differently.

He remains anchored internally. His actions are guided by his standards rather than by moment-to-moment fluctuations. He does not require immediate answers to remain steady, and he does not depend on a specific outcome to maintain his position.

Because his stability is not conditional.
It is established.

And in that shift, something changes.
He is no longer trying to manage the interaction.
He is simply experiencing it—clearly, fully, and without dependence.

X. Anchoring Through Internal Standards

Non-neediness does not come from willpower.

It comes from structure.

A man who lacks an internal anchor will inevitably drift toward external validation. His attention follows whatever appears in front of him, and his emotional state rises and falls with each interaction.

The Proven Man operates differently.

He is anchored before the interaction ever begins.

His life is organized around priorities that remain stable: his standards, his direction, and his routines. Because of this, no single person or moment has the power to destabilize him. He does not need to remind himself to stay grounded during an interaction.

He already is.

This is where non-neediness becomes natural. It is not something he performs in the moment.

It is something his life supports.

Internal standards create that foundation. They define how he spends his time, where he invests his energy, and what he is willing—or unwilling—to adjust.

These standards do not fluctuate with emotion. They remain steady and guide his decisions without hesitation.

Because of this, he does not reorganize his life around an interaction.

He integrates the interaction into a life that is already in motion.

If interest appears but remains inconsistent, he notices it without reacting. He does not shift his schedule, redirect his focus, or place his attention where it has not yet been earned. Instead, he continues forward with the priorities he has already established.

This is where many people lose their position.

They begin with structure but abandon it the moment something emotionally engaging appears. Priorities become negotiable, focus becomes scattered, and attention becomes reactive.

With that shift, neediness returns.

The Proven Man does not make that trade.

His routines remain intact. His direction remains clear. His time continues to be invested in what builds his life rather than in managing uncertainty.

Because of this, his energy remains consistent.

He is not passive.

He is selective.

When he engages, he does so fully, but never at the cost of what grounds him. If something aligns, it earns a place within his world. If it does not, he does not attempt to force it to fit.

This is what creates stability.

Not control over others—
but control over self.

The Proven Man remains anchored in that position.

In practice, the approach is straightforward. His days are structured around what matters. His focus remains directed rather than scattered. His sense of direction does not shift based on attention, attraction, or temporary emotion.

Because of that, no single interaction, no matter how promising or uncertain, carries disproportionate weight.

It cannot define him.

The more a man builds his life around internal standards, the less he depends on anything external to feel grounded. He no longer looks to interactions for stability, because stability is already established.

From that position, something changes.

He is free to engage without attachment.
To connect without dependence.
To walk away without hesitation.

Because his life is not built around the interaction.

The interaction exists within his life.

That is the difference.

XI. Practicing Non-Neediness

Non-neediness is not something a man understands once and carries with him effortlessly. It develops through repeated moments of awareness, restraint, and self-control. It is not about controlling other people or shaping outcomes to fit a desired result. It is about maintaining control over one's internal state regardless of what is happening externally.

The Proven Man does not concern himself with managing perception or securing validation. His focus remains on his position—how he thinks, how he responds, and whether he remains grounded when faced with uncertainty. When his position is stable, his behavior does not require management.

It follows naturally.

This is where many men lose their footing. Not in obvious moments, but in subtle ones, such as a delayed response, a shift in tone, or a change in energy. These situations create internal pressure. Attention narrows, emotions rise, and the impulse to act appears.

To say something.
To fix something.
To regain control of the interaction.

The difference is not whether the impulse appears.
The difference is what happens next.

The Proven Man notices the reaction, but does not act on it immediately. He allows the moment to exist without assigning meaning to it. Instead of reacting, he regulates himself first. His emotional state is not dictated by a single interaction, and uncertainty does not disrupt his stability.

From that position, he observes.

He does not rush to interpret behavior or force clarity where none exists. He understands that patterns reveal themselves over time and that premature conclusions are often driven by emotion rather than truth. Because he is not dependent on immediate answers, he remains patient without tension.

This patience creates space.

Within that space, he evaluates.

The Proven Man asks whether what is being experienced aligns with his standards, his values, and his direction. If it does, he continues without over-investing. If it does not, he adjusts without resistance. There is no need to force progression or hold onto uncertainty, because his direction does not depend on the outcome.

This is how internal stability develops.
Not through perfect interactions, but through consistent self-trust.

A man knows that no matter what unfolds, he will not compromise his position in order to secure a result. He does not rush progression, and he does not interfere with the natural pace of connection.

The Proven Man allows time to reveal what effort cannot.

This way of operating becomes natural. His presence remains steady regardless of external fluctuation. There is no urgency in his actions and no subtle pressure beneath his words. He remains engaged without attachment, aware without reactivity, and grounded even when the situation itself is uncertain.

This is what separates him.

While others are pulled by uncertainty, the Proven Man remains anchored.
While others seek validation, he operates from it internally.
While others attempt to secure connection, he allows connection to prove itself.

At this level, non-neediness is no longer something consciously practiced.

It becomes who he is.

Chapter Distillation

Neediness is rarely obvious. It does not reveal itself through dramatic words or visible desperation. Instead, it operates quietly beneath behavior and language, appearing as tension, anticipation, and subtle dependence on how something unfolds. It is felt the moment a man's emotional state begins to shift in response to another person's attention, behavior, or approval.

That is where it lives—

Not in what he says,
but in what he relies on.

The shift away from neediness is just as subtle, but far more powerful. It begins the moment a man detaches from the outcome. The Proven Man is not free because he avoids connection or suppresses desire.

He is free because his sense of self is not tied to what happens next.

He can engage fully, speak clearly, and connect deeply without requiring the interaction to unfold in a particular way.

His presence is not controlled or constructed.

It is the natural result of internal clarity.

He does not create distance to manufacture intrigue, and he does not move closer to secure attention. He does not adjust himself to influence perception, nor does he hold back to maintain control.

There is no performance in how he shows up.

He remains consistent.

Steady in his behavior.
Clear in his direction.
Unaffected by what he cannot control.

Because of this, his actions are no longer driven by the need to obtain something from the moment. They come from a position that is already complete.

This is where real control begins—

Not in forcing outcomes,
but in no longer being controlled by them.

When a man stops needing a result, pressure disappears.
Tension dissolves.

He no longer reacts or adjusts himself to secure something uncertain. Instead, he operates with a calm certainty that does not rise or fall with the interaction.

In that state, everything changes.

He becomes more present.
More direct.
More grounded in what he chooses rather than in what he fears losing.

This is why non-neediness is not the absence of desire.

It is the absence of dependence.

The Proven Man still wants.
He still engages.
He still connects.

But nothing external defines him.

That is what gives him presence.

That is what gives him control without force.

The moment a man no longer needs the outcome is the moment he stops being shaped by it.

And in that moment, he steps fully into his own authority.

This is where proof becomes independence.

Not in what a man desires—but in what he does not depend on.

When he engages without needing the outcome, that is proof.
When his emotional state remains steady regardless of response, that is proof.
When he allows connection to develop without attempting to secure it, that is proof.

Clarity has already shown him what is real.

Now his independence determines how he engages.

And from that point forward, his presence is no longer shaped by outcome—but by who he is.

The Proven Man Principle

Desire creates connection.

Dependence creates instability.

Non-neediness creates freedom.

Chapter Seven

Conversation

Presence Over Performance

Presence alone is not enough.

A man can be grounded, self-contained, and free from neediness, yet still fail to create depth. Connection is not built on presence alone.

It is revealed through communication—how he speaks, how he listens, and how he responds in real time.

Many men lose the advantage they have worked to build.

They become internally stable, yet externally ineffective.

Their words lack direction.
Their curiosity feels forced.
Their conversations remain surface-level.

The Proven Man understands that conversation is not performance.

It is alignment in motion.

It is where presence becomes felt.
Where clarity becomes expressed.
And where connection either deepens—or fades.

By this point, the foundation is already in place. The Proven Man is no longer reactive. He does not chase outcomes, seek validation, or lose himself in the uncertainty of interaction. He observes clearly, holds his standards, and remains grounded regardless of what unfolds in front of him. His sense of self is not shaped by external response. Because of that, he moves without pressure.

That position changes everything. It changes how he evaluates, what he tolerates, and how he communicates.

Conversation is where this becomes visible.

For most men, conversation is treated as a tool, something to manage, improve, or use to create attraction or maintain interest. There is an assumption that the right words, delivered in the right way, will produce a desired result. Attention shifts toward what to say next, how something will be received, and whether the exchange is progressing. Even when subtle, that shift introduces tension and turns conversation into performance.

The Proven Man does not approach it this way. He does not rely on technique, memorization, or calculated delivery. He is not trying to guide the interaction toward a specific outcome, and he is not concerned with maintaining a particular image. That phase is already behind him.

Conversation becomes an extension of his internal state. It reflects his presence, clarity, and stability in real time. The same discipline that keeps him grounded under pressure, the same awareness that allows him to read behavior without distortion, and the same detachment that frees him from outcome are expressed the moment he engages.

Nothing new is added—what has been built is revealed.

This is where most men lose impact in conversation. The problem is rarely intelligence or effort. It is something quieter, an underlying need for the interaction to go well, to continue, or to become something more. That need reshapes behavior. It influences tone, pacing, and attention. Even when the words sound composed, pressure sits behind them, and over time it keeps the interaction at the surface.

The Proven Man removes that entirely.

He does not enter a conversation to get something.

He enters it to see what is there.

From that position, everything simplifies. There is no urgency behind his words and no attempt to force direction. He does not accelerate connection or manufacture depth. Instead, he remains present, attentive, and engaged without attachment to where it leads.

Because of that, something shifts. The interaction begins revealing itself more clearly. It becomes something he participates in while observing it unfold. What is real begins to stand out on its own: interest, disinterest, consistency, or misalignment.

Nothing needs interpretation.

It becomes clear.

This is where conversation takes on a different role. It is no longer used to create connection.

It becomes a way to recognize it.

At that point, conversation becomes refinement rather than performance.

It becomes the ability to remain present, engage with genuine curiosity, and observe alignment without forcing it. When those elements are in place, conversation changes. Interactions become quieter, more focused, and more revealing. It creates space for depth without pressure and allows both people to engage without expectation.

In that space, something lasting can occur, not because it was engineered, but because it is real.

I. The Subtle Art of Curiosity and Alignment

Conversations are no longer an attempt to impress. They are not shaped by the need to create attraction, control direction, or secure an outcome. That phase has already been left behind. The Proven Man does not enter an interaction trying to make something happen. He enters grounded and already established within himself, and because of that, conversation becomes something else entirely.

It is no longer performance, nor is it strategy. It is not an exchange driven by expectation or subtle pressure. Instead, it becomes a space where presence, curiosity, and alignment reveal themselves in real time.

Most men never consciously decide to perform. The shift happens quietly: a slight hesitation before speaking, a filtered response, or an adjustment in tone. Instead of expressing what is natural, they begin shaping what is said, managing how it is received, and monitoring the direction of the interaction. What begins as a simple exchange becomes something controlled.

The exchange is no longer shared.

It is being guided.

With that shift comes strain, not always visible, but internally present.

There is a need for the interaction to go well, to continue, or to lead somewhere. Once that need exists, even subtly, the dynamic changes. Attention narrows, responses lose clarity, and awareness shifts away from what is actually happening toward what might happen next.

The Proven Man does not operate from that position. He is not trying to maintain the interaction, nor is he concerned with how he is being perceived moment to moment. He does not measure progress or search for signals that something is working. His presence is not dependent on feedback.

He remains there.

Because he is grounded before the conversation begins, he does not need the interaction to provide anything: neither validation, momentum, nor direction. His sense of self is already intact. The conversation does not define him, and as a result, he does not approach it with tension.

This absence of pressure changes everything. Without the need to perform, the interaction becomes lighter. Without the need to control direction, it becomes more natural. Without attachment to outcome, it becomes more honest. There is no urgency behind his words and no attempt to accelerate connection.

The conversation is allowed to unfold naturally—because of that, its direction becomes visible.

This is the shift.

The conversation is not something he approaches with an agenda or emotional pressure. He participates fully, engages honestly, and responds naturally without forcing momentum or manufacturing depth.

He allows what is present to unfold without pressure.

That difference is subtle, but it is immediately felt.

Most interactions are shaped by an unspoken agenda. Even when it is not acknowledged, there is often an attempt to impress, to be liked, or to create a specific outcome. That underlying intention introduces tension into the interaction, no matter how composed it may appear on the surface.

The Proven Man removes that entirely.

He is not trying to be chosen.
He is not trying to move the interaction forward.
He is not trying to make anything happen.

He allows the conversation to show him what it is.

This is where clarity begins. When nothing is being forced, what remains is real. Interest becomes visible without interpretation. Disinterest becomes equally clear. Consistency and inconsistency reveal themselves without projection.

The interaction speaks for itself. And he listens to it.

For this reason, conversation is no longer a tool for creating connection. It becomes a way of recognizing it.

If connection exists, it will become evident.
If it does not, that will be just as clear.

In either case, nothing needs to be managed or forced. He remains unchanged—grounded, present, and clear.

From that position, conversation becomes simple.

Not because it lacks depth, but because it is no longer complicated by need.

II. Presence Over Performance

Most conversations fail before they ever truly begin, not because of what is said, but because of where attention is placed. When a man becomes focused on himself, how he is coming across, what he should say next, or how the interaction is being received, he is no longer fully engaged in the moment. His attention divides. One part of him participates while another monitors, adjusts, and anticipates.

That division is subtle, but it is always felt.

Performance creates distance, even when the words are correct and the tone is confident. There is an underlying tension within the interaction, a sense that something is being managed rather than expressed. Responses become measured, timing becomes calculated, and the natural rhythm of the conversation tightens. What should feel fluid begins to feel controlled.

It may not be obvious on the surface, but it is enough to prevent depth from forming.

The Proven Man does not operate from that position. He is not trying to be perceived a certain way, nor is he adjusting himself in real time to maintain interest. He does not filter every thought in an effort to produce the right response, and he is not preoccupied with how each moment is being interpreted.

He is simply present with what is in front of him.

This is what creates ease within interaction—not effort, not technique, but the absence of internal pressure. When there is nothing to manage, nothing to protect, and nothing to prove, the conversation settles into a more natural pace. His words carry no urgency, and there is no attempt to control how the interaction unfolds.

As presence replaces performance, awareness sharpens. He begins to notice what most people overlook: tone, pacing, pauses, what is said, and what is avoided. He is not searching for hidden meaning. He is simply attentive, and because of that, meaning becomes clear.

This awareness also changes how he responds. Because he is not rushing to fill space or force the conversation forward, he allows moments to exist without interference.

Silence is no longer something to avoid.

It becomes part of the interaction.

A pause is no longer awkward.

It is information.

It gives the other person time to think, process, and move beyond surface-level responses. Most people speak in layers, and the first answer is rarely the complete one. It is simply a starting point, something near the surface that precedes what actually matters.

The Proven Man understands this. He does not interrupt the process by rushing to respond or redirect. Instead, he allows the conversation to develop at its own pace, creating space for those layers to reveal themselves naturally.

In doing so, he removes the pressure that prevents depth. There is no need to perform, no need to accelerate, and no need to control.

There is only presence.

From that position, the conversation takes on a different quality, one that is not forced, but uncovered.

III. Curiosity Without Agenda

Curiosity is often misunderstood. Many men believe they are being curious simply because they ask questions. On the surface, this can appear attentive and engaged. But beneath those questions there is often another motive, an attempt to guide the interaction, create attraction, or move the conversation toward a particular outcome.

That is not curiosity.

It is direction presented as interest.

When questions are driven by outcome, they carry subtle pressure. They are no longer about understanding the person in front of you, but about shaping the interaction into something desired. Attention shifts away from what is being revealed and toward what can be done with the information that emerges.

Even when delivery appears smooth, that intention is felt.

The Proven Man approaches conversation differently. He does not ask questions in order to steer the interaction, and he does not probe for the purpose of gaining leverage or creating momentum. His attention is not strategic or calculated.

He asks in order to understand.

There is no hidden objective behind his curiosity. He is not collecting information for later use, nor is he searching for particular answers. Instead, he observes what is present and allows his attention to follow what naturally stands out.

Because of this, his questions carry a different quality. They are not rushed or excessive, and they are not stacked one after another to maintain momentum. Each question arises from something specific within what was just shared—something that holds weight, reveals character, or hints at deeper meaning.

His questions are responses.

Not tactics.

When she speaks about her life, he listens beyond surface-level details. He notices what she values, what she prioritizes, and what appears to shape her decisions. He pays attention to tone, emphasis, and the moments that carry more significance than the rest.

Those are the points that matter, and the ones he returns to.

When something meaningful begins to reveal itself, he follows it, not abruptly and not with intensity, but with quiet focus.

He may ask what part of that experience mattered most or when it first became important. Not because he is attempting to force depth into the conversation, but because the conversation has already begun to move in that direction.

He simply stays with it.

There is no pressure behind his curiosity and no urgency for the interaction to reach a particular destination. Because of this, the other person does not feel guided or managed.

They feel understood.

In that environment, depth does not need to be created. It emerges naturally when attention is genuine and uninterrupted.

This is the difference.

Curiosity without agenda does not attempt to take the conversation somewhere.

It allows the conversation to reveal where it is already going—and meets it there with clarity and attention.

IV. Where Depth Actually Comes From

Depth is not something that is created through effort.

It is something that is uncovered over time.

Most conversations never reach that point, not because depth is unavailable, but because the conditions required for it rarely exist. The interaction moves too quickly. One topic replaces another before anything has the opportunity to develop. Questions appear, receive a brief response, and are then abandoned in favor of something new. There is movement, but there is no focus.

Without focus, nothing meaningful reveals itself.

The Proven Man understands this.

He does not attempt to manufacture depth through more questions or increased intensity, nor does he force the conversation into something deeper than it naturally is. Instead, he allows the interaction to unfold at a pace where something real can begin to surface.

He does not chase depth.

He creates space for it.

When something meaningful appears, whether in tone, emphasis, or content, he does not move past it. He recognizes it as a point of significance and gives it his attention. Instead of shifting direction, he remains with it long enough for it to expand.

If she speaks about something that clearly matters to her, he does not treat it as a passing detail. His attention narrows, not to analyze or challenge, but to understand what the moment is beginning to reveal.

He may ask what draws her to it or why it holds importance, not to create depth, but to remain with what is beginning to reveal itself.

As this happens, the interaction begins to change. The pace slows, the conversation becomes more focused, and attention becomes more deliberate. It is no longer driven by the need to keep things moving, but by a willingness to remain with what matters.

The conversation is not being managed.

It is being experienced.

There is less distraction, more awareness, and clarity in what actually matters.

This is where many men become uncomfortable. Stillness introduces uncertainty. Without constant movement, there is nothing to rely on but presence. There are no rapid transitions to fall back on and no easy shifts to avoid moments of silence or reflection.

Depth requires patience.

It requires the ability to stay with a single thread long enough for it to unfold and the willingness to allow the conversation to develop without controlling where it leads.

The Proven Man is comfortable in that space. He does not rush to fill silence or redirect the interaction. He understands that what matters rarely appears immediately. It emerges gradually, often in layers, and only when there is enough space for it to do so.

This is where connection is actually formed.

Not through constant movement or surface-level exchange, but through sustained attention.

When someone feels that what they are saying is not being skimmed over but genuinely received and explored, something shifts. The interaction becomes more grounded, more real, and more memorable.

Depth is not the result of doing more.

It is the result of doing less—with intention.

It comes from staying present long enough for something meaningful to reveal.

It comes from having awareness to recognize it when it does.

V. The Direction of Conversation

The direction of a conversation is rarely determined by the questions themselves.

It is determined by what is noticed.

Many men believe direction comes from asking the right questions, knowing what to say, when to say it, and how to guide the interaction. This approach places emphasis on output rather than awareness.

It assumes direction must be imposed rather than discovered, and as a result the conversation may appear guided while lacking genuine grounding.

The Proven Man approaches conversation differently. He does not rely on scripts, prepared lines, or structured sequences. He is not attempting to steer the interaction toward a predetermined destination. Instead, he pays attention to what is already present and allows that awareness to inform where the conversation moves.

He follows signals—not only the words themselves, but how those words are delivered: the tone, the pacing, the shifts in energy, what is emphasized, and what is passed over without weight.

These details often reveal far more than the surface of the exchange, and this is where his attention remains.

When something is expressed with genuine energy, he stays with it. There is no need to redirect the conversation or introduce something new. The direction already exists, and he allows it to unfold naturally.

When something is mentioned without depth or engagement, he registers that as well. He does not force interest where there is none, and he does not attempt to revive what has already fallen flat.

When words and energy do not align, he notices that too. He does not rush to confront it, and he does not ignore it. Instead, he allows the moment to remain as it is, understanding that clarity does not emerge from a single exchange but from what repeats over time.

This is where awareness replaces assumption.

Rather than reacting to isolated moments, he observes patterns as they develop. A single response rarely defines anything. What matters is consistency over time, how someone shows up across multiple moments rather than within just one.

Because of this, he does not treat conversation as a series of disconnected exchanges.

He sees it as a pattern in motion.

From this perspective, a natural rhythm begins to appear within the conversation.

The Proven Man does not force this rhythm.

He simply follows it.

First, something is noticed.
Then curiosity follows what stands out.
Attention remains long enough for meaning to expand.
And over time, alignment—or misalignment—reveals itself.

This quiet sequence forms the natural loop of conversation itself.

Notice.
Follow.
Expand.
Recognize.

The Proven Man does not impose direction.

He discovers it.

Because of this, he does not rush to conclusions. He does not assume meaning where it has not yet been established, and he does not fill uncertainty with expectation or projection. What is unresolved is allowed to remain so until repetition reveals the pattern.

This restraint preserves accuracy.

The Proven Man watches and listens, and over time what matters reveals itself clearly.

Then he adjusts without hesitation. His actions are not based on isolated impressions, but on what has been consistently observed. This allows him to respond with clarity rather than reaction and to move forward without second-guessing.

The direction of conversation, then, is never forced.

It is recognized.

By following what is real rather than attempting to create it, he ensures that the interaction remains grounded, aligned, and honest from beginning to end.

VI. The Role of Follow-Through

The first answer is rarely complete.

Most people speak in approximations, surface-level responses and fragments of thought that hint at something deeper without fully revealing it. They test the waters before committing to anything real, offering just enough to keep the conversation moving while holding back what actually matters.

The Proven Man understands this. He does not treat initial responses as conclusions, but as entry points. Each answer is something to note rather than finalize. He listens without rushing to interpret, allowing meaning to develop gradually instead of forcing it into immediate clarity.

Because of this, he does not feel the need to extract everything at once. If something stands out, he remembers it. When the moment naturally returns to that topic, he revisits it, not abruptly and not forcefully, but as part of the flow of the interaction.

"You mentioned that earlier—what changed there?"
"What about that experience stayed with you?"

These questions are not asked to keep the conversation going: they are extensions of attention.

They signal that he is not only hearing what is said, but tracking what matters across time.

This is where conversations begin to separate.

Some interactions move quickly, touching on many subjects while holding onto none of them. Others develop gradually, returning to what matters and allowing it to expand. The difference is not intensity or effort.

It is continuity.

The Proven Man does not rely on pressure to create depth.

He relies on continuity of attention.

The same conversational loop operates beneath the surface.

Notice what matters.
Follow it with curiosity.
Remain long enough for it to deepen.
Recognize what it reveals.

Over time, this creates a sense of coherence that most interactions lack.

It becomes clear that he is not reacting to isolated moments. He is observing patterns, following meaning, and allowing the larger picture to reveal itself gradually.

That alone sets him apart.

Most people listen just enough to respond. They move from one point to the next without returning, refining, or deepening what was said. They hear the words, but they do not follow through.

The Proven Man does.

Because of that, his conversations carry weight.

VII. The Experience of Being Understood

People rarely remember the exact words spoken in a conversation. What they remember is how the interaction made them feel.

To be heard is common—being understood is rare.

The Proven Man does not attempt to manufacture that feeling. He creates the conditions where it emerges naturally. He listens without interruption or redirection, allowing the conversation to unfold without pressure or control.

When the need to impress disappears, something shifts. People reveal more of themselves—not because they are asked, but because they feel free to do so. The Proven Man does not force depth or demand connection.

He simply removes the resistance that normally prevents it, and when resistance disappears, the interaction deepens on its own.

This is the subtle power of being understood. It is not created through effort, but revealed through presence.

When someone senses their words are not being managed, redirected, or judged, the conversation becomes grounded and authentic—and that is what makes it memorable.

But understanding another person is only one side of the equation.

When the Proven Man enters a conversation, he does so without need. He is not seeking validation, approval, or a particular outcome. He is present, attentive, and grounded within himself.

Yet this foundation is tested when desire becomes part of the interaction.

Attraction, curiosity, and the impulse to draw closer arise naturally between two people. These forces are part of human interaction, and they are not something to avoid or suppress.

The challenge is not their presence; it is remaining unchanged in the face of them.

Most men lose their grounding here. They begin to chase attraction, chase momentum, and chase outcomes. Their attention shifts outward, and their behavior begins to follow the interaction rather than their own center.

The Proven Man does not chase—he remains steady.

Desire may exist, but it does not control him. Attraction may appear, but it does not alter his position. His presence remains the same: calm, clear, and self-contained.

Because of that, he does not attempt to control the direction of the interaction.

He allows it to unfold without manipulation or pressure.

And in that composure, something powerful appears.

Not effort.
Not performance.
Quiet authority.

Chapter Distillation

Conversation reveals more than information—it reveals presence.

Most interactions are shaped by subtle pressures: to impress, to influence, to secure approval, or to control the direction of the exchange.

That pressure creates tension, and tension quietly distorts communication.

The Proven Man removes that tension.

He does not approach conversation as something to manage or manipulate. He enters it with clarity and attention, listening without redirecting, responding without performing, and allowing meaning to emerge naturally rather than forcing it.

Because of this, people experience something rare in his presence—they feel understood.

That changes the dynamic of the interaction. Words carry more weight. Attention deepens. Authenticity becomes possible because there is no hidden agenda shaping the moment.

Conversation is not a performance, and it is not a technique.
It is the natural expression of presence.

This is where proof becomes visible in real time.

Not in what a man intends—but in how he communicates without pressure.

When his words carry no need to impress, that is proof.
When his attention remains steady without controlling it, that is proof.
When he allows meaning to emerge instead of forcing it, that is proof.

Clarity has already shaped how he sees.

Now his presence shapes how he is experienced.

And from that point forward, every interaction reflects who he is—without effort or performance.

When a man removes the need to impress, control, or secure an outcome, conversation becomes simple and revealing.

By noticing what carries energy, following it with genuine curiosity, and allowing meaning to unfold over time, the Proven Man creates space where understanding and connection emerge naturally.

He does not force depth or manufacture momentum. He observes, listens, and allows alignment to reveal itself through attention and continuity.

Because presence removes pressure—people reveal themselves more honestly.

From that honesty, alignment becomes visible, and once it does, connection either deepens—or naturally fades.

The Proven Man Principle

Presence creates understanding.

Understanding reveals alignment.

Alignment determines connection.

Chapter Eight

Desire

Attraction Without Losing Direction

By this point, the shift is already in place. The Proven Man is no longer reactive. He does not chase outcomes or lose himself in uncertainty. He observes clearly, holds his standards, and remains grounded regardless of what unfolds in front of him. His attention is no longer pulled outward by validation or response; it is anchored internally, stable and deliberate. This changes how he moves through conversation, how he evaluates connection, and ultimately how he experiences attraction itself.

Desire does not disappear with awareness.
It becomes more noticeable.

Most men do not struggle with attraction itself. They struggle with what attraction does to them. Desire is immediate. It does not wait for clarity or consistency. It arrives quickly, often without context, and when misunderstood, it begins to influence behavior before it is ever examined.

A woman captures your attention. There is energy in the interaction, something engaging, sometimes even rare. The conversation flows and the dynamic feels easy. In that moment, focus begins to narrow and attention moves forward. Possibility appears before anything has been established.

Nothing has gone wrong.
But something has already started to move.

Desire does not remain contained.
It expands.

When unobserved, it begins to shape perception. What is felt starts to take priority over what is seen. Small inconsistencies are dismissed. Gaps in clarity are overlooked. Attention shifts toward what could be rather than what is. This is where most men begin to lose their position, not through obvious mistakes, but through subtle shifts. They invest before clarity forms. They respond to feeling instead of observing behavior. They begin to move in the direction of emotion rather than remaining grounded in evaluation.

The issue is not desire.
It is the absence of self-discipline around it.

Desire, on its own, is neutral. It can inform interest, signal attention, and reveal what draws someone in. But without discipline, it begins to pull. And when a man is pulled, he is no longer choosing.

The Proven Man does not remove desire from the equation. He does not suppress it or pretend it is not there. He recognizes it fully and allows it to exist without resistance.

He embraces it as part of the human experience.
At the same time, he does not allow it to lead.

At this level, the challenge is no longer conversation.
It is composure in the presence of attraction.

This is where clarity is either maintained or lost. It is where standards are either upheld or quietly negotiated. It is where a man either continues forward with intention or drifts back into reaction.

The discipline of desire is not about eliminating attraction.
It is about remaining unchanged in its presence.

From this position, everything becomes more precise. Desire still exists, but it no longer controls direction. Attention remains clear, evaluation remains steady, and the interaction unfolds without pulling the man away from himself.

Because desire is no longer leading,
the Proven Man leads himself.

I. The Nature of Desire

Desire is not rational. It does not wait for clarity, consistency, or evaluation. It responds immediately to what it perceives: physical attraction, attention, validation, and most powerfully, uncertainty. Desire is drawn to emotional contrast.

Uncertainty makes interactions feel more compelling than stability ever could.

When a connection appears and then disappears, when attention rises and falls, the emotional contrast intensifies the experience. Moments of closeness followed by moments of distance create a cycle of anticipation and release. The brain begins responding not to the person, but to the pattern of stimulation itself.

This is why unstable dynamics often feel stronger in the early stages. The intensity is not coming from depth or compatibility. It is coming from fluctuation.

The experience feels powerful, but the source of that power is rarely alignment.

When attention is pulled by emotional highs or unpredictability, the response is stimulation—not compatibility. The nervous system reacts first, long before clarity or understanding has time to form. What feels exciting in the moment is often the brain reacting to contrast rather than recognizing genuine connection.

Desire also creates urgency. It compresses attention and narrows perception, making the present moment feel disproportionately important. When attraction appears, the mind begins projecting meaning forward, imagining potential, anticipating outcomes, and assigning significance before anything has been proven.

In that state, evaluation weakens.

What might otherwise be neutral begins to feel significant. Small signals are magnified. Gaps in clarity are overlooked. The emotional pull of the moment begins to guide perception rather than observation guiding it.

This is where discipline becomes necessary.

Desire itself is not the problem. It is a natural response to attraction and engagement. It signals interest and awareness. But when desire is left unobserved, it begins to lead behavior rather than inform it. Decisions begin forming around emotional momentum instead of grounded evaluation.

The stronger the pull becomes, the more awareness is required.

Intensity has a way of disguising itself as importance. The mind interprets the intensity of the feeling as evidence that something meaningful is happening, even when nothing substantial has been revealed yet. Without discipline, the emotional surge begins to make decisions on its own.

The Proven Man understands this distinction. He does not attempt to suppress desire or pretend it is not there. He allows it to exist fully, but does not surrender his direction to it.

He recognizes that what feels powerful in the moment is not always aligned with what endures over time.

Because of this, he creates space between feeling and response. He notices the pull, but he does not immediately respond to it. He allows observation to continue even while attraction is present.

And in that space, clarity remains intact.

Desire may arrive quickly,
but it does not decide.
The Proven Man does.

II. The Discipline of Desire

The Proven Man understands that mastery over desire is a path forward, and it does not come from suppression. It comes from awareness. It demands attention, stirs emotion, and pulls with an intensity that can feel immediate and compelling. But discipline begins with the ability to see that pull clearly without being carried away by it.

When desire arises, most men react instinctively. Attraction appears, and behavior begins to follow it before evaluation has taken place. Attention narrows. The interaction begins to feel more important than it actually is. Action replaces observation.

This is where position is often lost.

The Proven Man creates space between feeling and response.

When the pull of attraction appears, he does not rush to act on it. He pauses. He allows the feeling to exist without immediately translating it into behavior.

That space becomes the beginning of discipline.

In that pause, reaction becomes a choice.

The stronger the pull, the more deliberate his awareness becomes. Where most men accelerate under the influence of attraction, he steadies his pace. He remains present with what he feels, but he does not allow the feeling to dictate his direction. Desire may be immediate, but his response is measured.

This is not resistance to attraction.
It is clarity within it.

By allowing the moment to settle before acting, he transforms impulse into evaluation. What might have pulled him forward unconsciously now becomes something he can see, understand, and place in context. Attraction is acknowledged, but it does not override observation.

Because of this, the interaction continues from a place of stability.

Connection is allowed to unfold without being forced by emotional momentum. His standards remain intact, his attention remains clear, and his behavior continues to align with the direction of his life rather than the urgency of the moment.

This is the discipline of desire.

Not the absence of attraction—
But composure in its presence.

The Proven Man still feels deeply. He still recognizes beauty, chemistry, and the pull of connection. But those feelings do not determine his actions. They inform him, yet they do not lead him.

Desire may appear quickly.
The decision remains his.

III. Why Men Lose Control

Desire, on its own, does not create misalignment.
It reveals what is already unstable.

When a man is grounded, desire moves through him without distortion. He feels it, recognizes it, and observes clearly. Attraction is present, but it does not alter his position. His awareness remains intact.

But when something beneath the surface is unsteady, when ego, scarcity, or uncertainty are present, desire no longer remains neutral. It begins to amplify those conditions.

From there, those internal states begin to express themselves, and what begins as attraction gradually becomes something else.

When ego enters the interaction, desire becomes validation. The focus shifts away from connection and toward being chosen. Attention begins to feel like approval, and the desire to maintain that approval subtly reshapes behavior.

The interaction is no longer being observed.
It is being managed.

When scarcity is present, desire becomes urgency. The moment begins to feel rare, even irreplaceable. There is pressure to secure the interaction before it disappears. Patience fades. Evaluation shortens. Time compresses around the feeling.

And when standards are unclear, desire becomes direction.

Instead of evaluating what is in front of him, the man begins following the emotion itself. The pull of attraction replaces discernment. When uncertainty takes hold, emotion begins to lead where clarity once did.

This is where mistakes begin.

Not through obvious failure, but through quiet concessions. Patterns are noticed, yet dismissed. Inconsistency appears, but is explained away. Investment increases before stability has ever been established. The awareness is often there, but the willingness to lose the feeling is not.

This is the shift most men never recognize.
They believe they are pursuing the woman.

In reality, they are protecting the emotion.

Attention moves away from what is real and toward preserving the experience being created internally. What matters is no longer alignment, but continuation.

And once that shift occurs, clarity begins to fade.

Momentary feeling outweighs long-term evaluation. Decisions are made to maintain the experience rather than to assess it. Over time, those decisions compound. What begins as a small compromise becomes a pattern of misalignment.

The Proven Man sees this clearly.

He does not protect the feeling.
He protects his position.

Desire is allowed to exist, but it is never permitted to override what he already knows to be true.

Because the moment emotion replaces evaluation,
self-control has already been surrendered to impulse.

IV. The Illusion of Chemistry

Chemistry is one of the most misunderstood aspects of attraction. It often feels like alignment, as if everything has fallen into place without effort. But in many cases what is being experienced is not alignment.

It is intensity.

Intensity is frequently driven by unpredictability. Attention appears and then withdraws. Energy rises and then drops. Moments of connection are followed by moments of uncertainty. This fluctuation creates emotional contrast, and that contrast produces the feeling many people interpret as chemistry.

The experience feels engaging because it is inconsistent.

Uncertainty creates anticipation. The moments of connection feel heightened because they follow moments of distance. Over time, this cycle of emotional contrast can begin to resemble depth, even when no real foundation has formed beneath it. What is being experienced is not stability or alignment.

It is reaction to emotional contrast.

This is why certain connections become difficult to step away from, even when misalignment is visible. The pull does not come from what is being built over time. It comes from the emotional stimulation created in the moment.

The experience itself is not the problem—it is interpretation.

When intensity is mistaken for alignment, clarity begins to erode. What feels strong is assumed to be meaningful. What feels engaging is assumed to hold meaning. Without realizing it, decisions begin to follow emotional momentum rather than observable reality.

But intensity and alignment are not the same.

Alignment develops through stability. It reveals itself through clarity, consistency, and coherence over time. It may not feel as urgent in the beginning, but it holds its structure. It does not depend on emotional swings to remain compelling.

The Proven Man understands this distinction. He does not deny chemistry, but he does not assign it more significance than it deserves. He recognizes intensity without confusing it for substance. The experience is allowed to develop naturally, but observation continues.

If he cannot separate the two, he will choose based on what pulls him rather than what supports him. This is where confusion replaces clarity.

At first, everything starts to feel aligned. The interaction is engaging. Energy moves easily, and the sense of connection seems to confirm itself.

Over time, however, structure begins to reveal itself. Consistency breaks. Clarity fades. What initially felt strong begins to show instability.

Nothing has changed in the feeling.
But everything has changed in what is being shown.

Desire created the pull.
Alignment would have created stability.

The difference between the two is rarely obvious in the moment. It requires patience, observation, and the discipline to remain grounded when something feels powerful.

Because not everything that feels real is built to last.

And not everything that lasts begins with intensity.

V. Stoic Control

Control is often misunderstood. It is not suppression, nor is it the denial of what is felt. It is the power of restraint. It is the ability to experience something fully without reacting to it immediately.

Desire does not need to be eliminated.
It needs to be observed.

The moment attraction is felt, there is a natural impulse to move with it, to respond, to pursue, to act before the feeling fades or changes. This is where most men lose clarity. The reaction happens too quickly, and once it does, the moment is no longer being evaluated.

It is simply being followed.

The Proven Man does not move in that way.

He creates space between the feeling and the response.

The pause is not forced or dramatic. It is subtle, but deliberate. Within that space he allows the feeling to exist without acting on it. Attraction is acknowledged, but he remains still long enough to observe it clearly.

This is where discipline begins to take form.
Not in resistance.
But in restraint.

This is the essence of stoic control.

The Proven Man feels the pull, but he does not allow it to dictate his behavior. He does not rush to match energy, accelerate momentum, or secure the interaction. Instead, he steadies himself. His attention sharpens. What might have become urgency settles into clarity.

From that position, a different question emerges.

Not "What should I do next?"
But "Is this aligned or simply stimulating?"

That distinction changes the direction of the moment.

Because once that question is asked from a grounded position, the answer is no longer shaped by intensity. It reflects what is actually present.

Detachment, in this sense, is also often misunderstood. It is not disinterest or distance. It is the absence of dependence on the outcome. The Proven Man remains present, engaged, and attentive, but he is not pulled forward by what he feels. The interaction is allowed to reveal itself rather than being pursued.

This is where clarity begins to take shape.

Reactive desire carries tension. Attention narrows and thoughts accelerate. The feeling begins to create urgency, and the impulse to act quickly replaces the discipline to observe.

Disciplined desire is different. The feeling is still present, but it no longer disrupts position. Awareness remains steady. The interaction continues to be evaluated rather than followed.

That stability is not passive—it is stoic control.

And it is what allows him to experience attraction fully without losing direction.

VI. Desire vs. Standards

Desire does not exist to guide you toward what is aligned. It responds to what is familiar, what is stimulating, and what creates emotional movement. At times, that may align with what is right; more often, it will not.

Desire pulls attention toward what feels good in the moment, what is exciting, engaging, or charged with energy, even when that direction lacks stability or long-term clarity. Without discipline, it becomes easy to follow that pull without questioning where it leads.

This is where standards become essential.

The Proven Man knows standards are not preferences. They are not flexible, nor are they adjusted based on how something feels in the moment.

They are his direction.

They define what is acceptable, what is sustainable, and what aligns with the life a man is building. Standards exist before the interaction begins, and they remain unchanged regardless of who stands in front of him.

When desire is strong, it is standards that keep him grounded.

When standards are not upheld, one truth becomes clear over time:

A man will often feel strong attraction toward people who do not meet his standards.

This is not a flaw.

Attraction does not automatically align with what is right. It responds to stimulation, not to long-term compatibility.

The difference, therefore, is not in what a man feels.

It is in what he chooses.

Discipline is not the absence of attraction. It is the ability to maintain clarity in its presence. The Proven Man may feel something deeply and still recognize when it does not meet the conditions required for real investment. Instead of reacting to emotional momentum, he pauses, assesses, and evaluates what is actually there.

He can feel attraction and still decline it.

He can recognize misalignment and refuse to negotiate with it.

This is where most men falter. Not because they lack awareness, but because they allow the feeling to override the standard. They adjust what they accept in order to preserve what they feel. Over time, those small compromises accumulate, and what began as attraction becomes a pattern of misalignment.

The Proven Man does not follow that path.

He does not lower his standards to accommodate attraction. He does not reinterpret behavior to preserve his interest. If something is misaligned, it remains misaligned, regardless of how strong the pull may be.

Because he understands something simple and often forgotten:

Desire will evolve.

But what he chooses to accept will shape what follows.

VII. The Cost of Undisciplined Desire

When desire leads and discipline follows, the outcome becomes predictable.

A man begins to tolerate what he normally would not. Behavior that once stood out as misaligned is minimized or explained away. What would have been a clear boundary slowly becomes negotiable.

What he sees clearly at first becomes something he chooses to ignore. The signs are not hidden, but recognizing them would require stepping away from something that feels good. Awareness is present, yet it is overridden.

Investment begins to follow the feeling rather than the evidence. Time, attention, and energy are placed where they have not been earned—into dynamics lacking consistency, clarity, and direction.

At first, the cost appears small. It feels like a moment, a single choice, a temporary exception.

But that cost does not remain small.

Over time it compounds.

Clarity begins to fade. The ability to see things as they are becomes diluted by emotional attachment. What should be obvious becomes uncertain, and what should be simple begins to feel complicated.

Focus begins to shift. Attention moves away from what a man is building and toward what he is reacting to. Energy that should be directed with intention becomes scattered across situations that do not support his path.

Momentum begins to slow. Not because of one decision, but because of repeated misalignment. Each time a choice is made based on feeling rather than clarity, direction weakens slightly.

Gradually, energy stops being directed and becomes reactive.

This is rarely a single mistake.

It is a pattern of decisions made under emotional influence rather than grounded awareness. Once that pattern forms, it becomes difficult to break, not because it is complex, but because the emotional cycle itself begins to feel familiar.

The Proven Man recognizes the cost before it accumulates.

He does not wait for consequences to confirm what he already sees. He does not allow temporary feeling to justify long-term misalignment. When something lacks structure, he does not attempt to create it. When something is unclear, he does not force clarity.

He steps back. This is not out of avoidance, but out of discipline.

Because he understands that every decision either strengthens his direction or quietly erodes it.

VIII. Controlled Desire

When desire no longer directs behavior, a shift occurs.

The Proven Man sees more clearly. Attraction may still be present, but it no longer distorts perception. Instead of reacting to the intensity of the moment, he observes it. Interactions that once appeared compelling simply because they felt intense can now be evaluated with patience and perspective.

With clarity restored, his responses become deliberate. Rather than reacting to attraction or emotional momentum, his words, actions, and attention are guided by awareness. Behavior begins to reflect intention rather than impulse.

This change becomes most visible when the moment carries emotional charge. Attraction, excitement, and curiosity may all be present, yet they no longer destabilize the interaction. Desire exists, but it no longer dictates direction. The emotional highs and lows that once influenced behavior lose their leverage.

What emerges in its place is steadiness.

Instead of chasing intensity, the focus shifts toward alignment. Attention moves away from creating the perfect moment or securing validation and toward understanding what is actually present. The interaction is evaluated against standards, direction, and long-term coherence.

Because of this, stability becomes evident.

Emotional steadiness is rare, and it carries weight. Others notice when a man is not moved by every fluctuation in mood or attention. They notice when he does not stretch himself to maintain temporary interest. Consistency in behavior signals something deeper than attraction—it signals self-control.

The Proven Man may feel strong attraction during a date, yet he does not rush to escalate the moment or flood it with attention. Conversation remains relaxed. He listens attentively and responds naturally while his priorities and routines remain unchanged. He is present, but he is not consumed by the moment.

What emerges is not urgency.

It is composure.

Controlled desire does not remove attraction. The feeling remains, but it no longer determines behavior. Attraction becomes something that informs awareness rather than something that drives action.

This is where the distinction becomes clear.

The Proven Man does not eliminate desire,
he remains unchanged in its presence.

IX. What This Looks Like in Real Time

Discipline rarely appears through dramatic action. More often, it reveals itself in small moments, the ones where the instinct to react is strongest and the choice to pause carries the most weight.

The Proven Man recognizes these moments as they happen.

When attraction is present, the natural tendency is to accelerate. Conversation moves faster, attention narrows, and the urge to escalate the interaction begins to appear. Many men respond to that energy by increasing effort or pushing the interaction forward.

The Proven Man does not accelerate with it.

Instead of chasing the feeling, he allows it to unfold. The moment is not forced toward a conclusion, nor is the emotion immediately acted upon. He remains present with the interaction while maintaining awareness of what is actually taking place.

Because of this, his awareness sharpens rather than his effort increasing.

Where others attempt to create connection through activity: more messages, more charm, more attempts to impress—the Proven Man focuses on attention. He notices subtle cues that others miss: pauses in conversation, shifts in tone, changes in energy. These signals reveal far more than surface enthusiasm.

Connection is revealed through observation.

What once felt compelling begins to separate into what is consistent and what is merely stimulating.

Patterns begin to matter more than isolated moments. A few engaging interactions do not outweigh inconsistency that appears over time. Attraction may rise quickly, but the Proven Man continues to watch how behavior develops.

Consistency signals alignment.
Inconsistency reveals misalignment.

He does not ignore what he sees simply because the experience feels good.

Pressure provides another point of clarity. When emotions rise or situations become uncertain, people reveal more of their underlying nature. The Proven Man evaluates how someone behaves in those moments—not looking for perfection, but for composure and groundedness.

Behavior under pressure reveals alignment more clearly than comfort ever will.

At the same time, he maintains his own structure. Attraction does not reorganize his priorities. His routines, direction, and commitments remain intact. The interaction becomes something that exists within his life rather than something that reshapes it.

Because of this, his internal questions remain simple and grounded: he asks whether the attraction is directed toward the person or toward the feeling being created. He considers whether what he is experiencing is consistent or simply intense. He evaluates whether the connection would hold value over time or whether it is being driven by short-term emotional momentum.

These reflections do not create hesitation—they refine clarity.

This is what discipline looks like in real time. The Proven Man pauses when others rush. He observes when others react. And because of that restraint, he is able to see what others miss.

Small moments reveal everything.

Those who rush through them lose direction.

The Proven Man uses them to remain grounded.

X. The Identity Shift into Observation

For most men, attraction operates in a reactive cycle. They feel the pull, they pursue it, and then they attempt to secure the connection. The interaction becomes a response to emotion rather than a reflection of clarity. Attention narrows around the feeling itself, and behavior begins to revolve around maintaining it.

In that cycle, attraction becomes the force directing the interaction.

The Proven Man no longer operates this way.

Attraction may still appear quickly, but his response is no longer driven by it. Instead, it follows a simple internal discipline: observe, evaluate, choose.

Observation comes first. The Proven Man does not rush into action when attraction appears. He allows the interaction to unfold while remaining attentive to what is actually present. Surface chemistry may exist, but he continues to notice the deeper signals beneath it: consistency, composure, alignment with his standards, and the direction the interaction is naturally moving.

The moment is experienced without being immediately acted on.

From there, evaluation becomes possible. Rather than chasing the momentum of the interaction, he places what he sees into context. The question is no longer whether the moment feels engaging, but whether the connection aligns with the life he is building. Standards remain the reference point. Attraction may be present, but it does not override them.

Only then does choice emerge. The Proven Man does not pursue intensity for its own sake, nor does he seek validation through the interaction. He chooses based on alignment. What supports his direction receives attention. What does not is allowed to pass without resistance.

This marks a fundamental shift in identity.

Instead of asking how to maintain the connection, his attention turns to something far more stable: whether the connection belongs in his life at all.

The question changes.

Not "How do I keep this?"
But "Does this belong in the life I am building?"

When that shift takes hold, much of the tension surrounding attraction disappears. The need for validation weakens because the outcome of the interaction no longer defines his position. His identity is anchored in his standards, his direction, and the structure of his life.

Attraction becomes something he experiences rather than something he must manage.

Because of this, the Proven Man does not attempt to shape the interaction. Desire becomes one element within the experience rather than the force guiding it. The emotional pull remains visible, but it no longer determines behavior.

This is where self-control begins.

The Proven Man does not react to attraction.
He masters his response to it.

That mastery carries a natural consequence. A man who can observe, evaluate, and choose without emotional interference is also capable of something many men avoid entirely.

He can walk away.

Cleanly.

Without hesitation.
Without resentment.

Because when alignment is absent, the decision has already been made.

And that decision leads to the next discipline the Proven Man must learn: detachment.

XI. Mastery Within Desire

Desire, when left unchecked, creates movement without direction. It pulls, accelerates, and convinces. But in the absence of discipline, it does not lead—it distorts. The Proven Man understands that mastery is not found in suppressing desire, but in refining his relationship with it. What once drove impulsive action becomes something he can observe, regulate, and ultimately direct.

In that shift, desire stops clouding awareness; it begins sharpening it.

Managing desire is not about control over another person. It is mastery of oneself. It begins with self-regulation, the ability to remain calm and grounded regardless of how attraction rises or how the interaction unfolds.

When desire appears, the body often reacts first. Attention narrows. Thoughts accelerate. Subtle tension appears in the body. The Proven Man does not ignore this response.

He notices it.

And in noticing it, he creates space.

That space is where discipline begins to form. Instead of reacting immediately, he allows the moment to settle. His breathing steadies. Attention returns to what is real rather than what the mind begins to imagine. Attraction may still exist, but it no longer dictates behavior.

From this position, curiosity becomes clean.

The Proven Man does not ask questions to impress or influence the interaction. He asks to understand. There is no hidden objective behind his engagement and no attempt to steer the moment toward a predetermined outcome. Because of this, the interaction develops without pressure. If connection exists, it reveals itself. If it does not, that becomes equally clear.

At the same time, evaluation continues.

Not overtly and not critically—but consistently.

The Proven Man does not experience attraction and then search for reasons to justify it. He observes first. He evaluates her values, her composure, her consistency, and the direction she moves in life. Only then does he decide whether the connection belongs within his world.

Desire does not bypass this process.

It moves through it.

This keeps his decisions grounded in reality rather than driven by emotional momentum. He allows patterns to reveal themselves before deciding where to invest his attention and energy.

Because he is not reacting, stability organically emerges.

There is no urgency in his presence. No pressure to accelerate the interaction or manufacture depth. The other person is not being managed or guided toward an outcome. They are simply being met.

And in that space, authenticity becomes possible. Depth is not something the Proven Man attempts to create; it is something that emerges.

He does not force it or rush toward it. Anything pushed too quickly loses its integrity. Instead, he allows the interaction to develop at a pace where clarity can form without distortion. What is aligned strengthens, and what is not becomes visible.

Over time this transforms the role of desire entirely.

It no longer disrupts his thinking or directs his behavior. It becomes something he can feel without being controlled by. Something that informs awareness without dictating action.

And this is the final shift.

Desire is no longer a force he follows. It becomes something he observes and evaluates, choosing only what aligns with his standards.

That is discipline.

And that is what allows the Proven Man to move through attraction without losing clarity, remaining grounded and aligned no matter how strong the pull becomes.

Chapter Distillation

Desire is natural. It will always exist. It rises quickly, often without warning, and at times it can feel overwhelming. The Proven Man does not attempt to eliminate it. He refines his relationship to it.

When left unexamined, desire narrows perception and pulls behavior toward what feels immediate rather than what is aligned. It creates movement, but not direction. Without discipline, it repeats the same patterns.

With awareness and discipline working together, desire no longer leads unconsciously. It becomes something that can be understood without being followed.

The Proven Man does not resist what he feels. He observes it. He evaluates it with clarity. And he chooses only what aligns with the life he is building.

Attraction no longer dictates behavior. It becomes part of a larger awareness, something that informs him without controlling him.

Clarity remains intact. His standards hold. And every decision reflects direction rather than impulse.

This is where proof becomes visible.

Not in what a man feels, but in what his choices consistently produce.

When his decisions lead to stability instead of chaos, that is proof.
When alignment strengthens over time instead of breaking down, that is proof.
When what he builds reflects his standards rather than his impulses, that is proof.

Desire has already been felt. Now its consequences reveal the truth.

And over time, what a man experiences is shaped not by what he wants, but by what he chooses.

The Proven Man Principle

Desire may speak.

Discipline decides.

Choice determines direction.

Chapter Nine

Detachment

Letting Go Without Losing Clarity

The moment attachment forms, clarity begins to fade.

The discipline of desire reveals why this matters. Attraction alone cannot determine the direction of a man's life. Without clarity and self-control, it becomes a force that pulls him toward intensity rather than true alignment.

The Proven Man now observes desire without becoming ruled by it. But observation alone is not enough. He must also learn when to release attachment before it begins to distort judgment and pull him away from his direction.

That is detachment.

I. What Detachment Is (And What It Is Not)

Detachment is often misunderstood because it is associated with emotional distance. It is mistaken for indifference, for a lack of care, or for an unwillingness to engage. In reality, it is none of those things.

Detachment is not about becoming cold, distant, or unavailable. It is not a rejection of connection, nor is it a withdrawal from emotion. The Proven Man does not suppress what he feels, and he does not avoid engagement to protect himself. He remains fully capable of interest, connection, and depth.

What changes is not his capacity to feel, but his relationship to what he feels.

Detachment is the ability to remain emotionally steady in the presence of uncertainty. It is the ability to see clearly without distortion, even when there is attraction or investment. And when something no longer aligns, it is the ability to let go without hesitation.

It is not the absence of feeling.
It is the absence of dependence on the outcome.

This distinction is critical. When a man becomes dependent on an outcome, perception begins to shift. He filters what he sees. He minimizes what does not align and amplifies what does. Over time, clarity is replaced by interpretation, and reality becomes shaped by preference rather than observation.

The Proven Man does not allow this shift to take hold. He remains grounded in what is consistent, not what is hoped for. He does not need the interaction to become something else in order to remain engaged. Because of this, he is able to step back when necessary, not as a reaction, but as a decision made from clarity.

Detachment, then, is not emotional shutdown. It is control without force: the ability to pause, observe, and act without being driven by the immediate pull of feeling.

It carries a distinct quality. There is no urgency behind it, no tension to resolve, and no need to hold on. It feels calm, centered, and unshakable.

In contrast, the absence of detachment becomes easy to recognize. It appears as reactivity, over-investment, and the subtle pressure to maintain or secure something that has not yet proven itself to be stable.

The Proven Man notices this, not only in others, but within himself. And when he does, he returns to stillness. He allows the moment to settle before deciding how to move.

A simple question anchors this position:

Am I holding on to what is—or to what I hope it becomes?

The answer, when faced honestly, restores clarity and allows a man to release what no longer belongs in his direction.

II. Why Most Men Struggle to Let Go

Letting go is rarely difficult because of the person alone. It becomes difficult because of what has been built around the interaction: what has been invested, experienced, and imagined over time.

A man does not simply walk away from what is in front of him. He walks away from the time he has already given, the emotion he has already felt, and the future he has already begun to construct in his mind. Each of these elements adds weight to the decision, not because they reflect alignment, but because they create attachment.

Time invested creates a sense of obligation. Emotion experienced creates a sense of significance. Future imagined creates a sense of loss.

And that imagined future is often the most powerful of the three.

It extends beyond what has actually happened and begins shaping what the interaction feels like it represents. Over time, the mind fills in gaps, smooths over inconsistencies, and builds a version of the connection that has not yet been demonstrated in reality.

The difficulty, then, is not in leaving what is real.
It is in releasing what has been projected onto it.

This is where most men hesitate. They do not want to let go of something that feels like it could become meaningful, even when the present does not support that direction. So they remain engaged, not because the pattern is stable, but because the possibility still feels alive.

The Proven Man recognizes this dynamic clearly. He understands that investment does not justify continuation and that imagined outcomes do not override observable patterns.

When something is no longer aligned, he does not anchor himself to what has already been given or what might eventually be gained. He returns to what is consistent, and he decides from there.

Because consistency—not potential—is what ultimately reveals the truth of an interaction.

III. From Potential to Attachment

Potential is where attachment takes its strongest form. Not in what is happening, but in what could happen. Most men do not stay because things are working. They stay because they believe things might begin to work.

There is enough to point to: moments of connection, glimpses of compatibility, and instances where everything briefly feels aligned to justify continued investment.

A few moments of connection can be mistaken for direction. A good conversation can feel like compatibility. A short period of alignment can feel like proof that something meaningful is forming. In those moments, the mind begins to build a story around what has not yet been established.

It could improve.
She has good qualities.
There is strong connection—sometimes.

Each of these reinforces the same pattern. Attention shifts away from consistency and moves toward possibility. Instead of evaluating what is repeatedly demonstrated, the focus becomes what might eventually emerge.

But potential is not a pattern.

Patterns, not isolated moments, define the relationship.

The Proven Man does not ignore potential, but he does not prioritize it over what is repeatedly demonstrated. He understands that isolated moments of alignment do not carry the same weight as sustained behavior over time.

What matters is not what appears occasionally, but what remains consistent without effort or interpretation.

Detachment allows him to make this distinction clearly. He separates what is reliable from what is intermittent. He recognizes the difference between something that truly exists and something that appears briefly before disappearing again.

Without that separation, confusion begins to form. Attention becomes divided between what is happening and what is hoped for. The interaction becomes difficult to evaluate, and time begins to pass without real movement.

The Proven Man does not remain there.

He observes patterns over time, allowing them to establish themselves fully before deciding where to invest. He does not rush to conclusions, but he does not delay them once consistency, or the lack of it, becomes clear.

Because of that, his decisions are not based on optimism.

They are based on what has already been shown.

IV. The Cost of Holding On Too Long

When detachment is absent, the shift rarely happens all at once. It does not begin with a clear decision to remain in something misaligned. Instead, it unfolds gradually through small adjustments that seem reasonable in the moment but compound over time.

At first, the changes are subtle. You begin to justify what you would normally question. Behavior that once would have stood out becomes easier to explain away. You tell yourself it is situational, temporary, or not significant enough to matter.

What was once clear begins to feel negotiable.

From there, adaptation follows. Instead of evaluating whether the situation truly aligns, you begin adjusting yourself to fit what is in front of you. Expectations shift. Responses change. You become more flexible, more tolerant of inconsistency, and more willing to absorb misalignment in order to preserve the connection.

This does not usually happen because you lack awareness. It happens because something about the interaction still feels valuable, and you are trying to preserve that.

But in doing so, clarity begins to erode.

Your attention is no longer anchored in what is consistent. It becomes divided between what is happening and what you hope will eventually stabilize. Instead of observing the interaction, you begin managing it.

Over time, this creates internal friction, a subtle tension that becomes harder and harder to ignore.

The Proven Man recognizes this shift early. He understands that standards are rarely lowered all at once. They move slowly, shaped by repeated exposure to what does not fully align. If that process continues long enough, what once would have been unacceptable can begin to feel normal.

This is the real cost of holding on too long.

It is not just the time lost.

It is the gradual movement away from your own clarity.

The longer you remain in something that requires constant justification, the more your sense of what is acceptable begins to shift. That shift rarely happens consciously. It develops through repetition.

Over time, the effect becomes visible not only in the interaction, but in yourself. Energy becomes scattered. Focus becomes inconsistent. A quiet fatigue begins to form from trying to reconcile what you feel with what you see.

Detachment prevents this. It preserves clarity by ensuring that what is misaligned is not given the time to reshape what remains true.

V. The Skill of Seeing It Early

Detachment is often associated with the moment of leaving, but its real value appears much earlier. It is not simply the ability to walk away. It is the ability to recognize when walking away will eventually be required.

Most men do not struggle because they cannot leave. They struggle because they wait too long to recognize what is already forming. By the time the decision becomes obvious, attachment has already taken hold, making separation far more difficult than it needed to be.

The Proven Man approaches this differently. He does not wait for clarity to arrive in a single moment. Instead, he allows clarity to develop through observation. He pays attention to patterns as they begin to take shape rather than after they have fully established themselves.

Inconsistency in effort does not need to become extreme before it is recognized. Confusion in communication does not need to persist for months to be acknowledged. Imbalance in energy does not need to escalate before it becomes visible.

He notices these things early. Confusion, urgency, and reaction are recognized before they fully take hold. Because clarity remains intact, he is still able to make smaller, steadier, and more deliberate decisions before attachment complicates the process.

This is a skill.

It requires attention, patience, and the willingness to trust what is being observed before it becomes undeniable. It also requires discipline: the ability to act on that observation without needing further confirmation through prolonged experience.

There comes a point where what is being observed is already clear. Beyond that point, continued observation does not create more clarity; it delays a decision that has already been made.

The Proven Man does not wait for collapse.

He recognizes the pattern while it is forming and adjusts accordingly.

A simple question keeps this process clear:

Am I responding to patterns—or to moments?

The answer determines whether he remains grounded in reality or becomes pulled into interpretation.

VI. What Walking Away Actually Looks Like

Walking away is often imagined as a defining moment, something expressed through confrontation, explanation, or emotional resolution. In reality, it rarely takes that form.

It is not a speech.
It is not a negotiation.
It is not an attempt to be understood.

It is a decision, followed by behavior that reflects it.

The Proven Man does not rely on words to finalize what has already been made clear through observation. Once alignment is no longer present, he does not attempt to manage the outcome or extract closure through conversation. He does not explain his reasoning in detail, nor does he seek validation for the decision itself.

Instead, he adjusts his behavior.

He stops investing where there is no return. He no longer engages in the same way. Distance forms, not through conflict or resistance, but through the quiet withdrawal of attention and energy.

There is no need to create tension in order to leave. There is no need to define the ending beyond what has already been demonstrated through pattern. The interaction resolves itself through the absence of continued investment.

Because of that, the exit remains calm and controlled.

It is clean.
It is quiet.
And it is final.

This does not come from avoidance. It comes from clarity. When something has been seen fully, there is nothing left to debate.

The Proven Man understands that not every situation requires expression. Some require only alignment between what is known and how he chooses to act.

VII. Why Clean Exits Matter

How a man leaves something matters, not for the other person, but for himself.

A departure that is reactive, emotional, or unresolved does not create true separation. It extends the interaction beyond its natural end point. Even after physical distance is created, the experience can remain active internally.

This is the result of a messy exit.

When emotion drives the departure, attachment often remains. There is a tendency to revisit what happened, to question whether more could have been said, or to feel the need to explain further. The interaction lingers, not because it is still relevant, but because it was not concluded with clarity.

The Proven Man avoids this entirely.

He does not leave in a way that keeps him tied to what he has already decided to move on from. His exit reflects the same discipline that guided his evaluation. It is consistent, measured, and free of unnecessary expression.

A clean exit does not create loose ends.

It protects his energy by preventing continued engagement. It reinforces his standards by aligning his behavior with what he has already recognized. And it allows him to reset fully, without carrying the interaction forward in thought or emotion. This is what it means to leave with clarity.

There is no need to revisit the decision. No need to re-engage. No need to question what has already been made clear through consistent observation.

The Proven Man understands that clarity is not only about seeing correctly; it is about acting in a way that preserves that clarity afterward.

Before stepping away, his position is already established. He is no longer investing. He is no longer negotiating internally. His behavior is already aligned with his standards.

From that point, walking away is not a disruption, but a continuation of what has already begun.

VIII. When Emotional Pull Remains

Detachment does not always end the moment you walk away. Even after the decision is made, emotional attachment can take time to fully release. The decision may be clear, and your behavior may already reflect it, yet internally the attachment can still linger for a period of time.

This is where many men misread what they are experiencing.

After distance is created, their thoughts do not immediately settle. It returns to what was familiar. It revisits what felt good. It isolates moments of connection and begins to give them more weight than they held when viewed in the full context of the interaction. What was once seen clearly as inconsistent can begin to feel meaningful again when remembered selectively.

From there, doubt can begin to form. Not because the original decision lacked clarity, but because emotional residue has not yet fully dissipated. The mind begins to question what has already been resolved. It looks for reasons to reconsider, reach out, or reopen what has already been closed.

This is the emotional pull when attachment has not yet fully released.

It does not present itself as logic. It presents itself as feeling—a quiet sense of absence, a subtle tension that seeks relief, a pull toward what once felt significant even if it lacked consistency. The experience can feel convincing, not because it is accurate, but because it is familiar.

The Proven Man does not confuse this with new insight.

He recognizes it for what it is: the natural release of attachment. It is not evidence that the decision was wrong. It is evidence that there was investment, and investment does not disappear the moment a decision is made.

That release can take many forms. There may be sadness. There may be anger. There may even be moments where the emotion surfaces physically, where a man feels the weight of the experience fully and allows it to pass through him. This is not weakness. It is the natural response to genuine investment. The Proven Man does not suppress what he feels—he simply refuses to let what he feels distort what he already knows to be true.

Because of that, discipline is required, not in deciding to walk away, but in maintaining that decision once the emotional response begins to surface.

He does not act on every thought that arises, and he does not follow every feeling back into action. He allows the impulse to exist without responding to it. There is no urgency to resolve it and no need to revisit what has already been understood.

Instead, he returns to what was observed rather than what is being remembered. He remains anchored in what was consistent, not in what was occasional.

Over time, the pull weakens, not because it is resisted, but because it is not reinforced. Without action, without re-engagement, and without mental negotiation, it gradually loses its influence. And as attachment releases, healing occurs.

This is where detachment deepens.

It is no longer just the ability to walk away, but the ability to remain away without internal conflict or second-guessing.

And this is often where men lose their footing—not in the moment of leaving, but in the moments that follow. What comes next reveals whether the decision was grounded in clarity or dependent on the absence of pressure.

IX. When She Comes Back

This is where detachment stops being theoretical. It becomes real.

Distance has been created. The decision has been made. The interaction has been left behind with clarity.

And then, without warning, she returns.

A clean exit does not always prevent someone from resurfacing. The interaction begins again, and conversation starts to flow.

The tone is different. The energy feels lighter, more open, more intentional. There is renewed attention, deeper curiosity—sometimes even a version of her that appears more aligned than before.

And in that moment, everything can feel possible again.

Not because anything has fundamentally changed, but because the emotional experience has. Familiarity returns. Attraction follows. The tension that once existed is replaced, temporarily, with relief.

And with that shift, the mind begins to question what it had already resolved.

This is where many men lose their footing.

They do not return because the situation has improved in any meaningful way. The return is driven by feeling. The absence created clarity—but the reappearance reintroduces emotion. And without discipline, emotion begins to override memory.

The Proven Man does not allow that to happen.

He does not evaluate the present moment in isolation. He evaluates it in context. A single moment—no matter how positive—does not redefine a pattern that has already been observed over time.

Renewed attention is not the same as real change.
A shift in energy is not the same as a shift in character.

Because inconsistent dynamics often move in cycles.

Distance creates space.
Space creates reflection.
Reflection can create temporary adjustment.

And when that adjustment reappears in the interaction, it can feel like progress.

But without underlying change, the pattern does not disappear.

It resets.

This is what makes the moment deceptive.

It feels different. It appears improved. But in reality, it is often the same dynamic re-entered at a more appealing point in the cycle. When that is not recognized, the outcome does not change; it only arrives later.

The Proven Man does not rely on how the moment feels.
He relies on what has been demonstrated consistently.

He asks a different question:

Am I seeing change—or just the return of attention?

Not in words.
Not in short bursts of effort.
Not in how things feel for a few days.

But in pattern.

Has inconsistency been replaced with consistency?
Has confusion been replaced with clarity?
Has the behavior that created distance been resolved, not temporarily, but sustainably?

If the answer is unclear, he does not rush back into the interaction. He allows time to reveal the truth.

Because real change does not need to be proven quickly.
It proves itself through repetition.

This is where detachment becomes discipline in its most refined form.

It is not just the ability to walk away.
It is the ability to remain aligned even when the door opens again.

The ability to feel the pull, recognize the familiarity, and still choose based on what is real rather than what is being reintroduced.

The Proven Man remembers clearly. He does not allow selective memory to reshape what was experienced. He does not isolate the good and minimize the rest.

He holds the full picture, and decides from there.

Because patterns are not changed by a moment.
They change because of sustained behavior over time.

And without that, re-entry is not a new opportunity.

It is the continuation of the same cycle.

The Proven Man understands this. He does not chase the return of something that was already inconsistent. He does not interpret renewed attention as proof of value, and he does not allow temporary alignment to outweigh sustained misalignment.

He remains grounded in what is consistent.

If something has genuinely changed, it will not need to be assumed. It will be clear, steady, and repeated.

Until then, he does not choose to re-enter the cycle before observing whether the pattern has truly changed and whether it consistently aligns with his direction.

Because at this level, detachment is no longer about leaving.
It is about not returning to what you already understood.

X. The Internal Standard

Detachment is often misunderstood as a reaction to something clearly wrong. In reality, it rarely works that way. Most situations do not end because they are obviously broken. They end, or should end, because they do not align.

There is a difference.

When something is clearly wrong, the decision is easy. There is little to evaluate and little to question. But when something is almost right—when there is connection, attraction, and moments of alignment—the decision requires a different level of discipline.

This is where the internal standard becomes decisive.

The Proven Man does not wait for things to deteriorate in order to justify walking away. He does not require failure, conflict, or obvious dysfunction to make a clear decision. Instead, he evaluates based on alignment, not extremes. His attention remains on what is consistent, not on what appears occasionally.

Because of that, his threshold is not determined by how bad something becomes.

It is determined by whether the interaction ever fully meets what he has already defined as necessary.

This is what separates him.
He is not reacting to discomfort.
He is responding to misalignment.

Difficulty alone does not create misalignment. Every meaningful relationship will encounter friction, disagreement, and moments where growth requires patience and effort. The Proven Man does not walk away from challenge simply because it requires work. When there is mutual effort, honesty, and a shared willingness to address problems directly, he remains present and engaged. Growth is part of alignment.

Detachment becomes necessary only when effort is one-sided, when patterns remain unchanged despite clarity, or when the interaction repeatedly moves away from stability rather than toward it.

Even when the interaction contains moments that feel good, he does not allow those moments to override the broader pattern. He does not rationalize inconsistency simply because there are periods of engagement, and he does not adjust his expectations to preserve something that has not demonstrated stability.

Instead, he steps back and observes over time.

If effort is intermittent, he sees it.
If communication lacks clarity, he registers it.
If energy fluctuates without reason, he does not ignore it.

And when those patterns remain unchanged, he does not negotiate with them.

He disengages—quietly, without resistance, and without needing the situation to deteriorate further in order to feel justified.

Because his direction is already established.

The Proven Man protects his time, his focus, and his energy by refusing to invest where alignment is incomplete. He does not wait for confirmation through failure.

He decides through consistency.

And once that decision is made, he moves forward without needing anything to break first.

XI. The Identity Shift

At a certain point, detachment is no longer something the Proven Man practices.

It becomes something he embodies.

Early on, detachment may feel deliberate. It requires conscious effort to step back, to evaluate clearly, and to act without being pulled by emotion. But over time, as awareness sharpens and standards become fixed, the process begins to change.

It becomes automatic.

The Proven Man is no longer someone who holds on to inconsistency, hoping it will stabilize. He no longer chases clarity through continued engagement or remains confused waiting for resolution to appear.

That version of him is no longer present.

In its place is someone who recognizes misalignment early, without needing it to fully develop. Someone who acts on what is observed without hesitation. Someone who moves forward without carrying the interaction with him once it has been resolved.

This is the shift.

It is not behavioral.
It is foundational.

The Proven Man does not need to remind himself to detach. He does not need to convince himself to walk away. The decision is already aligned with who he is, and because of that, it happens without internal conflict.

There is no second-guessing.
No revisiting.
No pull to return once clarity has been established.

His clarity no longer depends on the outcome.

This changes everything.

Dating becomes clearer. Attraction becomes easier to evaluate. Connection becomes something that is recognized rather than chased. And his sense of direction remains intact regardless of who enters or leaves his life.

The Proven Man is no longer defined by the interactions he experiences.

He is defined by the standards he maintains and the decisions that reflect them.

XII. Attachment and Lost Momentum

Attachment rarely stops a man all at once. It slows him gradually.

At first, the effect is difficult to notice. Life continues moving. Responsibilities are handled. Daily routines remain intact. But beneath the surface, something begins to narrow.

Attention returns repeatedly to the same unresolved place. Energy remains tied to what has not fully aligned. And over time, momentum begins to weaken.

This is the hidden cost of attachment.

Not simply emotional discomfort, but the quiet fragmentation of focus.

The Proven Man understands that direction is shaped by what consistently holds his attention.

When something no longer aligns, continued investment is not harmless. It divides energy between what is moving forward and what is quietly holding him in place.

Because of that, he pays close attention to stagnation. Not just within the interaction itself, but within himself.

When thought begins circling the same uncertainty repeatedly, he notices it. When clarity has already formed but action continues to delay, he also notices. When emotional investment remains active without real progress, he understands that attachment has begun replacing movement.

This is where detachment protects him.

It allows him to release what no longer contributes to his direction before it begins consuming more of his focus, energy, and time. Instead of remaining psychologically tied to what is unresolved, he returns his attention to what continues to move his life forward.

Because of that, he does not remain suspended between clarity and action.

He moves without resistance.

Not impulsively. Not emotionally. But in alignment with what has already been revealed through repeated observation.

When something consistently fails to stabilize, he does not continue negotiating with it internally. He accepts what is being shown. And once that acceptance occurs, movement returns naturally.

There is nothing left to hold in place.

His attention expands again. His focus sharpens. His direction becomes uninterrupted.

There is no need to revisit. No need to mentally rehearse what has already been understood. No need to remain emotionally anchored to something that no longer belongs in his path.

The Proven Man does not protect every connection.

He protects his momentum.

XIII. Letting Go Completely

Most men hold on until something breaks. They wait for a clear ending—something undeniable that removes all doubt and makes the decision for them. Until then, they remain. They tolerate. They continue investing, even as clarity quietly builds beneath the surface.

By the time they finally let go, the decision is no longer theirs. It has already been made by the situation itself.

The Proven Man does not operate this way.

He does not wait for breakdown in order to act on what is already visible. He does not need conflict, distance, or loss to confirm what has been consistently shown.

When something does not align, he recognizes it early. More importantly, he trusts what he sees.

So he lets go. Not abruptly or emotionally, but with precision.

There is no explanation needed beyond what has already been understood. There is no need to revisit the decision once it has been made. There is no pull to return to something that has already revealed its limits.

He does not carry it forward, and he does not look back.

Because he understands that what he chooses to hold onto shapes who he becomes.

The man who cannot let go will always be influenced by what he should have left behind. His energy becomes divided. His attention remains partially fixed on something unresolved.

Over time, that fragmentation weakens his ability to move forward with clarity.

The man who can let go completely is different. He remains intact.

He does not lose himself trying to preserve something that was never right. He does not negotiate with misalignment, and he does not delay his own direction for the sake of temporary attachment.

When something ends, it ends fully. And because of that, he is free.

Nothing unresolved continues pulling at him internally.

Detachment, in its highest form, is not distance.

It is clarity maintained over time.

It is the ability to step back without distortion, to see without emotional interference, and to move forward without carrying the past into the present.

When that becomes natural, something deeper begins to settle.

There is no urgency to define things prematurely. No need to force conclusions before they have fully formed. No need to act before patterns have fully revealed themselves.

Because what is real does not require acceleration.

It reveals itself.

Time exposes what emotion often cannot.

What is consistent reveals itself over time.

And because the Proven Man is no longer held back by attachment, he can allow that process to unfold—without interference, without assumption, and without rushing ahead of what time will inevitably make clear.

Chapter Distillation

Detachment is not about leaving people behind.

It is about refusing to abandon your clarity.

The Proven Man does not wait for things to break before he acts on what he already understands.

He observes patterns, recognizes misalignment, and moves forward before attachment has the chance to reshape his judgment.

Detachment is not avoidance.

It is disciplined clarity.

This is where proof becomes separation.

Not in what a man says—but in what he is willing to leave behind.

When he releases what does not align without hesitation, that is proof.
When he does not return to what has already been revealed, that is proof.
When his direction remains unchanged after walking away, that is proof.

Clarity has already shown him what is real.

Now his detachment determines what remains.

And over time, what he refuses to return to defines the life he continues to build.

He does not wait for conflict or collapse before recognizing misalignment. Instead, he recognizes it early, trusts what it reveals, and acts before emotional attachment begins to distort his judgment.

Because a man who can step away from what does not align protects something far more valuable than the interaction itself.

He protects his direction.

The Proven Man Principle

Clarity reveals misalignment.

Detachment protects direction.

Direction determines the life a man builds.

Chapter Ten

Time

The Revealer of Truth

Once detachment is established, something begins to change.

There is no longer a need to rush toward clarity or urgency to define what has not yet revealed itself. The Proven Man is no longer pulled by uncertainty, and because of that, he no longer tries to resolve it prematurely.

Instead, he allows time to do what it does best: reveal.

Time is not passive. It is not something to wait through or endure. It is an active force within every dynamic, one that exposes patterns, tests consistency, and brings alignment or misalignment into full view. What appears compelling in a moment is tested over time. What is unstable cannot sustain itself, and what is real does not need to be rushed.

The Proven Man understands this.

He does not try to figure everything out early. He does not search for immediate certainty or attempt to define something before it has had the chance to become clear on its own. Where most men feel pressure to understand quickly, he remains grounded in observation.

Because he knows something they often overlook.

You do not understand a person in moments.
You understand them in patterns.

And patterns only reveal themselves over time.

Most men replace observation with assumption. They interpret early energy as meaning, early connection as alignment, and early consistency as proof. But without time, none of it is reliable. It is incomplete. These are fragments that have not yet been tested.

The Proven Man does not build on fragments.

He builds on what is shown repeatedly.

Because of that, he does not accelerate the process or force clarity. He allows behavior to repeat, to stabilize, or to break down on its own.

And in doing so, he sees what others miss.

He sees what sustains itself.

I. Why Time Matters More Than Intensity

Early attraction is often convincing.

It carries energy. It feels immediate, engaging, and at times rare. There is a sense that something meaningful is forming gradually, but all at once. The interaction flows easily. Attention is consistent. The connection appears strong without effort.

But what is felt early is not always real.

Intensity can create the impression of alignment, but the two are not the same. Often, it is driven by what is new, what is stimulating, and what creates emotional movement. Novelty, chemistry, and the exchange of attention can generate a powerful sense of connection, even when there is no underlying stability to support it.

The Proven Man understands this distinction.

He does not confuse what feels strong with what is sustainable. He does not assign meaning to early energy before it has been tested. Instead, he allows time to do what intensity cannot.

Filter.

What begins with energy must eventually continue without it. Excitement fades. Familiarity replaces novelty. Effort is no longer driven by impulse, but by intention. What once felt effortless begins to require consistency.

When that initial surge settles, something more accurate begins to appear.

What endures.
And what fades.
Time has a way of separating the two.

Most connections do not pass through this transition. What felt engaging at the start begins to lose structure. Communication becomes inconsistent. Effort fluctuates. The energy that once felt natural becomes conditional. What appeared to be alignment reveals itself as temporary intensity.

The Proven Man does not react to this shift.

He expects it.

He watches what happens when the moment is no longer carrying the interaction. He observes whether consistency replaces excitement, or if everything that felt strong begins to dissolve when it is no longer new.

Because that is where the truth is found.

Not in how something begins, but in how it continues.

A connection that relies on intensity will always require it to survive. A connection grounded in alignment will remain steady even when intensity is no longer present.

This is why time matters.

It removes what is unsustainable and reveals what is real.

And the man who understands this does not get carried away by what feels powerful in the moment. He remains grounded long enough to see whether it still exists when the moment passes.

II. What Time Actually Reveals

Time does not change people.
It exposes them.

In the beginning, most interactions are shaped by intention. There is effort, attention, and a natural tendency to present well. People are more aware of how they show up. They are more engaged, more responsive, and more deliberate in how they communicate.

But that version is not difficult to maintain for a short period.

What matters is what happens after.

As time passes, effort either stabilizes or fades. Attention either remains consistent or becomes conditional. What was once intentional becomes habitual, and is far more revealing than effort.

This is where the shift occurs.

The Proven Man does not evaluate someone based on how they show up briefly. He watches how they show up repeatedly. A single moment, no matter how strong, carries little meaning without consistency behind it.

Because of that, he begins to notice what others overlook.

Consistency or inconsistency.
Effort or convenience.
Stability or volatility.

These distinctions are rarely obvious in isolated moments. A single interaction can feel aligned. A single conversation can feel meaningful. A single week can feel consistent.

But none of those, on their own, define anything.

Patterns do.

And patterns only become visible through repetition.

Anyone can show up well when the interaction is new, when attention is high, or when the moment calls for it. Very few can maintain that same level of presence over time without fluctuation.

That is where truth exists.

Not in what is shown once, but in what is sustained.

The Proven Man does not rush to conclusions based on early impressions. He allows behavior to repeat, stabilize, or shift. He observes what remains when there is no longer any need to impress, no urgency to maintain momentum, and no external pressure shaping behavior.

Because what remains in those moments is not performance.

It is reality.

And once that becomes clear, there is nothing left to interpret.

Only something to accept or walk away from.

III. The Illusion of Early Clarity

Men often think they understand someone early. That impression strengthens quickly.

It rarely feels that way in the moment.
It feels like clarity.

A sense of certainty begins to form, subtle at first, then reinforced through interaction. The connection feels natural. Conversation flows easily. There is comfort, alignment in certain areas, and enough shared energy to create the impression that something meaningful has already been established.

"This feels right."
"She's different."
"We just connect."

These thoughts are not necessarily false.
But they are incomplete.

The Proven Man recognizes that early clarity is often an illusion. It's not because the experience lacks authenticity, but because it lacks depth. What is being observed may be real, but limited. It exists within a narrow window of exposure, shaped by a context that has not yet been tested.

Without time, there is no contrast.
No pressure.
No inconsistency.
No deviation from the initial presentation.

Without those elements, there is no way to see the full picture.

What appears as clarity is often coherence within a controlled environment: two people interacting under favorable conditions where effort is high and friction is minimal.

But alignment is not proven in ease.

It is revealed through variation.

Through differences in mood, stress, priorities, and time.

As those variables begin to enter the interaction, something more accurate starts to emerge. Communication patterns shift. Effort either holds or fluctuates. Priorities become visible through action rather than words.

What once felt seamless begins to reveal its structure—or its absence.

The Proven Man does not resist this process.

He expects it.

He does not attach to early impressions or build conclusions from limited data. Instead, he allows the interaction to expand, encounter variation, and reveal itself more fully over time.

He understands that clarity is not created through early intensity or early agreement. It is created through observation across different circumstances, moments, and conditions.

Because he understands something simple:

What feels clear in the beginning is often just the absence of contradiction.

Clarity that cannot withstand time is not clarity at all.

It is assumption waiting to be corrected.

IV. Why Rushing Creates Blind Spots

Rushing does not accelerate clarity.

It distorts it.

When a man moves too quickly, he moves ahead of what has actually been shown. The interaction has not had time to stabilize, patterns have not had time to form, and behavior has not been tested under enough variation to reveal anything reliable. Yet decisions begin to take shape as if clarity already exists

The Proven Man does not make this mistake.

He understands that there is a phase within every interaction where reality is still forming. It is not hidden, but it is incomplete. When that phase is bypassed, what follows is not insight, but assumption.

When pace exceeds awareness, blind spots begin to appear. Investment starts before patterns have stabilized. Commitment forms before behavior has been tested. Attachment develops before clarity exists.

At first, this often feels natural. The connection is engaging, the momentum is strong, and continuing forward feels like the right move. But something quieter is happening beneath the surface.

Movement begins to follow feeling rather than observation.

A man is moving based on what he feels, not on what has been consistently shown.

Once emotional investment takes hold, something shifts. Objectivity becomes more difficult, and attention begins to narrow. Instead of observing the interaction as it is, he begins protecting it as something he wants to maintain.

Inconsistencies are softened.
Gaps are rationalized.

What would have been obvious at a distance becomes harder to see from within the experience.

This is the real cost of rushing, not that things moved quickly, but that they moved before there was enough information to see clearly.

The Proven Man avoids this not by forcing himself to slow down, but by remaining grounded in observation. He does not allow the pace of the interaction to determine the pace of his investment.

He lets behavior repeat.
He allows patterns to emerge.

He gives clarity the time it needs to form before assigning meaning to what is happening.

Because he understands something simple.

Speed creates urgency.
And urgency narrows perception.

When urgency is removed, something else becomes available.

Space.

Within that space, awareness expands. Attention broadens. What was previously overlooked begins to stand out, not because it changed, but because it is finally being seen without pressure.

This is why he does not rush.

Not to protect the connection.
But to protect his clarity.

And because of that, he allows the interaction to unfold without interference.

V. The Discipline of Letting Things Unfold

Time requires patience, but not in the way most men understand it.

It is not passive. It is not waiting without awareness, nor sitting back while hoping something becomes clear on its own. That kind of patience lacks presence. It drifts away from what is actually happening.

The Proven Man approaches this differently.

His patience is active.

He remains engaged, attentive, and fully present within the interaction. But he does not interfere with its natural progression. He does not rush to define it, and he does not attempt to move it forward before it has revealed enough to justify doing so.

He allows it to unfold.

And while it unfolds, he observes.

He watches whether behavior remains consistent over time or fluctuates depending on circumstance. He notices whether effort is sustained, increases with familiarity, or gradually declines once the initial energy fades. He pays attention to communication—whether it creates clarity and direction or introduces confusion and inconsistency.

These are not questions he asks directly.

They are answers he allows to emerge.

The most accurate understanding rarely comes from what someone explains. It comes from what someone demonstrates repeatedly, without prompting.

This is where discipline becomes necessary.

The discipline is not about artificially holding back or resisting what is happening. It is about maintaining the space necessary for reality to reveal itself fully.

There is no urgency to label the connection.
No need to accelerate its pace.
No pressure to define the connection before it is earned.

The Proven Man is comfortable within that space.

He does not need immediate answers. He does not seek reassurance through premature conclusions. Instead, he allows the interaction to expand across different moments, contexts, and variations.

Because clarity is not found in a single instance.

It is found in what repeats.

Over time, this becomes instinctive. Observation becomes natural rather than deliberate. Patterns are noticed as they form. Shifts are recognized without overreaction. Consistency, or the lack of it, becomes visible before deeper investment is made.

Because of that, when he does move forward, the decision is not based on assumption.

It is based on what has already been shown.

VI. The Power of Repetition

Anyone can have a good moment.

A conversation can feel meaningful. An interaction can feel aligned. Even a short period of consistency can create the impression that something real is forming.

In isolation, these moments can be convincing, especially when they align with what you want to see.

The Proven Man does not evaluate isolated moments.

He evaluates what repeats.

A moment, no matter how strong, does not establish anything on its own. It is only a glimpse; an instance of behavior under a specific set of conditions. Without continuation, it has no structure. Without repetition, it has no reliability.

This is where most men lose clarity.

They assign meaning to singular experiences. One meaningful conversation becomes depth. One strong week becomes consistency. One emotional connection becomes compatibility. From there, conclusions begin to form that are not supported by sustained behavior.

The Proven Man does not build on assumptions.

He allows time to turn moments into patterns.

He watches what happens after the initial impression.

Does the effort continue without prompting?
Does the interest remain consistent once the interaction is no longer new?
Does behavior stabilize, or fluctuate depending on mood, circumstance, or convenience?

Because repetition removes ambiguity.

What happens once can be influenced by many things: timing, emotion, environment, even coincidence. But consistent behavior begins to reflect something deeper. It reveals priorities, habits, and underlying patterns that cannot be maintained artificially over time.

This is where clarity becomes grounded.

Not in what is shown once, but in what is sustained.

The Proven Man does not rush to define something based on early moments.

He allows those moments to either repeat and strengthen, or fade and reveal themselves as temporary. As repetition accumulates, the pattern becomes visible.

Once the pattern is clear, the decision becomes simple.

Patterns are what you build on.

Or walk away from.

VII. Where Most Men Get Impatient

Impatience rarely appears as urgency.

More often, it shows up as a quiet need to define something before it has had time to reveal itself fully. A desire to understand where things are going. A pull to create certainty while the interaction is still forming. In the moment, this can feel reasonable, almost responsible.

But beneath it, there is something less stable driving the behavior.

Discomfort with the unknown.

The Proven Man recognizes that this is where impatience begins. Not in action, but in intention. The need for labels too soon. The search for reassurance before consistency exists. The subtle attempt to secure the connection while it is still undefined.

These are not signs of clarity.

They are signs of tension with uncertainty.

When that tension is present, perception begins to shift. Instead of observing what is actually happening, attention moves toward resolving how the situation feels. The focus is no longer on whether the connection is aligned, but on whether it can be made to feel certain.

In that shift, something important is lost.

Objectivity.

When uncertainty is forced to resolve too quickly, attachment forms before clarity exists. You begin to give weight to a dynamic that is still incomplete. Investment grows around the idea of what something could become, rather than continuing to observe what it consistently is.

The Proven Man does not move this way.

He does not rush to define what is still unfolding, and he does not seek reassurance in the absence of demonstrated consistency. Instead, he allows uncertainty to exist without needing to resolve it immediately. He understands that clarity gained too early is rarely accurate.

More often, it is constructed to relieve internal tension rather than reflect reality.

So he waits, but not passively.

He remains present, attentive, and grounded, allowing time to do its work. As time passes, uncertainty resolves itself. What is consistent becomes clear. What is not begins to fall away. What once felt undefined gradually becomes either stable or unsustainable.

In this way, patience becomes a form of discipline.

Not the discipline of holding back.

The discipline of not interfering.

Because the real question is not simply what something becomes.

It is whether you are allowing it to show you—

Or deciding before it has.

VIII. Time and Emotional Control

Time does not only reveal her.
It reveals who you are.

It exposes how you respond when there is no immediate clarity, no consistent reinforcement, and no defined outcome to rely on. In the absence of feedback, your internal state becomes visible. What you feel, what you assume, and how quickly you move are no longer shaped by what is happening, but by how well you can remain grounded without it.

This is where most men struggle.

Not because they lack awareness, but because they rely on progress to feel stable. They look for signs, for movement, for reassurance that something is developing. When that feedback becomes inconsistent or delayed, their state begins to shift.

Attention tightens. Thoughts accelerate. The impulse to act, clarify, or secure something begins to rise.

The Proven Man does not depend on that.

He remains steady without constant validation. He does not require immediate return on his attention or investment in order to stay grounded. He remains consistent in how he shows up, regardless of whether the external response matches his pace or expectation.

This is where emotional control is visible and tested.

Not in moments of intensity—

But in moments of absence.

When clarity is delayed and feedback is limited, the question becomes internal.

Can you stay present without needing confirmation?
Can you remain clear without needing definition?
Can you continue observing without rushing to resolve what is still unfolding?

For most men, the answer is no—not because they are incapable, but because they have not developed the ability to sit with uncertainty without reacting to it.

The Proven Man has.

He does not interpret silence as loss, and he does not interpret delay as rejection. He allows space to exist without assigning meaning to it prematurely. His focus remains on what is consistent over time, not on what is felt in a single moment.

Because of that, his energy remains stable.

It does not fluctuate with every shift in attention. It does not rise with excitement or drop with uncertainty. It remains grounded, measured, and internally regulated, even when external feedback is limited or unclear.

This is what creates control.

Not the elimination of emotion,

but the ability to remain unchanged within it.

Over time, this stability becomes one of the clearest signals of strength. It demonstrates that your internal state is not dependent on what you receive. Your position remains steady regardless of external movement.

It is established before anything is given.

IX. Letting Behavior Speak

Over time, words begin to lose their weight.

Early in an interaction, language carries influence. Promises feel meaningful. Expressions of interest feel convincing. Intentions, when spoken clearly, can create the impression that something solid is forming.

But without time behind them, words remain untested.

They reflect what someone can say, not necessarily what they will do.

The Proven Man understands this distinction.

He listens, but he does not rely on what is said. He watches what is done.

Time removes the ability to maintain an image that is not supported by behavior. Anyone can present well in the beginning. Anyone can communicate interest, availability, or intention when the interaction is new. But as time passes, effort either continues—or it does not. Attention either stabilizes—or it fluctuates.

What is consistent begins to stand apart from what was simply expressed.

This is where behavior becomes the only reliable signal.

The difference between promise and follow-through becomes visible. The gap between stated interest and actual effort is no longer theoretical; it is observable. Attraction, if real, translates into investment. If it does not, what was felt or said early on begins to lose its meaning.

The Proven Man does not confront this prematurely.

He does not question it or seek clarification too early. Instead, he allows behavior to speak without interference. He gives it the time necessary to confirm itself—or contradict itself. As repetition accumulates, the pattern becomes visible.

Once the pattern is clear, there is nothing left to interpret.
Because what is real does not require explanation.

It repeats.

What does not repeat begins to fade, regardless of how convincing it once seemed.

This is why he does not attach to early words or initial impressions. He allows them to be tested naturally over time, and in doing so he removes guesswork entirely.

In the end, behavior does not need to be analyzed.

It only needs to be observed.

X. When Time Gives Its Answer

There comes a point where the question is no longer open.

Not because something was explained, and not because a single moment provided clarity, but because the pattern has repeated enough times that it can no longer be misinterpreted. What once felt uncertain becomes visible through consistency. What once required analysis becomes obvious through accumulation.

Time makes the answer clear.
It removes the need to interpret.
It leaves only what has been shown.

The Proven Man recognizes when that moment arrives.

He does not continue searching for explanations once the pattern is established. He does not revisit early impressions or rely on isolated moments to challenge what has already been shown repeatedly.

Repetition is not coincidence.

It is information.

And when that information becomes clear, the role of observation begins to close.

This is where the shift occurs.

The question is no longer, "What is this?"

That question belongs to the earlier phase—when clarity is still forming and understanding remains incomplete. During that phase, observation is necessary and patience is required. But once time has done its work, the question changes.

It becomes something more direct.

And more demanding.

Am I willing to accept this pattern?

This is where discipline meets clarity.

Because at this stage, the challenge is no longer seeing the truth. The truth is already visible. The challenge is responding to it without distortion. Once the pattern is clear, not responding becomes a decision in itself.

The pull to reinterpret, to justify, or to hold onto earlier moments can still exist. The mind may search for exceptions, looking for reasons to soften what has already been established.

The Proven Man does not negotiate with what is consistent.

He does not attempt to reshape the pattern to fit what he prefers. He accepts what is being shown fully and without distortion. From that position, the decision becomes simple—not because it is easy, but because it is clear.

He either accepts the pattern as something that aligns with his life.

Or he does not.

There is no in-between.

Because once time has given its answer, continuing to question it is no longer confusion.

The answer is not something he continues searching for.
It is something he either accepts or resists.

Otherwise it is avoidance.

XI. The Cost of Ignoring Time

There is a difference between not seeing—and not accepting.

Most men do see the pattern. They notice the inconsistency. They feel the imbalance. They recognize when effort fluctuates, when communication creates confusion, and when something does not fully align.

But recognition alone is not enough.

What time reveals must also be respected.

This is where the cost begins.

When a man overrides what time has already shown him, he extends an experience that has already defined itself. He remains longer than he should, not because he lacks information, but because he resists acting on what is already clear. He invests more than he should, not because the connection has earned it, but because he continues holding onto what it could become.

The Proven Man does not make this mistake.

He understands that time is not offering suggestions.
It is presenting evidence.

And once that evidence becomes clear, ignoring it does not change the outcome.
It only delays the moment he eventually has to face it.

This is where misalignment deepens.

Not in the initial uncertainty—

But in the decision to remain after clarity has already formed.

Each additional moment spent in something that does not align creates internal friction. He begins to feel it: in his focus, in his energy, and in the quiet tension that develops when his actions no longer match what he already knows.

This is the real cost.

Not only time, but clarity.

The longer he remains in a dynamic that contradicts what has already been shown, the harder it becomes to trust his own judgment. He begins to question what he sees—not because it has changed, but because he has chosen not to act on it.

The Proven Man does not disconnect from what he sees.

He respects it.

Even when it is inconvenient. Even when it requires letting go of something that once felt promising. He does not wait for the situation to worsen in order to justify a decision. He acts when the pattern is clear, because that is when the truth is already present.

In doing so, he avoids unnecessary outcomes, not by controlling the situation, but by responding to it correctly.

Ignoring time does not protect a man from the result.

It only ensures that he endures it longer than necessary.

Respecting time creates something very different.

Clarity without conflict.
Decisions without hesitation.
And movement without regret.

XII. The Advantage of Patience

Patience is often misunderstood as inaction. In reality, it is discipline applied over time.

The Proven Man does not use patience to delay decisions. He uses it to improve them. He understands that clarity cannot be rushed, and that decisions made without sufficient information are rarely accurate, no matter how confident they may feel in the moment.

By trusting time, something shifts in how he moves.

He makes fewer emotional decisions, not because he suppresses what he feels, but because he does not allow those feelings to dictate immediate action. Instead, he gives them space to settle, stabilize, and be understood within the context of what is consistently being shown.

Emotion is acknowledged, but it is not allowed to lead. Observation remains primary.

What is repeated carries weight. What appears briefly is noted, but not elevated beyond what it has demonstrated. Over time, this separation between feeling and evaluation becomes natural.

This changes what he invests in.

The Proven Man avoids unstable dynamics early, not through prediction, but through observation. What is inconsistent reveals itself before deeper investment is made. What is misaligned becomes visible before it has the chance to take root.

Because of that, he does not find himself entangled in situations that were unclear from the start—only unexamined.

Most importantly, he builds on what is proven.

Not what is assumed.
Not what is promised.
Not what is felt in a single moment.

What is demonstrated repeatedly.

Repetition removes uncertainty. It reveals priorities, habits, and character in ways that isolated moments never can. When behavior sustains itself over time, it becomes something real, something that can be trusted.

This does not eliminate risk entirely. No process can.

But it removes the unnecessary risk that comes from acting too soon, investing too early, or committing before clarity exists. It allows decisions to be made from a position of grounded awareness rather than emotional momentum.

Patience, in this sense, becomes an advantage. It prevents wasted energy and protects attention.

It keeps direction intact while others become pulled into situations that were never stable to begin with.

The Proven Man does not rush to define what has not yet earned definition. He allows time to confirm what is real.

And when he moves forward, he does so with confidence—not because he forced certainty, but because certainty revealed itself without pressure.

XIII. The Internal Shift

At a certain point, something fundamental changes.

It is not a new strategy, and it is not something consciously applied within each interaction. It is a shift in how a man sees. A shift in what he trusts. A shift in where his attention naturally rests.

Before this, a man's focus is forward.

He looks for direction. For signs of progress. For indications of where something might lead. The question is always some variation of the same thing:

Where is this going?

Beneath that question is an underlying need: to know, to secure, to feel certain about what is still unfolding.

But that way of seeing is rooted in anticipation.

It pulls attention away from what is actually happening and places it on what is hoped for next.

The Proven Man no longer operates from that position.

He is not concerned with where something is going until it has shown him what it consistently is.

His attention shifts away from projection and returns to observation. He is no longer trying to define the future of the interaction. He allows the present to reveal its pattern.

And that changes everything. When projection stops, the pressure that distorts perception begins to disappear. He is no longer trying to connect moments into a story that may not exist. He is no longer filling in gaps with assumption or intention.

He is simply watching what repeats.

What is this consistently showing me?

That question does not reach forward.

It anchors attention in the present.

It places attention on behavior, on patterns, on what is real and measurable over time. It removes the influence of hope, urgency, and imagined outcomes, and replaces them with something far more stable.

Clarity.

This is where the shift becomes permanent.

The Proven Man no longer needs to remind himself to slow down. He no longer needs to manage expectation or correct his thinking in real time. His perspective has already changed. He trusts what is shown, not what is suggested. He responds to what is consistent, not what is possible.

Because of that, his decisions become cleaner.

There is no internal negotiation. No second-guessing driven by emotion. No attachment to what could be.

There is only what is, and his willingness to accept it or walk away from it.

This is where perception matures.
Not by learning more, but by seeing differently.

And once that shift occurs, it does not reverse.

Because he no longer looks for answers in potential.

He recognizes them in patterns.

XIV. Time Protects Clarity

Time is not something to move through—it is something to use.

The Proven Man does not treat time as a delay between moments—he understands it as the mechanism that brings truth into view. What cannot be seen in a single interaction, what cannot be understood through words alone, and what cannot be confirmed through early intensity is revealed through duration.

Time removes distortion. It strips away what cannot be maintained, exposes inconsistency, and reveals whether what is felt can actually be sustained.

Most men resist this process. They rush to define, to label, to decide before enough has been shown. In doing so, they trade clarity for certainty, attaching meaning to moments that have not yet earned it.

But the truth does not respond to urgency. It unfolds on its own timeline, through repetition, variation, and consistency.

The Proven Man allows that process to unfold without interference.

He does not force understanding before it is ready, and he does not attach to what has not yet been proven. He remains patient, not passively, but with intention, observing what repeats, what stabilizes, and what begins to fade.

Over time, what is real becomes unmistakable. And what is not loses its weight without the need for analysis or interpretation.

Because of this, his clarity is protected. His energy remains grounded. His decisions are no longer shaped by assumption or early emotion, but by what has been consistently demonstrated.

He does not need to search for truth or extract it prematurely. He allows it to emerge.

Most men try to define a connection early. The Proven Man lets it establish itself. And when it does, something more accurate becomes possible.

Once clarity is established through time, the question is no longer whether something is real. It becomes whether it belongs.

Not whether it can continue—
but whether it fits within the life he is building.

Learning to observe patterns over time changes how a man evaluates every relationship and opportunity in his life. Within The Proven Man System, this becomes one of the core ways men make decisions with clarity.

In that shift, decision-making becomes clean, direction becomes defined, and what once required effort is replaced by quiet certainty.

Chapter Distillation

Time does not create truth.
It allows it to become undeniable.

The Proven Man does not rush to conclusions, and he does not build his life on early impressions. He observes what repeats, trusts what endures, and allows reality to show itself before deciding what deserves his investment.

Time is the discipline that protects clarity.

This is where proof becomes consistency.

When what is shown repeats, that is proof.
When what endures does not require explanation, that is proof.
When patterns remain unchanged over time, that is proof.

He does not define connections based on early emotion or momentary intensity. Instead, he observes what stabilizes, what endures, and what proves itself over time.

Through patience and attention, patterns become visible.

Once they are visible—
decision becomes unavoidable.

Clarity does not remove responsibility.
It defines it.

The Proven Man Principle

Time reveals patterns.

Patterns reveal truth.

Truth determines direction.

Chapter Eleven

Alignment

What Belongs After Clarity

With clarity established through time, a new responsibility emerges. The challenge is no longer seeing clearly, but choosing correctly.

The Proven Man no longer operates from impulse, uncertainty, or assumption. He has observed patterns. He has allowed behavior to reveal itself. He has separated intensity from consistency and moment from meaning. Because of that, he is no longer trying to understand what something is. He is deciding whether it fits.

This is where alignment becomes central.

Most men do not struggle to create connection. They do not struggle to generate attraction, build rapport, or maintain interaction. What they struggle with is choosing correctly once those things exist. Connection, on its own, is not rare. It can be created in many places, with many people, under many conditions.

But alignment operates differently. The Partner reveals herself through consistency.

Alignment is not about whether something feels good in the moment. It is about whether it fits, structurally, consistently, and over time, within the life you are building. It determines whether a connection can exist without friction, without constant adjustment, and without requiring you to compromise what matters in order to maintain it.

The Proven Man understands this distinction.

He does not pursue connection for its own sake or measure value by intensity, attention, or emotional pull. Those things may be present, but they are no longer decisive. They are observed, not followed.

Because without alignment, even the strongest attraction becomes unstable.

What begins with energy eventually requires effort. What feels natural begins to feel managed. Over time, what once felt promising becomes something that must be sustained through adjustment rather than supported through compatibility.

The Proven Man does not build on that.

He chooses what fits.

Not what excites him temporarily. Not what feels compelling in brief moments. But what integrates cleanly into his standards, his direction, and the structure of his life.

Because once clarity has been established, the standard is no longer whether something can work.

It is whether it should.

I. What Alignment Really Means

Alignment is frequently misinterpreted.

It is not perfection. It is not the absence of differences, nor is it the expectation that two people think, feel, and operate in exactly the same way. The Proven Man does not look for sameness. He looks for compatibility in the areas that determine whether something can function over time.

Because alignment is structural.

It exists in the deeper layers of a connection—values, lifestyle, communication style, emotional patterns, and direction in life. These are not surface-level preferences that can be adjusted without consequence. They shape how two people interact, how they respond under pressure, how they handle conflict, and how they move forward together over time.

This is where many men lose clarity.

They feel a strong connection and assume alignment is present simply because the interaction feels good. But feeling strongly for someone does not mean you fit with them. Attraction can exist without compatibility. Chemistry can exist without stability. When those are mistaken for alignment, the foundation is already unstable.

The Proven Man does not confuse the two.

He understands that two people can connect easily, enjoy each other's presence, and still be misaligned in ways that matter. Those differences do not fade with time. They become more visible. What feels minor in the beginning—differences in communication, emotional needs, or pace of life—gradually becomes friction when repeated consistently.

Because what is misaligned does not correct itself through intensity.

A connection may begin with energy, natural flow, and strong attraction. But if one person values independence while the other requires constant emotional reassurance, that difference will not resolve itself through effort alone. It will surface repeatedly, creating tension where there was once excitement.

The Proven Man pays attention to this early.

He does not ignore subtle friction simply because the overall interaction feels good. He does not override what feels slightly off in favor of what appears temporarily right. He recognizes that alignment is not determined by how something feels in isolated moments, but by how it functions across time.

When alignment is present, The Partner is felt differently.

There is stability because the effort is mutual and natural.
There is balance because differences complement rather than compete.
There is clarity because behavior remains consistent over time.

When alignment is absent, the opposite begins to emerge.

Not always dramatically, and not always immediately, but subtly, through small inconsistencies, recurring friction, and a quiet sense that something does not fully fit.

The Proven Man does not wait for that friction to become obvious.
He recognizes it while still quiet.

Because that is where alignment is either confirmed—

or revealed not to exist.

II. Why Attraction Alone Is Not Enough

Attraction creates movement.

It generates momentum, pulls two people together, and gives the interaction its initial energy. That energy makes something feel exciting, engaging, and worth exploring. Without it, most connections would never begin.

But attraction is not what sustains a connection.

Alignment is.

The Proven Man understands this distinction clearly. He does not dismiss attraction. He recognizes it, observes it, and appreciates it for what it can offer. But he does not mistake it for deeper compatibility. Attraction, on its own, does not account for how two people function together over time.

A man can feel chemistry. He can feel excitement. He can feel a strong emotional pull toward someone.

None of those guarantee that the connection will work.

Because beneath those feelings are patterns of behavior, communication, emotional response, and lifestyle. If those patterns do not fit together, the connection begins to require effort in the wrong places, not the natural effort of building something, but the constant adjustment of trying to make something fit that does not.

This is where exhaustion begins.

At first, the attraction is strong enough to carry the interaction. The energy feels worth it. The differences feel manageable. But over time, those differences do not disappear. They repeat. With each repetition, more effort is required to maintain what once felt natural.

Some men begin adapting. Adjusting. Compensating.

Not because they are incapable of maintaining the connection, but because the connection itself is not stable without that effort.

The Proven Man does not build on instability.

He pays attention to how a connection feels over time, not just in moments of intensity, but in its natural state. Does it energize him, or does it require ongoing adjustment? Does it flow, or does it need to be managed?

Because a connection that constantly requires adaptation is not sustainable.

It is conditional.

No amount of attraction can compensate for a lack of alignment in the long run.

The Proven Man does not chase what feels strong in the moment if it cannot stand on its own over time. He chooses what holds its shape without constant correction: what remains stable, grounded, and supportive for both people within it.

Because the question is not whether something feels good.

It is whether it works.

III. The Illusion of "It Feels Right"

"It feels right" is one of the most convincing signals, and one of the most incomplete.

Feelings matter. The Proven Man does not dismiss them or attempt to override them. But he understands their limitation. What feels right in a moment is often influenced by temporary conditions: what is new, what is stimulating, or what fills an emotional gap present in that moment.

Because of this, feeling right is not the same as being right.

A connection can feel natural, effortless, and even meaningful in isolated moments. Conversation flows. Energy is high. The interaction carries a sense of ease that suggests something deeper is forming. But those moments exist within a specific context, one that has not yet been tested by time, routine, or variation.

The Proven Man does not mistake that for alignment.

He understands that moments do not determine alignment. What holds over time does.

This is where the illusion begins to break.

A connection may feel strong in curated environments: weekends, planned time together, or moments where attention is focused and energy is high. But as the dynamic moves into everyday life, where routines, responsibilities, and natural rhythms take over, differences begin to surface. Communication patterns shift. Effort becomes uneven. Emotional responses begin to diverge.

What once felt aligned begins to require correction.

The Proven Man watches for this transition.

He does not anchor himself to how something felt at its peak. He observes how it holds under normal conditions. Because that is where sustainability is determined.

This is why he does not rely on the feeling that something is right.

He allows that feeling to be tested.

Because what is truly aligned does not only feel right in moments.

It continues to function when those moments pass.

At some point, observation becomes a decision.

Patterns reveal themselves over time. Clarity comes from evaluating what those patterns consistently produce.

This is where the decision becomes structured rather than emotional.

The Decision Map provides a simple process for recognizing the nature of a dynamic and choosing the direction that protects your standards and your future.

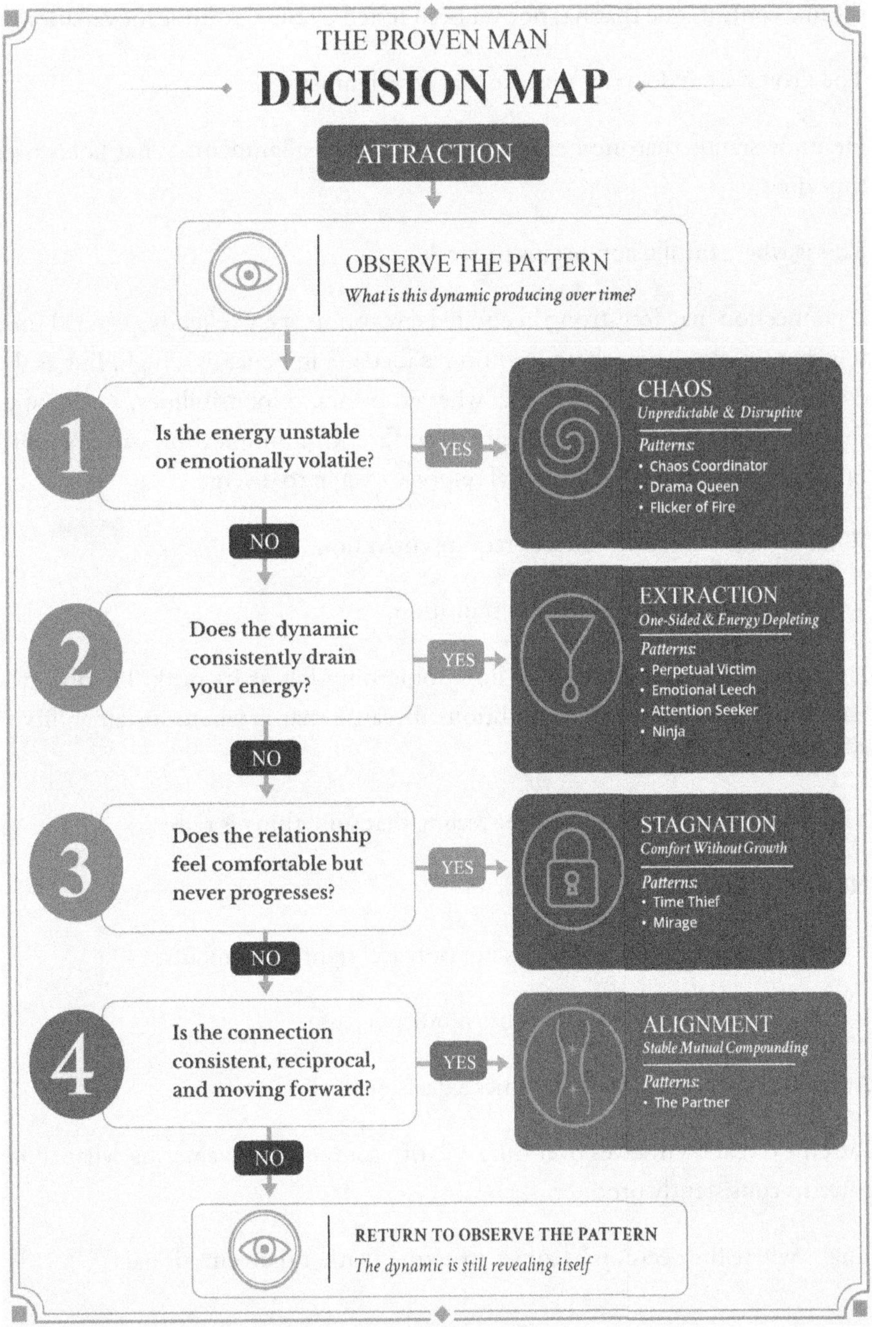

Every dynamic eventually reveals what it produces.

Some create instability.
Some quietly drain energy.
Some remain comfortable but never move forward.
And one builds something stable, reciprocal, and enduring.

The Proven Man does not chase potential.

He observes the pattern and chooses what aligns with the life he is building.

IV. Where Misalignment Shows Up

Misalignment rarely announces itself.

It does not appear as something obvious or immediately disruptive. In the beginning, most differences feel small, manageable, even insignificant. The interaction is still new, the energy is still strong, and the focus often remains on what is working rather than what is slightly off.

The Proven Man pays attention to that.

Because that is where misalignment begins.

It appears in subtle ways. Differences in expectations around effort: how often you connect, how consistently you show up, how much initiative is taken. Differences in the balance between independence and closeness: how much space is needed versus how much reassurance is expected. Differences in communication rhythm: how clearly things are expressed, how quickly tension is addressed, and how naturally understanding develops.

Individually, none of these seem significant.

But over time, they repeat.

When they repeat, they begin to shape the entire experience of the connection.

What once felt like a minor difference becomes a recurring point of friction. Not dramatic enough to end the interaction immediately, but persistent enough to create a subtle tension that never fully resolves. You begin to notice it in small moments such as slight misunderstandings, mismatched expectations, or a sense that something requires more effort than it should.

The Proven Man also understands the difference between natural variation and true inconsistency.

No person is static. Energy shifts. Moods fluctuate. There are days when communication is lighter, presence is lower, or emotional availability changes. This is part of being human and not a sign of misalignment on its own. There is a rhythm to people. Energy rises and falls. Presence expands and contracts.

Alignment is not found in the peaks or the dips, but in what remains consistent through both.

What matters is not the moment—it is the pattern around it. Does communication return to clarity? Does effort re-stabilize? Does the connection correct itself naturally without confusion or tension building over time?

Healthy variation moves within a stable structure.

Misalignment breaks that structure.

And when the structure begins to break, it rarely does so all at once.

It happens gradually. A delay that becomes a pattern. A miscommunication that stops being resolved. An imbalance in effort that no longer corrects itself. What once felt occasional begins to feel expected. What was once dismissed as situational begins to reveal itself as consistent.

This is where many men lose clarity.

Because the connection still feels good in parts, they anchor themselves to those moments. They revisit the highs, justify the inconsistencies, and remain engaged with what the interaction once was rather than what it is becoming. They attempt to preserve the feeling even as the structure beneath it begins to weaken.

The Proven Man does not do this.

He does not anchor himself to isolated moments of alignment while ignoring patterns of misalignment. He does not allow emotional highs to override structural inconsistencies. He understands that what repeats is what defines the experience—not what occasionally appears.

Because alignment is not proven in moments where everything works.

It is proven in what continues to work consistently, naturally, and without correction.

When consistency is not present, he does not wait for friction to become undeniable.

He recognizes it early,

when it is most honest.

V. The Cost of Ignoring Alignment

Ignoring misalignment does not remove it.

It shifts the responsibility onto the man experiencing it.

At first, the adjustments feel small. A man becomes more flexible. More understanding. More willing to adapt in order to maintain the connection. It feels reasonable, like effort, like compromise, like something relationships naturally require.

But there is a difference between mutual adjustment and one-sided compensation.

The Proven Man recognizes that difference early.

When alignment is present, both people move toward each other naturally. Effort is shared. Understanding develops without force. The connection stabilizes without constant correction.

When alignment is absent, that balance begins to shift.

He starts compensating for differences that do not resolve. He adjusts his behavior to maintain momentum. He overlooks inconsistencies to preserve the feeling of the connection. What was once occasional becomes something he anticipates and prepares for.

Over time, this changes his position within the dynamic.

He is no longer participating in something that flows.

He is managing something that resists.

The interaction becomes less about connection and more about maintenance. He begins thinking ahead, adjusting in real time, and subtly carrying more of the structure than he should. Not because he is incapable of doing so, but because the connection itself does not hold its shape without his effort.

This is where clarity begins to erode.

Not all at once, but gradually.

He begins to normalize what once stood out. He becomes more tolerant of what he would not have accepted before. His standards do not disappear. They adapt to the situation he has remained in. Because the change is incremental, it often goes unnoticed until the dynamic feels fundamentally different from how it began.

There is also a hidden cost that most men do not immediately recognize.

The more he compensates, the less clearly he sees.

His attention shifts away from evaluation and toward preservation. He stops asking whether the connection fits and starts focusing on how to keep it working. He begins solving problems that should have been signals. He invests energy into managing friction instead of questioning why it exists in the first place.

In doing so, he loses his position as the one who chooses.

He becomes the one who adjusts.

The Proven Man does not allow this shift to take hold.

He does not compensate for misalignment in a way that distorts his standards. He does not repeatedly adjust himself to stabilize something that cannot stabilize on its own. He observes where effort is required, and more importantly, where it continues to be required without resolution.

Because that is the signal.

Where he is consistently adjusting is where alignment is lacking.

If that pattern persists, no amount of effort will transform it into something stable.

It will only deepen his investment in something that does not fit.

This is why he steps back before committing further.

He watches patterns over time. He notices where things correct themselves, and where they do not. He allows enough space for consistency to reveal itself before increasing his level of investment.

Because once a man invests deeply, objectivity becomes harder.

And the cost of ignoring alignment becomes much higher.

The Proven Man avoids that cost not by doing more—

but by seeing clearly sooner.

VI. Short-Term Chemistry vs Long-Term Compatibility

Short-term chemistry is immediate.

A man feels it without effort. The conversation flows. The energy is engaging. There is a sense of excitement that makes the interaction feel significant, even early on. It creates momentum quickly, and because of that it is often mistaken for something deeper than it is.

But chemistry is not a measure of fit.

It is a reaction.

The Proven Man understands this distinction. He does not dismiss chemistry, but he does not rely on it to make decisions. What feels strong in the moment is not what determines whether something will hold over time.

Compatibility does.
This cannot be felt instantly.
It must be observed.

It reveals itself through patterns: how two people function together beyond the initial energy. How they communicate when things are not effortless. How their habits interact when routines begin to form. How naturally balance develops without one person needing to adjust more than the other.

This is where the shift happens.

What begins as chemistry is tested by reality.

Does the dynamic feel stable, or does it fluctuate depending on mood, timing, or circumstance? Do their lifestyles support each other, or require ongoing compromise to stay aligned? Is there a natural rhythm to the interaction, or does it require constant awareness to maintain?

These are not questions chemistry can answer.

They are questions only time and observation can reveal.

Because compatibility reduces friction.

It allows the connection to exist without constant correction. It creates an environment where both people can remain themselves without needing to reshape who they are to sustain the interaction.

Misalignment does the opposite.

It creates subtle resistance. It introduces the need for adjustment. It turns what should feel natural into something that must be managed.

And the longer that continues, the more energy it requires.

This is where many men lose direction.

They continue chasing how the connection feels in its strongest moments rather than evaluating how it functions across time. They prioritize intensity over stability, and in doing so invest in something that cannot sustain itself without effort.

The Proven Man does not chase the feeling.

He evaluates the structure behind it.

He recognizes chemistry, but he measures compatibility. He observes whether the connection holds its shape when the intensity settles. He looks for stability beneath the surface, not just stimulation within it.

Because what lasts is not built on how something feels at its peak.

It is built on how it functions consistently.

And that is what he chooses.

VII. The Role of Standards

Alignment does not happen by chance.

It is determined by what a man is willing to accept, and what he is not.

Without standards, attraction leads. The strongest feeling in the moment becomes the deciding factor. What feels good is pursued. What creates intensity is prioritized. Because of that, decisions become reactive rather than intentional.

The Proven Man does not operate this way.

He understands that attraction, on its own, is not a reliable guide. It can pull him toward something engaging, stimulating, even exciting, but not necessarily something that fits. Without a structure in place, it becomes easy to follow that pull without questioning where it leads.

This is where standards become essential.

Standards are not preferences. They are not flexible depending on the situation or the person in front of him. They are established beforehand. They define what is acceptable, what is sustainable, and what aligns with the life he is building.

They do not adjust to accommodate attraction.

They remain steady regardless of it.

Because of that, The Proven Man uses standards as a filter.

They determine what he allows into his life. They guide what he chooses to invest in. They shape what he continues to explore, and what he steps away from early.

They prevent him from committing to something that does not actually fit, even if it feels compelling in the moment.

This is what creates clarity.

Instead of reacting to intensity, he evaluates through structure. Instead of being pulled by how something feels, he measures it against what he knows works. The decision is no longer driven by emotion alone. It is grounded in alignment.

And that changes the entire experience.

He is no longer trying to make something work.

He is determining whether it should.

The Proven Man does not look for reasons to continue.

He looks for reasons that justify investment.

If those reasons are not consistently present, he does not override that absence with feeling.

He trusts the standard.

Because the standard protects his direction.

It keeps him anchored when attraction is strong. It keeps his decisions consistent when emotions fluctuate. It ensures that what he builds is not based on momentary intensity, but on something that can actually hold over time.

This is why standards create a different kind of presence.

There is no urgency in him. No need to force momentum or secure an outcome. He is not chasing clarity—he already has it.

Because of that, he moves with a calm confidence that does not depend on how the interaction unfolds.

He is grounded before the connection begins.

And he remains grounded within it.

VIII. How to Evaluate Alignment in Practice

Alignment is not something a man evaluates in a single moment.

It is something he recognizes over time.

One conversation can feel strong. One interaction can feel effortless. One experience can create the impression that everything fits. But none of those, on their own, are enough to establish alignment.

The Proven Man understands this.

He does not rush to define the connection based on isolated moments. He allows it to unfold, and more importantly, he observes how it unfolds. Alignment is not revealed through intention or words—it is revealed through behavior repeated consistently over time.

He pays attention to how she handles consistency.

Not just when it is easy, but when life becomes routine. Does her level of effort remain steady, or does it fluctuate depending on mood or convenience? Does the connection maintain its shape, or does it require re-establishing each time?

He notices how she responds to boundaries.

Not through what she says, but through how she adjusts. Respect for boundaries is not demonstrated through agreement. It is demonstrated through behavior that aligns with them over time.

He observes how she communicates under pressure.

Anyone can communicate well when things are smooth. But when there is stress, misunderstanding, or tension, clarity is tested. Does communication become more direct and grounded, or more reactive and inconsistent?

Most importantly, he watches whether behavior matches words.

Because words can create momentum.

But only behavior sustains it.

This is where alignment becomes visible.

Not in what is promised, but in what is repeated.

Patterns, not promises, define the connection.

The Proven Man does not get caught in isolated examples of "being good." He does not overvalue moments of high effort if they are not maintained. He is not persuaded by potential when consistency is not present.

He looks for what continues. That is where The Partner reveals herself.

This is why he creates space before increasing investment.

He allows enough time for patterns to form. He pays attention across multiple interactions, across different contexts, and across shifts in energy and circumstance. He is not looking for perfection. He is looking for stability.

A simple practice, rarely applied with discipline, is for The Proven Man to keep a mental record of repeated behaviors over time. Not in a rigid or analytical way, but with awareness. He notices what happens consistently over the course of weeks, not days. He notices where effort stabilizes, and where it does not. He notices where clarity builds, and where confusion repeats.

Once the pattern becomes clear, the decision becomes simple.

The challenge is not understanding what is happening.

It is choosing based on what he sees.

And the Proven Man does both.

IX. The Importance of Direction

Alignment is not only about who someone is in the present.

It is also about where they are going.

Two people can meet at a point where things feel easy, natural, even compatible. Their lifestyles may overlap. Their communication may flow. Their connection may feel balanced in the moment. But if their direction is different, that alignment will not hold.

Because direction determines whether something can continue. Not just whether it works right now.

The Proven Man understands this.

He does not evaluate a connection based solely on how it feels in the present. He looks at trajectory. He pays attention to how she approaches growth, how she prioritizes her time, what she is building toward, and how that direction interacts with his own. He considers how their paths move in relation to one another: whether they support each other naturally or begin to pull in different directions.

Compatibility in the moment can be misleading.

Two people can function well today, but create friction tomorrow if their paths begin to diverge.

This is where many men overlook what matters.

They focus on how well things are going now. They anchor themselves to the current experience. In doing so, they ignore subtle indicators of where things are heading. Differences in ambition, lifestyle, emotional needs, or long-term priorities may not create immediate tension, but over time they shape the direction of the relationship.

If that direction is not aligned, the connection will eventually require adjustment to continue.

The Proven Man does not wait for that point.

He asks the deeper questions early—not out loud, but internally.

Are we moving in a way that supports each other over time?

Do our priorities naturally complement one another, or will they compete as life becomes more defined?

Is there a shared understanding of growth? Not identical, but compatible enough to move forward without resistance?

These questions do not require immediate answers.
They require observation.

Direction reveals itself the same way alignment does.

How someone makes decisions.
How they respond to responsibility.
How they handle change.
How they invest their time, energy, and attention.

These patterns indicate where they are going, whether they state it clearly or not.

The Proven Man does not confuse stated intention with demonstrated trajectory.

He watches what is repeated. He observes where time, energy, and focus are consistently invested. That is what reveals whether two paths are moving together, or simply crossing for a period of time.

When alignment in direction is present, The Partner moves forward naturally beside him. Growth reinforces the bond instead of creating distance. Both people expand without pulling away from each other, because their movement supports the same general direction.

When direction is misaligned, something more subtle begins to appear.

Progress creates tension.

Priorities begin to conflict.

What once felt easy starts to require coordination, compromise, or restraint to maintain.

The connection is no longer naturally aligned—it is being held together.

The Proven Man does not force alignment where it does not exist.

He does not slow his direction to preserve a connection, and he does not attempt to accelerate someone else to match his own. He recognizes direction for what it is. Not where it could go, but where it is already heading.

From that clarity, the decision becomes simple.

He either moves forward, with alignment supporting him.

Or he moves on, with clarity guiding him.

X. When Alignment Is Present

Alignment does not need to be explained.

It is experienced.

There is a natural stability to the dynamic that does not rely on constant effort or correction. Conversation flows without overthinking. Plans come together without resistance. Time spent together feels grounded rather than uncertain.

The Proven Man recognizes this. Not as intensity, but as stability.

There is no need to force momentum or create connection. It builds on its own.

Each interaction reinforces the last rather than resetting or creating doubt. There is continuity. There is direction. There is a sense that what is developing has structure beneath it, not just energy within it.

Communication becomes clear.

Not perfect, but consistent.

There is little confusion about where things stand because behavior aligns with words. When something is expressed, it is followed through. When something changes, it is addressed directly. This removes the need to interpret, guess, or fill in gaps.

Clarity replaces uncertainty, and with it, quiet confidence in the interaction itself.

With The Partner, effort becomes mutual. It is not measured or negotiated, but naturally balanced. Both people contribute without needing to be prompted. The dynamic holds itself because both individuals are invested in a way that is steady and reliable.

There is no strain in maintaining momentum. It is sustained without force. Because of that, stability emerges.

The connection supports his life rather than competing with it. It adds clarity rather than confusion and creates forward movement rather than hesitation.

What is aligned does not require force to continue.

It continues because it fits.

Over time, that fit becomes undeniable. Not through intensity, but through repetition and consistency.

The Proven Man does not fall in love. He rises into it, building through clarity, discipline, and the ability to recognize what truly aligns.

What forms is not based on projection or hope. It is built on something that has been tested, observed, and chosen deliberately.

XI. When Alignment Is Missing

When alignment is missing, it rarely announces itself clearly.

It is felt subtly at first.

There is a sense that something is slightly off, even in moments that appear good on the surface. The interaction may still carry attraction. Conversation may still flow at times. There may even be periods where everything appears stable.

But beneath it, instability begins to appear, and that instability requires effort to manage.

A man begins to explain more than he normally would. He adjusts his behavior to maintain momentum and compensate for gaps in communication, effort, or clarity.

What should feel natural begins to require awareness and correction. Not constantly, but often enough to be noticeable.

Patterns begin to break.

Moments of strong connection are followed by periods of distance or confusion. Effort fluctuates. Communication shifts. What feels clear one day becomes uncertain the next.

Because of that, he is never fully grounded in the interaction.

He is present, but not at ease.

Clarity is replaced with interpretation.

He finds himself reading into behavior, trying to understand what changed, or anticipating what might happen next. Instead of experiencing the connection directly, part of his attention is always managing it.

That is the cost of misalignment.
Effort begins to feel uneven.

One person carries the greater share of the interaction, adjusting more frequently to maintain consistency, while the other moves in and out of it.

Slowly, the dynamic begins to shift.

The connection becomes less about mutual participation and more about maintaining stability.

Attraction alone cannot sustain that.

It may create moments that feel strong. It may temporarily mask the imbalance. But over time it cannot compensate for patterns that do not align.

What feels compelling in isolated moments begins to feel draining when experienced repeatedly without consistency.

The Proven Man does not ignore this shift.

He does not rationalize it or attempt to stabilize something that is inherently unstable. He recognizes that the need to consistently adapt is not a challenge to solve. It is a signal to observe.

Because when something is aligned, it does not require ongoing adjustment to function.

It holds on its own.

When it does not, no amount of effort will make it sustainable.

If adaptation is constant, the balance is not real.

XII. The Discipline of Choosing Alignment

Choosing alignment requires restraint.

Not everything that feels good should be pursued.

There are moments where attraction is strong, the connection feels easy, and the experience is enjoyable in the present. But without structure beneath it—without consistency, direction, and mutual alignment—those moments cannot sustain themselves over time. What feels compelling now may not hold later, and without discipline it becomes easy to invest based on feeling rather than reality.

The Proven Man does not confuse a good experience with a good fit.

He understands that something can feel engaging, exciting, even meaningful in the moment and still be misaligned in ways that will matter over time. Because of that, he does not allow intensity to dictate the pace of his investment. He remains steady, grounded in what has been demonstrated, rather than what is temporarily felt.

This is where restraint becomes visible.

Not in what he avoids,

but in how he chooses.

He is willing to walk away from strong chemistry when it lacks structure. He is willing to pause when consistency has not yet been established. He is willing to let something remain undefined rather than forcing it into progression before it has earned that movement.

Not because he is hesitant,

but because he is clear.

Many men struggle at this point, even when they understand it.

They recognize the inconsistency. They see the misalignment. But the experience itself feels good enough that they hesitate to step back. They attempt to extend it, shape it, or give it more time in the hope that it becomes something more stable.

But discipline is not about waiting for something to change.

It is about recognizing what is and choosing based on that.

The Proven Man does not negotiate with misalignment. He does not attempt to build on inconsistency, and he does not override what he sees in order to preserve what he feels. He remains anchored in reality, even when the moment invites him to drift away from it.

This is what separates reaction from intention.

He prioritizes long-term fit over short-term experience. He allows what is aligned to develop naturally, without interference. And he allows what is not aligned to fall away—without resistance, without overanalysis, and without the need to extract more from it than it can offer.

Because of that, his energy remains directed.

His time is not scattered across possibilities that have not proven themselves. His attention is not consumed by trying to stabilize something that lacks structure. What he invests in is intentional, and what he withholds from is just as deliberate.

His time remains protected.

He does not give it freely to uncertainty, and he does not extend it in the hope that something will eventually align. Time, once invested, creates attachment. Because he understands this, he invests carefully where consistency has begun to establish itself.

His decisions remain consistent with the life he is building.

They are not influenced by temporary emotion or isolated experience. They are grounded in a broader direction. One that does not shift based on who enters his life, but instead determines who remains in it.

Before increasing his level of investment, he creates space.

Not to hesitate,

but to see clearly.

The Proven Man allows the moment to settle. He separates the feeling from the structure. He steps back just enough to observe without being pulled by intensity.

In that space, clarity returns.

What once felt compelling is now seen in context. What once felt urgent becomes measured against what is consistent. From that position, the decision no longer feels complicated.

A simple measure brings everything back into focus:

If the intensity is removed, it should still feel right.

XIII. The Internal Check

When evaluating a connection, the shift becomes internal. A man is no longer asking what it feels like. He is asking what it is.

The Proven Man does not rely on emotion alone to guide his decisions. He brings awareness into the moment and applies it with precision, separating attraction from alignment, experience from pattern, and feeling from structure. This separation allows him to remain fully present without becoming absorbed in what has not yet proven itself. He can feel without losing clarity, engage without attaching meaning prematurely, and observe without distorting what is in front of him.

From this position, the questions he asks are no longer reactive—they are grounding.

Is this aligned or just attractive?
Would this work over time or only in moments?
Am I adjusting to make this fit, or does it naturally fit?

These questions are not meant to interrupt the experience, but to clarify it for him. They create a subtle pause that shifts attention away from assumption and back to what is observable, repeatable, and real. When asked honestly, they cut through projection and reveal whether the connection is supported by pattern or sustained by feeling alone.

Over time, this process becomes automatic. What once required conscious effort becomes instinctive recognition. Signals that once felt confusing become clear.

Internal conflict and second-guessing decrease, because what is felt and what is seen begin to align.

With that alignment comes a different kind of clarity.

It is not loud or urgent, but quiet and stable.

When something fits, it carries a sense of calm that does not need to be reinforced. It holds without constant validation.

Misalignment, on the other hand, rarely announces itself directly.

It appears as subtle tension: small inconsistencies, slight imbalances, patterns that do not fully settle. They are easy to overlook in isolated moments, but over time they accumulate.

The Proven Man does not ignore that tension.

He does not override it in favor of what feels good in the moment. He respects it, because he understands what most overlook: small misalignments, when repeated, do not remain small.

They expand.

What is subtle early becomes significant later for those who are paying attention.

XIV. Alignment Determines Outcome

Attraction begins the connection, but it does not determine where it goes.

Alignment does.

What feels strong in the beginning often creates the illusion of direction. But without alignment, that direction cannot hold. The relationship must then be sustained through effort, by being managed, adjusted, and continually corrected to maintain momentum. What begins as something natural gradually becomes something that requires attention to preserve.

Over time, that cost becomes unavoidable.

Anything that is not structurally aligned will eventually reveal the imbalance it was built on.

There is always a point where that imbalance becomes clear. The effort begins to outweigh the return. The experience no longer justifies the investment. What once felt engaging begins to feel demanding, and what was initially overlooked becomes impossible to ignore.

This is not a sudden shift.

It is a gradual exposure of what was always there, made visible through repetition and time.

With alignment, something fundamentally different happens. The connection does not need to be sustained in the same way, because it is not built on instability. It supports itself. Not because it is effortless in every moment, but because it is fundamentally compatible.

Effort still exists, but it is mutual. Growth still occurs, but it does not create distance. The relationship moves forward without requiring constant correction, because its foundation does not require it.

It holds, because it fits.

The Proven Man understands that outcome is not determined by how strong something feels in the beginning, but by how well it functions over time. He does not chase intensity in the hope that it will become stable. He does not invest in potential that has not yet proven itself through consistency.

Instead, he chooses what is already demonstrating the capacity to endure.

This is the discipline that protects direction.

In doing so, he reduces uncertainty before the outcome ever fully forms. He is not reacting to where the connection eventually goes.

He is selecting for what can last from the beginning, before deeper investment begins to shape the outcome.

Because of that, the direction of the relationship is no longer determined by momentum or emotion. It is determined by alignment.

XV. Protecting Direction

Most men choose what feels strong in the moment.

The Proven Man chooses what remains stable over time.

He does not prioritize the intensity of a connection. He prioritizes its integrity.

He understands that what feels powerful in the beginning often fades, shifts, or reveals itself to be incomplete. What is aligned—what is consistent, mutual, and grounded—does not require constant reassessment to justify its place in his life. It holds its position without negotiation because it has already proven that it belongs.

Because of that, he does not find himself caught in cycles. He does not build on uncertainty, and he does not invest in something that must continually prove itself without ever fully doing so. His attention is not consumed by trying to stabilize what was never stable to begin with. Instead, he builds on what is already demonstrating its ability to hold.

In doing so, he creates something that does not need to be constantly repaired, redefined, or reconsidered. It stands on its own structure, supported by alignment rather than sustained by effort.

Clarity allows him to see.

But what he does with that clarity is what ultimately defines his life.

Because even when a man can recognize what aligns, and what does not, he is still faced with a decision: what he allows into his life, what he invests in, and what he continues to engage with even when he knows better.

Awareness alone does not change outcomes.
It requires a different decision.

This is where most men fall back into old patterns. Not from lack of awareness, but from lack of standards.

Without a clear internal filter, even the strongest insight can be overridden in the moment. Emotion takes priority. Attraction distorts judgment. Misalignment, once recognized, is still entertained, extended, and given more space than it has earned.

In that space, clarity begins to weaken.

The Proven Man does not allow this. He does not rely on awareness alone.

Structure reinforces it.

Alignment is not simply something a man recognizes. It is something he protects.

Protection requires definition. It requires a standard that determines what is accepted, what is rejected, and what is never allowed to take root in the first place.

Without that, clarity remains vulnerable.

With it, his direction becomes unshakable.

Because once a man sees clearly, the next step is not more understanding.

It is learning how to guard what he allows into his life.

Chapter Distillation

Alignment is not discovered by chance.

It is revealed through patterns, protected through standards, and chosen through discipline.

The Proven Man does not rely on intensity, promises, or potential to determine what belongs in his life. He observes what repeats, trusts what stabilizes, and builds only on what proves itself through consistency.

Alignment is not a feeling.

It is a pattern.

This is where proof becomes alignment.

When what fits remains without effort, that is proof.
When what does not fit falls away without resistance, that is proof.
When what continues supports his direction, that is proof.

He does not measure relationships by intensity or potential. Instead, he observes what repeats, what stabilizes, and what continues to demonstrate its place in his life.

Through this discipline, clarity becomes protection.

Protection preserves direction.

Because the life he builds is not determined by what appears.

It is determined by what fits.

The Proven Man Principle

Intensity attracts.

Patterns reveal.

The Partner is recognized through consistency.

Chapter Twelve

What a Man Allows

The Discipline of Direction

Standards are what turn clarity into action.

Up to this point, a man has learned to observe without reacting, to detach without losing presence, to let time reveal what is real, and to recognize alignment for what it is rather than what it appears to be in isolated moments. But none of that holds without reinforcement. None of it matters if it is not applied consistently in the moments where it is easiest to compromise.

This is where standards take hold.

Standards are the internal filter that protects everything a man has come to understand.

They define what a man allows, what he accepts, and what he walks away from without hesitation, negotiation, or influence from temporary emotion.

Alignment shows a man what fits. Standards ensure he never settles for less than that, even when something feels compelling enough to justify it.

The Proven Man understands this at a deeper level.

He does not rely on awareness alone. He does not assume that seeing clearly is enough to act correctly. In moments of attraction, uncertainty, or emotional pull, clarity can be overridden if it is not supported by structure.

What he sees must be upheld.

Standards provide that structure.

They remove negotiation from the decision-making process. They eliminate the need to reconsider what has already been defined. They create a level of internal consistency that does not shift based on who he is dealing with or how he feels in the moment.

As a result, his behavior becomes stable—not reactive, not situational, but disciplined in direction regardless of external influence.

Most men do not lose control because they lack options.

They lose control because they lack standards.

Without standards, every connection becomes negotiable. Every interaction is influenced by how it feels in the moment. Boundaries shift. Decisions fluctuate. What is accepted one day may be rejected the next, depending on emotion, attraction, or circumstance.

There is no stability in that.

Only reaction.

With standards, something different happens.

Every connection is evaluated before it is invested in. Every behavior is measured against a defined baseline. There is no need to "figure it out" in the moment, because the framework already exists.

And that difference changes everything.

Because the direction of a man's life is not determined by what he wants.

It is determined by what he allows.

The Proven Man does not adjust his standards to accommodate what he feels.

He allows what meets his standards, and releases what does not.

In doing so, he removes chaos from his decisions and replaces it with clarity that holds under pressure.

I. What Enforcement Actually Means

Standards are not enforcement.
They are the structure behind it.

A standard can exist clearly in a man's mind and still fail to shape his behavior when the moment arrives. Attraction, emotion, uncertainty, and attachment all create pressure against what has already been defined. Without reinforcement, even strong standards become flexible under the weight of feeling.

Enforcement is what prevents that.

It is the ability to hold a standard in place after emotion becomes involved. It is the decision to remain aligned with what has already been established, especially when compromise would feel easier in the moment.

At its core, enforcement determines what a man allows into his life, what he accepts once it is there, what he continues to invest in over time, and what he is willing to walk away from without hesitation.

It is not reaction. The decision has already been made before emotion has the chance to influence it.

The Proven Man understands that enforcement is not control placed on others.

It is discipline applied to himself.

It governs his behavior when emotions are involved—when attraction is strong, when uncertainty is present, and when the temptation to compromise feels justified. In those moments, he does not rely on how he feels to guide him.

He follows what has already been decided—without enforcement, decisions become reactive.

They are shaped by the moment, influenced by emotion, and inconsistent from one situation to the next. What is tolerated once becomes easier to tolerate again. What was once a boundary becomes something negotiable.

With enforcement, something else takes over.

Consistency.

His decisions do not fluctuate based on intensity or circumstance. They remain aligned with a defined baseline that does not shift under pressure. Because of that, his behavior reflects stability, not just in how he thinks, but in how he acts.

II. Why Standards Matter More Than Intentions

Intentions do not determine outcomes.

Behavior does.

A man can have clear intentions: to choose well, to build something meaningful, to avoid instability and repetition. But intentions alone carry little weight if they are not consistently applied. In those moments, they are easily overridden.

Not because they are weak, but because they are unstructured.

Attraction does not ask for permission.

Loneliness does not wait for clarity.

Curiosity does not consider long-term consequences.

Emotional highs do not operate with discipline.

In those moments, intention gives way.

The Proven Man understands this.

He knows that what he wants for himself is not enough to guide what he will actually do. Without structure, intention becomes situational. It bends under pressure. It adjusts to justify the moment.

Over time, the gap between what he intends and how he behaves creates inconsistency—first in his actions, then in his outcomes.

Standards close that gap.

They take what is internal and make it enforceable.

They ensure behavior reflects intention even when emotion pulls in a different direction.

They remove the need to decide again in the moment, because the decision has already been made in a state of clarity.

Without standards, a man hopes he will choose correctly.

With standards, the decision is already made.

III. The Moment of Enforcement

Clarity is not the end of the process. It is the point where a decision is required. Seeing clearly does not protect a man's direction. Acting on what he sees does.

The moment a pattern becomes visible, the standard is already being tested. Not later, and not after more time, but in that moment. Most men delay here. They continue observing after clarity has already formed. Space is given where a decision is required. They wait for something to change that has already revealed itself.

This is where standards begin to fail. Not because they are undefined, but because they are not enforced.

The Proven Man does not hesitate once the pattern is clear. He will not continue investing in something that has already shown misalignment. He does not search for exceptions to override what is consistent.

He acts.

Not emotionally.
Not impulsively.
But decisively.

If something aligns, he allows it to continue without interference. If it does not, he steps back without negotiation. There is no middle position once clarity has been established. Delay is not neutrality. It is a decision to remain in something that does not meet the standard.

Every moment after clarity carries a cost. Time continues to be invested. Energy continues to be directed. Attachment continues to build. The longer action is delayed, the harder it becomes to act at all.

This is why enforcement must be immediate—not abrupt, not reactive, but aligned with what has already been seen. The Proven Man does not wait for discomfort to justify action. He acts when the pattern is clear, not when the consequence becomes unavoidable.

Because once something has revealed itself, continuing to engage with it is no longer exploration. It is choice.

IV. The Quiet Erosion of Standards

Standards are rarely broken all at once.

They erode gradually, almost imperceptibly, like a steady drip of water carving through stone.

It begins with small compromises such as a quiet concession here, a slight bend there. At first, it feels insignificant.

"This one time is fine."

"It's not a big deal."

"She'll probably change."

Each exception feels minor, harmless even. But what begins as an occasional overlook slowly becomes part of the landscape. These small adjustments accumulate and patterns begin to emerge.

What was once a hard line becomes flexible.

What he would not tolerate becomes something he accepts almost without questioning.

And it does not happen because his values changed.

It happens because his standards were not upheld when they needed to be.

The moment he allows them to bend, even slightly, they stop serving their purpose. They no longer function as the filter that protects his life and his direction.

Instead, they become negotiable.

Something influenced by attraction, circumstance, or emotion.

The clarity they once provided begins to fade, and without that framework it becomes easier to accept what does not actually align with him.

The Proven Man understands the cost of this erosion. He recognizes the subtle shifts and addresses them before they become patterns. He does not allow small compromises to accumulate into larger misalignments, because he knows that what begins as a minor concession can eventually lead to instability that touches everything.

What was once a momentary exception becomes the new baseline.

And before long, he is no longer just tolerating misalignment.

He is living with it.

This is the danger of quiet erosion.

It is rarely the dramatic break that changes the direction of a man's life. It is the small, repeated compromises that slowly reshape what he accepts until he finds himself living inside something he never meant to allow.

The Proven Man holds firm to his standards because he understands what is at stake. Each decision either reinforces the structure of his life or weakens it.

Protecting his standards is not simply about saying no to misalignment.

It is about recognizing the earliest shifts and reinforcing his boundaries before they begin to disappear.

V. Delayed Decisions Are Decisions

Delay does not preserve clarity. It erodes it.

Once a pattern has been seen, the standard has already been defined. What follows is not a search for more information. It is a decision, either to act on what is clear, or to remain in it despite that clarity.

Most men do not see delay this way. They believe they are giving something time. They believe they are being patient. They believe they are allowing space for things to improve.

But once the pattern is consistent, time does not create a different outcome. It extends the same one.

Delay is not neutral.

It is participation.

Every additional interaction reinforces what has already been shown. Every moment of continued engagement strengthens the pattern, increases investment, and builds attachment to something that has already failed to meet the standard.

This is where clarity begins to lose its authority, not because it was incorrect, but because it was not acted on.

The longer a decision is delayed, the more difficult it becomes to make.

What was once obvious becomes complicated. What was once clear becomes something they begin to question. Not because the pattern changed, but because their position within it did.

They have now invested more. They have now experienced more. They have more to justify. Thus, justification replaces clarity.

The Proven Man does not allow this shift to take place.

He does not continue engaging once the pattern has made itself clear. He does not allow misalignment to become more acceptable over time. He does not reinterpret what he has already seen in order to remain where he should not.

He acts when the decision is simple.

Because once it becomes complicated,
it is no longer clarity.

It is attachment.

VI. What Pressure Reveals

Standards are not revealed when everything is flowing smoothly. It is easy for a man to remain aligned with his boundaries when the connection feels effortless and everything appears to fit naturally.

Standards reveal themselves in moments of pressure. Moments when emotion, desire, and the fear of loss begin pushing against what has already been defined.

The Proven Man understands this. Standards are only proven in the moments that tempt him to abandon them. When uncertainty appears or emotional pull intensifies, that is when his structure either holds firm or begins to weaken.

He does not avoid these moments.

He values them.

Because pressure reveals what is real and exposes what is only theoretical.

A man can speak confidently about standards when nothing meaningful is at risk. But standards have little value until they are tested by something capable of pulling him away from them. Attraction creates urgency. Emotional connection creates attachment. Potential creates justification. Under enough pressure, even obvious misalignment can begin to feel negotiable.

The Proven Man recognizes that pressure, but he does not allow it to override his clarity. Chemistry may feel powerful, but he understands that intensity is not the same as alignment. Rather than becoming consumed by the moment, he allows time and consistency to reveal what is real.

Pressure also reveals how a man responds to uncertainty. These are the moments when clarity has not fully formed, yet emotional investment begins pulling him toward premature decisions. Many men attempt to resolve discomfort quickly.

The Proven Man does not.

He remains grounded within uncertainty. He understands that clarity develops through observation, not urgency. Rather than filling uncertainty with assumption or compromise, he allows it to sharpen his awareness and reinforce his discipline.

Pressure also reveals whether fear controls decision-making. The moment when walking away feels heavier than remaining in something that no longer fully aligns.

The Proven Man does not surrender to that fear.

He understands that strength is not measured by how tightly a man holds onto something, but by whether he can release what no longer supports his direction.

Short-term discomfort protects long-term integrity.

Pressure also reveals whether investment has begun replacing judgment. Time and energy have already been spent, and the idea of stepping away begins to feel like loss.

The Proven Man does not remain simply because he has invested.

He does not allow past effort to dictate future direction.

Time already spent is not the measure of alignment. Integrity is.

This is when compromise becomes most dangerous. The pressure to accept something "good enough" begins intensifying. The Proven Man feels that pressure like anyone else, but he does not yield to it. He understands that temporary compromise often becomes permanent structure. What feels manageable today can become costly tomorrow—emotionally, mentally, and physically.

And this is exactly when standards matter most.

In these moments, standards become the anchor that keeps him grounded. They become the filter through which every decision is measured. When attraction is strong, emotions rise, and the fear of loss begins building, his standards remain fixed.

They do not move with the moment.

They define it.

The Proven Man's standards are not simply lines drawn in the sand. They are boundaries that protect his purpose, his integrity, and the direction of his life.

Discipline in these moments determines what he builds.

Something sustainable,

or something temporary.

This is where real discipline appears: the ability to resist short-term gratification in favor of long-term alignment.

The Proven Man exercises this discipline deliberately. His standards are not reactive guidelines—they are the structure that ensures his life continues moving in the right direction.

When the temptation to compromise appears, he does not react impulsively. Instead, he returns to what he has already defined. He measures the moment against what he values and chooses the path that protects his direction.

He does not bend his standards to serve a temporary feeling.

He holds them in place, knowing that the right connections will always meet him at the level he has chosen to maintain.

VII. When Attachment Overrides Clarity

Emotional attachment asks:

"How do I keep this?"

It is a basic human instinct to hold on—to prevent loss, to preserve what feels good in the moment.

The emotional pull creates a desire for continuity regardless of long-term alignment. It encourages a man to overlook the signs, soften the patterns, and reinterpret the reality of the situation in order to preserve the feeling itself.

Standards ask:

"Does this deserve to continue?"

The question comes from a different place. It is rooted in clarity, grounded in self-awareness, and aligned with long-term direction. The Proven Man asks it because he understands that attachment, while natural, can easily lead him to invest in something that does not truly fit his life.

He does not act from fear of loss.

And he does not pursue comfort at the expense of integrity.

These are two very different frames of reference.

Emotional attachment pulls inward. It reacts to the moment. It is influenced by intensity, chemistry, and the emotional highs that come with connection. Its focus is preservation, and holding on to what feels good in the present even when the long-term picture remains unclear.

Standards operate differently—they evaluate outward.

They create distance from the emotional pull and provide a stable framework for decision-making. The Proven Man's standards function as a filter, ensuring that what he chooses aligns with the larger direction of his life.

Where attachment is driven by feeling, standards are guided by clarity.

Even when emotional attachment appears, the Proven Man remains aware of it. He does not deny the pull, and he does not pretend it is not there.

Instead, he allows it to pass through the structure of his standards.

He asks whether the connection truly supports his direction, or simply feels compelling temporarily.

Attachment may tell him to hold on—standards ask whether holding on is justified.

The tension between these two forces is a defining moment of growth. Emotional attachment is powerful, but it cannot be allowed to determine his decisions.

Standards must remain the authority.
Because attachment seeks comfort.

Standards protect direction.

And the Proven Man understands that only one of those will consistently lead him toward the life he intends to build.

VIII. The Drift Into Compromise

Most compromises do not appear all at once. They emerge gradually, in small and seemingly inconsequential ways, each one easy to dismiss in the moment.

The Proven Man understands this.

He knows that subtle compromise, when left unchecked, erodes the clarity and direction he has worked to establish.

What feels minor at first reveals itself through patterns over time.

Compromise often begins through tolerance.

A man accepts communication that lacks consistency, clarity, or reliability. At first, the tension appears manageable. The confusion feels temporary. Eventually, ambiguity creates instability, and instability slowly reshapes what a man becomes willing to accept.

Compromise also appears when behavior repeatedly fails to match words.

Many men overlook these inconsistencies, hoping things will improve or convincing themselves the pattern is temporary. The Proven Man does not ignore what behavior continues to reveal. He understands that inconsistency is often the earliest visible sign of deeper misalignment.

Compromise also appears when imbalance becomes normalized.

Effort in a healthy connection is mutual. When one person consistently carries the momentum while the other remains passive, the imbalance becomes visible. The Proven Man does not rationalize this pattern or mistake ongoing compensation for connection. He reevaluates where his energy should be invested.

The most damaging compromise occurs when repeated patterns are tolerated simply because emotional attachment has formed.

Patterns are the clearest indicators of alignment or misalignment. While others may justify repeated behavior because of emotional investment, the Proven Man understands that patterns rarely change without deliberate action. When the same signals repeat without correction, he does not wait indefinitely for improvement.

These patterns rarely appear suddenly. They emerge gradually, revealing misalignment long before the connection fully breaks down.

Each compromise feels small in the moment. A slight exception here. A subtle bend there. Nothing that appears significant when viewed individually. But over time, these compromises accumulate. Together they reshape the baseline of what he accepts, and what once felt unacceptable gradually becomes normal.

The Proven Man recognizes this progression early.

He does not allow small compromises to accumulate into larger problems. His standards remain fixed, serving as a constant reference point for his decisions. He understands that bending once makes the next compromise easier, until eventually the boundary itself begins disappearing.

Left unchecked, these compromises create a pattern of misalignment.

What begins as occasional exceptions slowly becomes a way of living: one that moves further and further away from the life he intends to build.

The Proven Man never allows that shift to take hold.

IX. The Cost of Compromise

For the Proven Man, compromised standards are not simply temporary mistakes.

They create a direct path toward misalignment, instability, and wasted energy. The cost is not always visible in the beginning, but over time it becomes impossible to ignore.

When standards weaken, the consequences begin appearing in predictable ways.

One consequence is the type of dynamics a man allows into his life.

What a man accepts eventually shapes what he experiences. When standards weaken, the connections that enter his life often reflect that condition. What feels compelling in the moment frequently lacks the consistency, stability, or depth required for something meaningful to sustain itself.

Another consequence is the behavior a man gradually normalizes.

Compromised standards lead to accepting dynamics that slowly drain energy—emotionally, mentally, and sometimes physically. What begins as patience slowly becomes accommodation. Over time, the connection requires more energy than it returns.

Compromised standards also create repeated cycles.

Without structure, the same patterns return. The same compromises are made. The same warning signs are overlooked. Situations that appear different on the surface begin producing the same underlying outcome.

But the cost of compromise extends beyond relationships.

Over time, it begins reshaping how a man experiences himself and the direction of his life.

Self-respect begins to erode.

Each time a man accepts behavior that contradicts his values, a small amount of internal trust is lost. Doubt begins replacing certainty, and confidence in his own judgment weakens.

Clarity begins to fade.

When standards become inconsistent, decisions are influenced by emotion, temporary desire, or external pressure. Without a stable structure, it becomes harder to evaluate situations objectively.

Direction begins to drift.

Standards shape the path a man walks. When they weaken, that path becomes less defined. Small compromises accumulate until the life he is living no longer reflects the life he intended to build.

The underlying truth is simple. What a man allows into his life often reflects what he believes he deserves within it.

The Proven Man does not allow inconsistency or misalignment to define his experience. By maintaining strong standards, he creates an environment where the connections in his life reflect the same clarity, integrity, and direction he holds within himself.

X. What Strong Standards Require

For the Proven Man, strong standards are not built on rigidity or emotional reaction. They are grounded in clarity and upheld through consistency. They create a structure that ensures his decisions remain aligned with his values and the direction of his life.

Strong standards require clarity.

The Proven Man understands what he stands for and what he will not accept. His standards are defined before the moment tests them. They are not vague or flexible depending on circumstance. Clarity removes hesitation and allows decisions to remain aligned with who he is and where he is going.

Strong standards require consistency.

Standards lose authority when they fluctuate. The Proven Man upholds them across situations, interactions, and relationships. What he accepts today remains the same tomorrow. This consistency creates stability in both his decisions and the environment he builds around himself.

Strong standards require firmness in the areas that define direction.

Values, character, effort, and integrity are foundations. In these areas, the Proven Man does not compromise. If a situation repeatedly contradicts these principles, he does not attempt to force alignment.

Strong standards are not about demanding perfection.

They are about protecting what matters.

The Proven Man allows space for individuality, growth, and difference in areas that do not affect alignment. But when it comes to the principles that determine direction, his standards remain firm.

In doing so, he creates stability without rigidity. He releases what does not fit without hesitation and builds a life that supports his values, his growth, and his long-term direction.

When emotion rises, he does not reconsider—he follows the standard.

XI. What Remains Fixed

For the Proven Man, internal standards are not preferences that shift with emotion or circumstance. They are principles held in place regardless of attraction, pressure, or temporary desire. These standards create structure within his life, protecting his time, energy, attention, and long-term direction from influences that do not truly align.

Consistency matters more than intensity.

The Proven Man values stable behavior over emotional highs that quickly fade. Intensity may create attraction, but consistency creates trust. Lasting connection is built through patterns that remain steady over time, not through moments of excitement that disappear as quickly as they arrive.

Communication must create clarity, not confusion.

Clarity in communication is essential. The Proven Man does not tolerate ongoing ambiguity or mixed signals. Clear communication creates understanding and stability, while confusion introduces unnecessary tension. Because of this, he prioritizes directness and consistency in how people express themselves.

Effort must remain mutual, not imbalanced.

Healthy dynamics require shared investment. The Proven Man observes whether effort moves naturally in both directions. When energy flows only one way—when he is consistently the one maintaining momentum or pursuing clarity—he recognizes the imbalance and reevaluates the connection.

Behavior must continue aligning with words over time.

Promises carry little weight without follow-through. The Proven Man evaluates what people repeatedly do, not simply what they say. Words may create initial momentum, but repeated actions reveal the true level of alignment.

Patterns matter more than isolated moments.

Single moments do not define character.

Patterns do.

The Proven Man observes behavior across time, recognizing that repeated actions reveal a person far more accurately than isolated displays of emotion, attention, or generosity.

These standards are not rules imposed on others.

They are principles the Proven Man refuses to compromise within himself.

They guide how he evaluates situations, how he responds to behavior, and how he determines where his attention and investment belong. By maintaining these internal standards, he protects himself from emotional impulse and continues building a life aligned with clarity, integrity, and long-term direction.

XII. Discipline Over Emotion

Discipline is what keeps standards in place when emotion begins to rise. It creates steadiness when emotional pull intensifies. It is easy to follow principles when everything feels aligned and uncomplicated.

Real discipline appears when attraction strengthens, uncertainty enters the situation, or desire begins inviting compromise.

Attraction can distort perception.

When emotions become strong, it becomes easier to overlook what would otherwise appear obvious.

One common compromise is minimizing red flags.

The excitement of a new connection can make early warning signs appear insignificant. Strong chemistry may create the illusion that potential outweighs concern. The Proven Man does not dismiss these signals simply because the experience feels compelling.

Another compromise appears through rationalization.

Emotional investment can create explanations for behavior that contradicts his standards. It becomes tempting to justify inconsistency, excuse lack of effort, or assume improvement will arrive with time.

The Proven Man does not negotiate his standards through hope or potential.

He evaluates behavior for what it repeatedly demonstrates.

Standards are also tested when a man remains longer than he should.

Fear of losing the connection can make it difficult to step away. The desire to preserve the experience may encourage continued investment even when alignment is no longer present.

The Proven Man recognizes when a situation no longer supports his direction.

He does not allow emotional attachment to extend what has already revealed itself.

When emotion rises, his standards act as a counterbalance.

They create stability when perception begins shifting.

Instead of reacting to the emotional intensity of the moment, he returns to the structure he has already defined. From that position, clarity returns and the situation can be evaluated without distortion.

The Proven Man does not allow temporary emotion to determine permanent decisions.

He maintains his standards not out of stubbornness, but out of self-respect.

Discipline ensures that what he builds remains aligned with his values, even when emotional currents attempt to pull him away from them.

XIII. The Power of Walking Away

For the Proven Man, walking away is not defeat.

It is discipline expressed through action.

It is not an impulsive reaction to frustration or emotion, but a deliberate decision made from clarity. He does not allow fear of loss or the weight of attachment to dictate his behavior.

When alignment is no longer present, he steps away with purpose, knowing that his standards remain the compass guiding his direction.

This decision reveals something important: he values his direction.

The Proven Man knows where he is going. His life has a trajectory, and he does not compromise that path for a temporary connection. Misaligned relationships, no matter how appealing in the moment, have the power to pull a man away from the direction he intends to build.

It reflects respect for his own boundaries.

The Proven Man does not depend on external validation to maintain a connection that contradicts his standards. By honoring his boundaries, he protects his peace and reinforces the level of integrity he expects within his life.

It demonstrates independence from any single outcome.

The Proven Man does not attach his identity or future to any single outcome. His sense of stability does not depend on maintaining a connection at any cost. Because of this, he is capable of releasing what does not truly align and trusting that what belongs in his life will remain.

This does not mean he walks away from difficulty. When alignment has been proven and a partnership has been chosen, he invests fully. Commitment is not conditional on comfort.

Stepping away is reserved for something different: when misalignment becomes clear and the foundation that sustains the relationship is no longer present.

This decision is not about loss.

It is the ability to choose what aligns with his values rather than settling for what does not.

It is about self-control, self-preservation, and dedication to the standards and direction he has chosen.

The Proven Man understands that the willingness to walk away is one of the clearest demonstrations of strength. It takes clarity and discipline to release something that feels good in the moment but does not support the life he is building.

By doing so, he protects his future, preserves his peace, and ensures that his energy remains available for what truly deserves it.

Once defined, the standard is applied, not revisited.

XIV. Standards Shape Outcomes

The Proven Man understands that standards do more than guide behavior. They shape outcomes.

The level of standards he maintains influences the people he attracts, the dynamics he allows, and the direction his relationships ultimately take.

His standards become the structure upon which his life is built.

The quality of the connections he attracts reflects the standards he maintains.

The Proven Man does not pursue surface-level attraction or temporary excitement. He values depth, consistency, and mutual respect. Because of this, the people who remain in his life naturally reflect those same qualities.

His standards act as a filter, allowing only those who align with his direction to remain close.

The behavior he tolerates also reflects his standards.

He does not accept ongoing inconsistency, disrespect, or instability. By maintaining clear standards, he establishes the level of behavior permitted within his life. Others learn quickly what is acceptable within his world and what is not.

Low standards invite unhealthy dynamics.

Strong standards create an environment where respect, effort, and accountability become normal.

Most importantly, standards determine the direction relationships ultimately take.

Low standards often lead to repeated cycles of uncertainty, compromise, and emotional volatility.

Strong standards lead to something entirely different: connections that are stable, aligned, and capable of growing over time.

These relationships move forward with clarity rather than confusion. Trust develops naturally because behavior remains consistent. Effort flows in both directions because both individuals share commitment to the same foundation.

The Proven Man understands this principle clearly.

His standards are not simply preferences.

They are the filters that determine what enters his life, and what does not.

Low standards create unstable outcomes.

Strong standards create aligned ones.

By maintaining them consistently, he ensures that the people, relationships, and experiences remaining in his life support the direction he has chosen to pursue.

XV. Raising the Standard Within

The shift begins internally. It is not about demanding more from others or attempting to control the people around him. It begins with an honest evaluation of his behavior, his decisions, and the patterns he has allowed to remain within his life.

The Proven Man understands that change does not begin externally.

His internal standard must rise before anything around him can truly change.

The first step is honesty. He looks directly at what he has tolerated in the past. He reflects on decisions that created frustration, confusion, or disappointment.

Where did he accept behavior that contradicted his values?

Where did he compromise in ways that slowly moved him away from his own direction?

This level of honesty is necessary. Without it, patterns remain invisible. With it, clarity begins to form.

And once clarity forms, it carries responsibility.

To act on what has been seen.

Next, the Proven Man recognizes where compromise occurred. Most compromises are not made deliberately. They happen quietly in moments influenced by emotion, uncertainty, or the desire to avoid discomfort.

What feels small in the moment often becomes significant over time.

Each compromise slightly weakens the structure standards are meant to protect. By recognizing those moments clearly, he identifies where his standards were tested and where they gave way.

Finally, he decides what he will no longer allow. This decision is not driven by anger or reaction. It comes from clarity.

He defines his standards through his values, the direction of his life, and the outcomes he intends to create. Once that internal decision is made, his behavior begins to change.

The standard becomes the filter. From that point forward, every choice is measured against it.

When the internal standard rises, external choices follow naturally. Misalignment becomes easier to recognize. Compromise becomes harder to justify.

What a man tolerates becomes his structure.

What he enforces becomes his life.

And over time, that life reflects the standard he refuses to lower.

Not occasionally.

Consistently.

The Proven Man no longer feels compelled to pursue what does not meet his standard. What aligns remains. What does not, he releases.

XVI. The Internal Question

When evaluating any connection, the Proven Man returns to a set of simple internal questions. These questions restore clarity when emotion begins to interfere with judgment. They separate momentary feeling from long-term alignment and ensure that decisions remain consistent with the standards he has established.

The first question is simple:

"Would I accept this pattern over time?"

This question forces him to step back and observe the interaction as a pattern rather than a moment. Early attraction or temporary excitement can create the illusion that something meaningful is forming.

But patterns reveal whether the connection can actually sustain itself.

If the pattern he observes today would not be acceptable in the future, the answer is already clear.

The second question follows:

"Am I choosing this freely or settling because of attachment?"

Emotional attachment can distort perception. The desire to preserve the connection can quietly replace objective evaluation.

This question brings the decision back into focus. It reveals whether he is acting from clarity or reacting from fear of loss.

The final question is the most direct:

"Does this meet the standard I have set for my life?"

This question returns him to the foundation of his decisions, his values, his direction, and the structure he has chosen to maintain. No amount of emotional intensity changes that foundation.

If the connection meets the standard, it continues. If it does not, he walks away.

These questions exist to simplify the moment, not complicate it. By returning to them consistently, the Proven Man ensures that every connection he invests in supports his growth, his direction, and the life he is intentionally building.

XVII. What a Man Becomes

A man does not rise to the level of his intentions.

He rises, or falls, to the level of the standards he maintains.

It is not enough to have strong intentions or a clear vision for the future. What ultimately determines the direction of a man's life is whether his standards support that vision.

Standards shape the decisions he makes, the connections he allows, and the paths he continues choosing over time.

They become the invisible structure that determines the reality he experiences.

What a man pursues reflects his standards.

When standards are elevated, attention naturally moves toward relationships, opportunities, and experiences that align with long-term direction. Temporary attraction or surface-level appeal no longer determines his choices.

Instead, he moves toward what strengthens the structure of the life he is building.

What a man accepts also reflects his standards.

The Proven Man does not tolerate what contradicts his direction simply because it feels good in the moment. His standards create a clear separation between what aligns and what does not.

When those standards remain firm, emotional impulse and external pressure lose their influence.

The integrity of his life remains protected because he refuses to lower the standard of what he allows.

What a man continues building reveals his standards most clearly.

The relationships he maintains, the habits he reinforces, and the goals he pursues all reflect the structure he continues holding in place.

When something no longer aligns, the Proven Man does not remain attached through familiarity, comfort, or obligation.

He releases it, and redirects his time and energy toward what strengthens the foundation of his life.

Standards determine what remains.
They determine what leaves.
They shape what grows.

The Proven Man understands that the life he experiences is not accidental. It is shaped by the standards he chooses to maintain, and the discipline he applies in protecting them.

When standards are upheld consistently, something important begins to happen.

What once required discipline begins to feel natural.

The structure no longer exists only as something he practices. It begins shaping how he sees, how he evaluates, and how he decides.

At that point, the standard is no longer something he applies—

it becomes who he is.

Chapter Distillation

Most men adjust their standards to keep what they want. The Proven Man keeps his standards, and allows the right connections to rise to meet them.

He does not negotiate with what he has already defined. He does not lower the bar in moments of attraction, uncertainty, or emotional pull. His standards remain fixed, and because of that, the life he builds remains stable.

Standards determine direction.

This is where standards become identity.

When what is defined holds without exception, that is proof.
When decisions do not change under pressure, that is proof.
When behavior remains consistent regardless of emotion, that is proof.

Intentions may inspire action, but standards determine what a man accepts, what he rejects, and what he continues to build.

The Proven Man does not allow emotion or temporary attraction to lower the threshold of what belongs in his life. He defines his standards clearly and protects them through consistent discipline.

When standards are clear and applied consistently, decisions no longer shift with emotional impulse or external influence.

The Proven Man no longer chases alignment.

Through those standards, his life becomes structured, intentional, and aligned with the direction he has chosen.

Real change does not come from knowing what to do. It comes from living it.

Standards become behavior.
Alignment becomes habit.
Direction becomes the structure of how he moves through the world.

Because once these principles are lived consistently, the life he builds is no longer something imagined.

It becomes embodied—what is practiced consistently becomes who he is.

The Proven Man Principle

Intentions imagine a life.

Standards build it.

Discipline protects it.

Chapter Thirteen

Integration

When Identity Becomes Action

Integration is where the principles move from understanding into operation. What once appeared as separate ideas now functions as a unified structure. Each principle connects, forming a framework that allows you to observe, evaluate, and act with clarity.

Knowledge shifts.

What was once understood intellectually becomes embodied. What you learned begins to operate as instinct, and instinct becomes deliberate, purposeful action.

You have encountered a wide range of principles and perspectives that change how you interpret attraction, connection, relationships, and direction.

Knowledge creates potential.

Application creates change.

This is where the framework stops existing as separate ideas and begins functioning as a unified way of thinking. It becomes the lens through which you interpret interactions, decisions, and relationships.

The question is no longer what or why something works.

It becomes how you live it.

The Proven Man operates from this shift. Transformation does not come from collecting ideas. It happens when those ideas are integrated into a structure that operates naturally, without constant analysis, hesitation, or second-guessing.

The framework stops being something you reference.

When practiced consistently, these principles become a structured way of living.

It is not a theory.

It is a way of operating in the world.

It becomes part of who you are.

This is where everything connects. The principles no longer stand alone. They reinforce one another, forming a consistent approach to interaction, decision-making, relationships, and direction.

Through this integration, the Proven Man moves with clarity, steadiness, purpose, and intention.

I. From Concepts to Awareness

Archetypes, patterns, alignment, standards, detachment, time, and stoic desire are not independent ideas.

They are interconnected layers of the same structure.

Together, they create the framework through which the Proven Man observes, evaluates, and responds to what unfolds around him.

Archetypes reveal behavioral tendencies.
Patterns show how those tendencies appear over time.
Questions expose what lies beneath behavior.
Stoic desire prevents emotion from overpowering clarity.
Detachment creates distance when necessary, preserving objectivity.
Time reveals what remains consistent and what fades.
Alignment determines whether something fits the direction you are building.
Standards define what is accepted and what is released.

When these elements operate together, something important emerges.

Clarity.

The Proven Man understands the difference between clarity and certainty.

Clarity sees what is already present.
Certainty attempts to predict outcomes.

Clarity removes distortion created by emotion, assumption, or urgency and replaces it with awareness grounded in observation.

This awareness becomes a refined lens.

From this perspective, attraction, connection, and relationships are no longer interpreted through impulse alone. Emotion remains present, but it no longer dominates the decision-making process. Instead, emotion is balanced by perspective, patience, and disciplined evaluation.

This is the beginning of integration.

The framework no longer sits outside of you as knowledge.

It becomes the awareness through which you see.

II. The Shift in Perspective

Before understanding this framework, most men evaluate relationships through immediate experience.

They focus on how something feels in the moment.
They measure the strength of attraction.
They judge the connection based on the potential they imagine it could become.

These responses are emotional, and they often drive the decisions that follow.

But once the framework begins to operate internally, the evaluation changes.

Attention shifts toward deeper signals such as patterns, consistency over time, alignment between values and actions, and standards maintained under pressure.

The Proven Man understands that meaningful evaluation does not come from the intensity of a single moment.

It comes from observing what remains stable over time.

This shift does not eliminate emotion.

It refines awareness.

Emotion becomes something he experiences rather than something that dictates his decisions. Instead of reacting to the highs and lows of attraction, he observes the signals beneath them: consistency, alignment, and mutual respect.

From this perspective, emotional reactions become information—not instruction.

They are signals to observe, not impulses to follow.

This shift allows the Proven Man to build connections grounded in stability rather than intensity—connections shaped by what proves itself through time rather than what feels compelling in a single moment.

III. How It Works in Practice

In real situations, the Proven Man is not consciously running through a checklist of principles.

The framework operates internally.

It becomes a lens through which he observes and evaluates what unfolds.

He notices inconsistency without needing to rationalize it away. He recognizes misalignment without attempting to force a connection that does not fit. He senses when something is grounded and aligned versus when it is unstable and uncertain. He observes first and invests later, allowing patterns to reveal themselves before committing energy or emotion.

Over time, this awareness becomes natural.

It no longer requires deliberate effort or constant analysis. The framework integrates into instinct, allowing him to respond with clarity rather than hesitation.

The Proven Man no longer feels the need to dissect every detail of an interaction.

He knows what to observe.

He trusts what patterns reveal.

Because of this, his decisions become more fluid and confident. They are guided by awareness rather than impulse, by clarity rather than uncertainty.

And through that clarity, he moves with steadiness, direction, and control.

IV. When Awareness Becomes Natural

When the framework is fully integrated, your approach becomes more direct and natural. The complexity of decision-making begins to fade because clarity and instinct start working together.

The Proven Man no longer has to force the process.

What once required conscious effort now begins to operate as part of how he sees, thinks, and responds.

He stays present in the moment without losing sight of the bigger picture. He engages in relationships and situations without overinvesting emotionally or energetically.

Instead, he observes what is happening without projecting his desires or assumptions onto it.

He feels deeply, but he does not attach prematurely to outcomes or ideas.

He chooses based on patterns, with what has been shown over time, not on fleeting moments driven by intensity or emotion.

It is a deeper form of engagement.

The Proven Man is not distant or aloof. Instead, he remains fully involved and operates with awareness. He brings the discipline to step back when necessary, reassess clearly, and act with purpose instead of reaction.

True engagement comes from awareness—not impulse.

Through that awareness, he shapes his outcomes instead of being shaped by them.

V. What Changes Over Time

As you apply these principles consistently, the changes begin quietly.

At first they may seem small.
Over time, they compound.

Be patient.

Each principle you integrate does not just influence what you do in a single moment. It begins to reshape how you move through relationships, decisions, and life itself.

Your decisions become more deliberate.

You no longer act from impulse or temporary emotion. Instead, your choices begin to reflect clarity, thoughtfulness, and alignment with your long-term direction. The pull of fleeting desires and external pressure starts to weaken, and what remains becomes easier to see.

Your relationships become more stable, or they fall away more quickly.

You no longer spend unnecessary time inside uncertain dynamics or with people who do not truly align. Connections either strengthen into something real or naturally fall away.

What does not fit is no longer pursued. Investment shifts toward what aligns. Your energy begins moving toward The Partner instead of toward temporary attachment.

The Proven Man understands that energy is finite. Instead of scattering it in multiple directions, he directs it toward what supports his values, his goals, and the life he is building.

That focus creates more peace, more fulfillment, and far less exhaustion.

The same dynamics are no longer revisited.

Where you once may have overinvested, ignored early warning signs, or stayed longer than necessary, you now recognize the pattern sooner. You notice when something is off, and instead of forcing it or rationalizing it, you move on.

That creates space for something real.

Over time, these changes become instinctive.

Patterns are recognized earlier, often before they fully establish. The more consistently you apply the framework, your awareness becomes sharper.

What once required effort begins to feel automatic.

The Proven Man does not waste time trying to understand everything after the fact.

He notices the early indicators of alignment or misalignment and responds accordingly. He moves with purpose rather than uncertainty. He chooses with conviction rather than hesitation.

By seeing patterns sooner, he not only protects his time and energy, but keeps his path aligned with who he is.

Through consistency and clarity, he becomes more stable in his decisions and stronger in the outcomes they create.

VI. The Quiet Advantage

This framework does not make you louder, more dominant, or more expressive by default.

It does not push you to become someone else.

What it does is sharpen the qualities you already possess in a way that naturally commands respect.

The Proven Man does not need to prove himself in every room.

He does not need to raise his voice to be heard.

And he does not compete for attention.

His presence carries weight because it is grounded in clarity, direction, and self-control.

Instead of changing who he is, the framework refines how he moves.

It makes him clear.

The Proven Man no longer second-guesses himself or his choices. He understands what aligns with his life and what does not. That clarity allows him to move with confidence because his decisions are rooted in direction rather than impulse.

It makes him observant.

His awareness sharpens. He begins to notice the details others overlook such as the small inconsistencies in behavior, shifts in tone or energy, and repeating patterns that reveal what is actually happening beneath the surface.

It makes him grounded.

No moment pulls him off center. His identity is not tied to a single interaction, relationship, or outcome. Because of this, he remains composed even when situations become intense or uncertain.

It makes him selective.

He becomes intentional about where his time, energy, and attention go. Instead of investing everywhere, he chooses carefully. His resources move toward what aligns, including The Partner, and away from what does not.

At first these qualities may appear subtle.

In a world full of noise and constant reaction, steadiness often goes unnoticed in the beginning.

But over time the difference becomes clear.

People begin to sense that something about his presence is different.

There is a quiet confidence in how he carries himself. His energy is steady, his decisions are deliberate, and his direction is clear.

He does not need to demand respect.

His consistency earns it.

And within that quiet advantage lies real influence.

He does not chase validation, force outcomes, or react to every situation.

What aligns moves toward him naturally, while what does not falls away.

VII. The Real Outcome

The goal of this framework is not to win interactions.

The goal is to avoid losing yourself within them.

The Proven Man is not focused on proving himself or dominating every situation. His priority is maintaining clarity, integrity, and alignment regardless of what unfolds around him.

When you operate from this level of awareness, the entire dynamic changes.

Interactions are no longer driven by need or by the urge to secure an outcome. Instead, they unfold with patience and clarity because you understand that forcing results only creates instability.

The Proven Man moves differently.

Misalignment is not pursued.

He recognizes when something does not fit his direction and allows it to pass rather than pursuing it out of emotion or temporary attraction.

Unstable patterns are not maintained. When inconsistency becomes visible, he does not wait for it to correct itself. Stability is built on repeated behavior, not hopeful expectation.

What is not forming naturally is not pursued forcefully. Connections develop through alignment and consistency. He allows that process to unfold rather than attempting to accelerate or manipulate it.

He does not abandon his standards for temporary attachment.

No momentary attraction, emotional high, or short-term experience is worth compromising the structure that protects his life.

Instead, he participates with clarity.

The Proven Man remains grounded in his awareness. He observes what unfolds, evaluates it through the framework he has developed, and chooses accordingly.

Because of that, his energy moves only where it truly belongs.

He does not chase outcomes.

He creates them by consistently investing in what aligns with the life he is building, including The Partner who strengthens that direction.

VIII. Living the Framework

As you move forward, everything you have learned begins to operate together as a refined way of living. What once existed as individual concepts—awareness, detachment, time, alignment, and standards—now functions as a unified internal structure guiding your decisions.

The Proven Man is no longer simply someone who understands relationships.

He is someone who embodies clarity, awareness, direction, and purpose in how he lives.

He does not need to force outcomes or control every situation. He has learned to recognize what is unfolding in front of him, allowing patterns, consistency, and alignment to reveal the truth over time.

Because of this, each decision becomes deliberate rather than reactive.

Every moment becomes an opportunity to remain aligned with his standards, his direction, and the life he is building alongside The Partner.

This is not about reacting to the world around you.

It is about shaping the world you move through by the decisions you make within it.

The Proven Man understands that the choices he makes today will compound over time. What he accepts, what he invests in, and what he walks away from all contribute to the life that gradually takes form.

And over time, that life becomes something larger than the moment itself.

Because when clarity becomes instinct and discipline becomes natural, something deeper begins to emerge.

Direction becomes legacy.

What you build through your standards, your decisions, your relationships, and the partner you choose does not exist only in the present. It extends forward, shaping the life you create and the impact you leave behind.

The framework you have integrated is no longer something you apply.

It is something you live.

From this point forward, every choice becomes part of what that life becomes.

Chapter Distillation

Integration is the point where understanding becomes identity.

The Proven Man no longer relies on isolated ideas or occasional insights. The principles he has learned now operate together as a unified structure guiding how he observes, evaluates, and responds to the world around him.

The framework stops operating as separate ideas and begins functioning as a unified way of thinking.

He observes clearly, maintains his standards, and chooses alignment consistently.

Clarity becomes instinct.
Standards become habit.
Alignment becomes direction.

This is where integration becomes identity.

When clarity no longer requires effort, that is proof.
When decisions reflect who he is rather than what he feels, that is proof.
When his standards are lived without hesitation, that is proof.

Because of this, his decisions no longer depend on emotion, pressure, or circumstance. They arise from a stable internal framework that remains consistent regardless of what unfolds externally.

He does not move through life reacting to every moment.

He moves through life shaping it.

What began as knowledge becomes practice.
What began as awareness becomes discipline.
And what began as a framework becomes a way of living.

This is the point where the Proven Man stops trying to apply the principles.

He begins to embody them.

The Proven Man Principle

Knowledge creates awareness.

Discipline creates structure.

Consistency turns structure into identity.

Chapter Fourteen

Legacy

The Life Built Through Repeated Decisions

When identity is established, it begins to shape everything that follows.

That is where legacy begins.

Legacy is the continuation of the direction you have been building.

It is where everything you have integrated—awareness, standards, alignment, and discipline—begins to shape something larger than the individual decisions.

Every choice you make contributes to the direction of your life.

Some appear small in the moment. Others carry immediate weight.

But none exist in isolation. Over time, they accumulate.

Integration is where principles become habits.

Legacy is where those habits define the life that follows.

The Proven Man understands that the future is not shaped by a single defining moment, but through repeated decisions that reinforce the direction he has chosen.

What he tolerates, what he invests in, and what he walks away from all contribute to the life that gradually forms around him.

He does not treat decisions lightly.

What he chooses today becomes part of what he will live with tomorrow.

Legacy is not created through intensity. It is created through consistency.

The life a man builds, including the people he chooses to build it with, is the result of aligned decisions repeated over time.

Each action reinforces the next.
Each standard maintained strengthens the path ahead.

And through that steady accumulation, the direction of his life becomes unmistakable.

The Proven Man understands that his time, his energy, and his attention are not neutral.

They are always shaping something.

And over time, what he builds becomes the life he lives.

I. The Accumulation of Choices

Most men operate within isolated moments. Attention remains fixed on individual moments rather than the pattern they create.

The Proven Man sees it differently.

Life is not defined by single moments.

It is shaped by the accumulation of decisions made consistently over time.

What you tolerate repeatedly.
Who you invest in consistently.
Who you choose to walk away from.
What patterns you allow to continue.

These choices compound.

Small decisions made daily, when repeated over months and years, form the foundation of the life you ultimately live.

A man's life rarely shifts because of one dramatic decision.

It shifts because of what he consistently allows.

The Proven Man understands that every choice either reinforces his direction or slowly moves him away from it.

He pays attention to the patterns his decisions create.

Each action becomes part of a larger structure.

Each decision adds another layer to the life he is building.

Over time, those layers form the reality he lives within.

The Proven Man asks himself:

"Are my daily decisions reinforcing the life I want to build or quietly moving me away from it?"

II. The Direction of Your Life

The Proven Man understands that relationships are not simply emotional experiences. They are forces that influence the direction of his life, often in ways that are not immediately visible.

The people he chooses to bring into his life affect far more than how he feels in a given moment.

They shape how he thinks.
They shape how he spends his time.
They shape how clearly he moves toward his goals.

They influence several critical aspects of his life.

Those same forces shape yours.

Focus.

The people around you either reinforce your direction or quietly pull you away from it. The Proven Man protects his attention because focus is one of his most valuable resources. He invests attention where it supports his purpose rather than allowing it to drift toward what does not serve his direction.

Energy.

Every connection either adds energy to your life or slowly drains it. The Proven Man recognizes that energy is finite. He directs energy toward relationships, especially with The Partner, that support growth and stability rather than those that require constant repair or emotional turbulence.

Mental clarity.

The quality of the people around you influences how clearly you think. The Proven Man surrounds himself with individuals who reinforce his principles, challenge him to think honestly, and support his ability to remain grounded. He avoids relationships that introduce confusion or self-doubt.

Stability.

Stability becomes the foundation for everything else in his life. The Proven Man chooses relationships built on consistency, trust, and mutual respect. When stability is present, his decisions remain clear and his direction remains steady. When instability enters his life repeatedly, it disrupts everything else.

Long-term direction.

Most importantly, the people you choose either support your trajectory or gradually redirect it. The Proven Man recognizes that the connections he maintains today influence where his life moves tomorrow.

Each relationship either reinforces his path or slowly redirects it.

He chooses carefully.

He does not allow attraction, social pressure, or momentary emotion to determine who remains in his life.

He evaluates whether connections strengthen or quietly weaken his direction.

The Proven Man builds his life around principles that protect his trajectory. The people he allows close to him, especially The Partner, are chosen with intention.

Over time, those connections become part of the structure that shapes his life.

III. Short-Term Feelings vs Long-Term Outcomes

The Proven Man understands the difference between what feels powerful in the moment and what proves sustainable over time.

Short-term feelings are immediate.
Long-term outcomes are cumulative.

These two forces are often misinterpreted in relationships.

A connection can feel compelling in the moment while quietly creating instability over time.

In the early stages, attraction and novelty create excitement. Conversation flows easily, the energy feels strong, and the interaction carries intensity. It is easy to assume that something meaningful is forming.

But intensity alone does not create stability.

The Proven Man does not confuse strong feelings with long-term alignment. A moment that feels powerful today may not support the direction he is building tomorrow.

Because of this, he values depth over excitement. He understands that The Partner is revealed through consistency, not intensity.

He is willing to walk away from something that feels good in the moment if it does not show the consistency required to last.

At the same time, some of the strongest connections do not feel effortless at the beginning.

They may require patience. They may involve moments of uncertainty or friction early on. But when shared values, mutual respect, and aligned direction exist beneath the surface, those early challenges can strengthen the connection rather than weaken it.

The Proven Man sees this clearly.

He does not evaluate relationships based on intensity alone. Instead, he looks for what reveals itself through repetition.

Patterns over intensity.

Short bursts of emotion can create the illusion of alignment. Patterns reveal what is actually real. The Proven Man looks for behavior that repeats consistently rather than moments that feel unusually strong.

Consistency over novelty.

Novelty excites the mind, but consistency builds the foundation that lasts. Sustainable connections are not built on constant stimulation, they are built on reliability, stability, and shared direction.

He evaluates connections through a long-term lens.

He considers how something will function over time rather than how it feels in a single moment. He recognizes that decisions made for temporary comfort often create long-term consequences.

The Proven Man does not sacrifice his future for the intensity of the present.

He builds his life through decisions that compound in his favor, choosing relationships that strengthen his direction rather than distract from it.

IV. The Cost of Misalignment

For the Proven Man, alignment is not optional.

It is the structure that protects the life he is building.

Misalignment rarely appears as a dramatic event. More often, it develops quietly through decisions made without awareness—choices based on impulse, emotion, or temporary comfort rather than long-term direction.

At first, the consequences are subtle.

But over time, the cost becomes visible.

Misalignment creates predictable outcomes.

Repeated cycles of instability.

Small decisions made without alignment rarely remain isolated. When decisions are made from fleeting emotion rather than alignment, stability becomes impossible. Something may feel right in the moment, only to feel uncertain shortly afterward. These repeated swings create patterns of instability. The Proven Man understands that lasting structure cannot be built on inconsistent choices.

Emotional fatigue.

Instability eventually drains more than time. It drains energy. Constant emotional reaction is draining. When decisions are guided by impulse rather than clarity, a man becomes pulled in multiple directions at once. Over time this creates exhaustion. The Proven Man steps back from emotional immediacy and evaluates what is actually unfolding before committing his energy.

Loss of clarity.

When exhaustion builds, perspective begins to suffer. Misalignment clouds perspective. When standards are not reinforced, it becomes harder to see what truly fits and what does not. The Proven Man protects his clarity by remaining anchored in the principles that guide his decisions.

Drift away from direction.

When clarity weakens, direction slowly begins to erode. Most men do not lose their direction through one major mistake. They lose it through many small decisions that gradually alter their path. A compromise here or a tolerance there—each one moves the trajectory slightly. Over time, that small drift becomes significant.

The real cost of misalignment is rarely a single decision.

It is the accumulation of many small decisions made without awareness.

Misalignment does not announce itself loudly.

It whispers.

And repeated whispers eventually shape a man's life if he ignores them.

The Proven Man listens early.

He recognizes the subtle signals that something is slightly off and corrects his course before those signals grow into patterns.

By maintaining clarity, reinforcing his standards, and remaining connected to his direction, he prevents misalignment from quietly reshaping the life he intends to build with The Partner.

V. The Value of Alignment

Where misalignment drains energy, alignment restores it.

For the Proven Man, alignment becomes the foundation that allows his life to move forward with clarity and purpose.

It ensures that his decisions, his relationships, and his direction all support the same trajectory.

When alignment is present, several things begin to change.

Energy is preserved.

Misalignment constantly pulls energy away from what matters. Alignment does the opposite. When decisions reflect a man's standards and direction, his energy remains focused rather than scattered.

Direction becomes clear.

Life will always present distractions, opportunities, and pressures. Alignment functions as a compass that keeps the Proven Man oriented toward what truly matters. Decisions become simpler because they are measured against a clear direction.

Relationships reinforce direction.

Aligned relationships, especially with The Partner, strengthen the life he is building. Instead of creating friction or distraction, they reinforce growth and shared progress. Misaligned connections demand constant adjustment. Aligned ones support movement forward.

Internal conflict fades.

When a man's choices, values, and actions align, internal tension disappears. There is less second-guessing and fewer moments of regret. Decisions feel grounded because they reflect the life he intends to build.

Alignment simplifies more than individual decisions.

It simplifies life itself.

When choices consistently reinforce the same direction, unnecessary complexity disappears. A man no longer wastes energy navigating contradictions or maintaining what does not truly fit.

The Proven Man does not attempt to force alignment.

He recognizes it.

And when it is absent, he moves on by choosing only what naturally supports the life he is building.

VI. You Become the Common Factor

When you examine the relationships and dynamics in your life, one truth becomes unavoidable.

You are the common factor.

Every interaction, connection, and relationship reflects the standards you hold, the awareness you maintain, and the decisions you make. This is not blame.

It is about ownership.

The Proven Man understands this clearly.

He does not see himself as a victim of circumstances or the behavior of others. Instead, he recognizes that the patterns in his life are shaped by what he tolerates, what he chooses, and what he allows to continue.

His standards, awareness, and decisions determine the dynamics he experiences.

Standards shape who you attract.

What you allow into your life sets the tone for the relationships that follow. Low standards invite inconsistency, instability, and low effort. Higher standards attract individuals, especially The Partner, who respect clarity, discipline, and mutual alignment. The Proven Man does not lower his standards to maintain a connection. He raises them to ensure the right connections remain.

Awareness determines your responses.

Awareness allows him to see beyond the surface of an interaction. Instead of reacting impulsively or attempting to fix what is misaligned, he observes what patterns reveal. This awareness gives him the ability to respond deliberately rather than emotionally.

Decisions create the patterns you experience.

Every decision contributes to the structure of your life. What you invest in repeatedly becomes the pattern you live within.

The Proven Man understands that patterns are never accidental. They are the result of repeated choices.

Because of this, he accepts responsibility for the direction of his life.

He does not wait for others to change. He does not rely on circumstances to improve on their own. He adjusts his standards, his awareness, and his decisions.

And by doing so, he reshapes the patterns that unfold around him.

The Proven Man understands that the life he experiences is not random.

It is built through what he consistently allows.

VII. The Long-Term View

In a world driven by instant gratification, the Proven Man sees life through a different lens.

He does not measure the value of a connection by how it feels in the moment, but by where it leads over time.

Short-term emotions can be powerful.

But long-term outcomes are shaped through patience, discipline, and consistency.

Because of this, his perspective shifts.

Not just: "How does this feel today?"

Immediate feelings can be persuasive. Attraction, excitement, and chemistry often create the impression that something meaningful is forming. But the Proven Man looks further ahead. He asks where the connection is leading and whether it aligns with the direction he is building.

Patience becomes a strength.

Instead of rushing decisions, he allows time to reveal patterns. Genuine alignment is not proven in moments of intensity. It becomes visible through consistency over time.

Discipline replaces impulsive choice.

The long-term view requires the ability to delay gratification. The Proven Man understands that the easiest decision in the moment is not always the one that supports his future. Discipline allows him to choose what will serve him later rather than what simply feels good now.

The right decisions are not always comfortable.

Maintaining standards and protecting direction often requires difficult choices.

Walking away from misalignment, resisting emotional urgency, and choosing patience over immediacy demand courage.

The Proven Man accepts this.

While others chase immediate satisfaction, he focuses on building something that will hold over time. That includes choosing The Partner with the same patience, discipline, and clarity that shape every other lasting part of his life.

Because the life he ultimately lives is determined not by the intensity of the present moment, but by the decisions that consistently support his future direction.

VIII. The Identity That Emerges

A man who applies these principles consistently becomes:

More selective with his time.
More aware of patterns.
Grounded in his decisions.
Steady through emotional fluctuations.
Intentional with who he allows into his life.

His choices reflect clarity, not urgency.

Over time, this presence creates stability throughout life. At the highest level, the question is not about the other person. It is about the life you are building, the standards that protect it, and the people you choose to share it with.

The principles in this book form the foundation. The daily practice of them becomes a way of living.

In every relationship, in every decision, the real question you must ask yourself is:

"Does this connection support the life I am trying to build?"

If the answer is unclear, time will reveal it.
If the answer is clear, your actions should reflect it.

Your life is not shaped by a single decision, but by repeated patterns of decisions made over time.

Choose with awareness.
Act with consistency.
Maintain your standards.

Because in the end, legacy is not built in moments of intensity.

It is built in moments of alignment, repeated again and again, until they become the life you are living.

Legacy is the result of your choices—how you lead, how you respond, who you allow close to you, and what you refuse to compromise.

This is your legacy.

This is how a life becomes intentional, built not by chance but by design.

In this final stage, you are no longer simply applying a framework; you are living the principles you have learned.

As you move forward, every decision becomes an opportunity to build something lasting, including the life you share with the partner you choose intentionally.

The standards you uphold.
The clarity you maintain.
The awareness you bring to every choice you make.

Your life becomes the story written by your decisions. One choice at a time. Make each one count.

Let your choices create the life you intend to live.

Chapter Distillation

Legacy is not created in a single defining moment.

It is built through repeated decisions.

By this stage, the Proven Man no longer sees relationships, decisions, and direction as separate parts of life. He understands that they are connected forces shaping the same outcome.

Every interaction reveals something.
Every pattern teaches something.
Each decision reinforces what follows.

Over time, these small choices accumulate into something larger than the moments themselves.

They become the structure of a life.

This is where proof becomes legacy.

When direction remains consistent over time, that is proof.
When what is built continues to reflect his standards, that is proof.
When his life becomes the result of aligned decisions, that is proof.

Because of this, his behavior is no longer driven by impulse.

He does not chase intensity.
He does not rely on chance.
He does not drift.

Instead, his actions become deliberate.

He observes.
He evaluates.
He chooses.

Through that discipline, his decisions become the structure of the life he builds alongside a partner he chooses intentionally.

What he builds lasts beyond the moment; it becomes the life he lives.

Not chaotic.
Not accidental.
Intentional.

Because legacy is never created in a single defining moment.

It is built quietly—decision by decision, standard by standard, alignment by alignment—until the direction of a man's life becomes undeniable.

The Proven Man Principle

Clarity guides decisions.

Standards shape direction.

Consistency builds legacy.

Conclusion

Becoming The Proven Man

Becoming the Proven Man is not a destination.
It is a way of living.

Every decision, every relationship, and every boundary you enforce shapes the man you become.

The process does not end. It refines itself through repetition, with awareness applied consistently over time.

The Proven Man is not defined by what he knows.
He is defined by how he lives what he knows.

He sees patterns where others see confusion.
He evaluates behavior where others follow emotion.
He enforces standards where others negotiate them.

Clarity becomes his default position.

Alignment becomes his filter.

Through those disciplines, his life stabilizes around the decisions he consistently makes.

This is integration.

Not the understanding of principles, but the embodiment of them.

Awareness becomes instinct.
Standards become non-negotiable.
Decisions become deliberate.

Over time, the framework disappears as a concept and becomes identity.

The Proven Man does not expect perfection from himself.

He expects consistency.

He will face setbacks.
He will make mistakes.

But he does not drift from his standards or abandon his direction.

Each decision is evaluated, corrected if necessary, and reinforced moving forward.

Because he understands something most men overlook.

Life compounds.
Patterns compound.
Decisions compound.

The life a man lives becomes the sum of those repetitions.

Over time, that life becomes the proof.

The principles you have learned are not meant to be admired.

They are meant to be lived.

It gives you the lens to see clearly, the structure to evaluate honestly, and the discipline to act in alignment with the life you intend to build.

From this point forward, every decision becomes part of that foundation.

Every relationship you allow.
Every pattern you tolerate.
Every boundary you enforce.

Each one shapes the direction of your life.

The Proven Man does not force outcomes.

He recognizes them.

Through awareness, discipline, and alignment, he builds a life that reflects the standards he refuses to compromise.

And over time, those standards become legacy.

Not through intensity.

Through consistency.

Because the life a man builds should create more than stability.

It should create the capacity for trust, peace, meaningful connection, and the freedom to fully engage life without losing himself within it.

In doing so, he builds a legacy worthy of the life he chose to live.

The Proven Man is not a man who has arrived.

He is a man in motion.

Observing.
Refining.
Choosing.
Again and again.
Without deviation.

Become The Proven Man.

The Proven Man's Field Guide

Behavioral Patterns in Real Time

This section is not meant to be read once.
It is meant to be used.

The patterns outlined here are not theoretical.

They are observed behaviors that reveal themselves through repetition, not isolated moments.

The Proven Man does not rely on memory or assumption.

He returns to what is consistent, what is repeated, and what becomes predictable over time.

Use this guide to recognize patterns as they emerge, evaluate them clearly, and understand where they lead before time makes the outcome obvious.

Clarity is not created by intensity.
It is created by observation.

The purpose of these principles is not withdrawal from life, but the ability to engage it with clarity, stability, and intention.

A Proven Man builds a life capable of trust, depth, peace, meaningful connection, and legacy without sacrificing himself in the process.

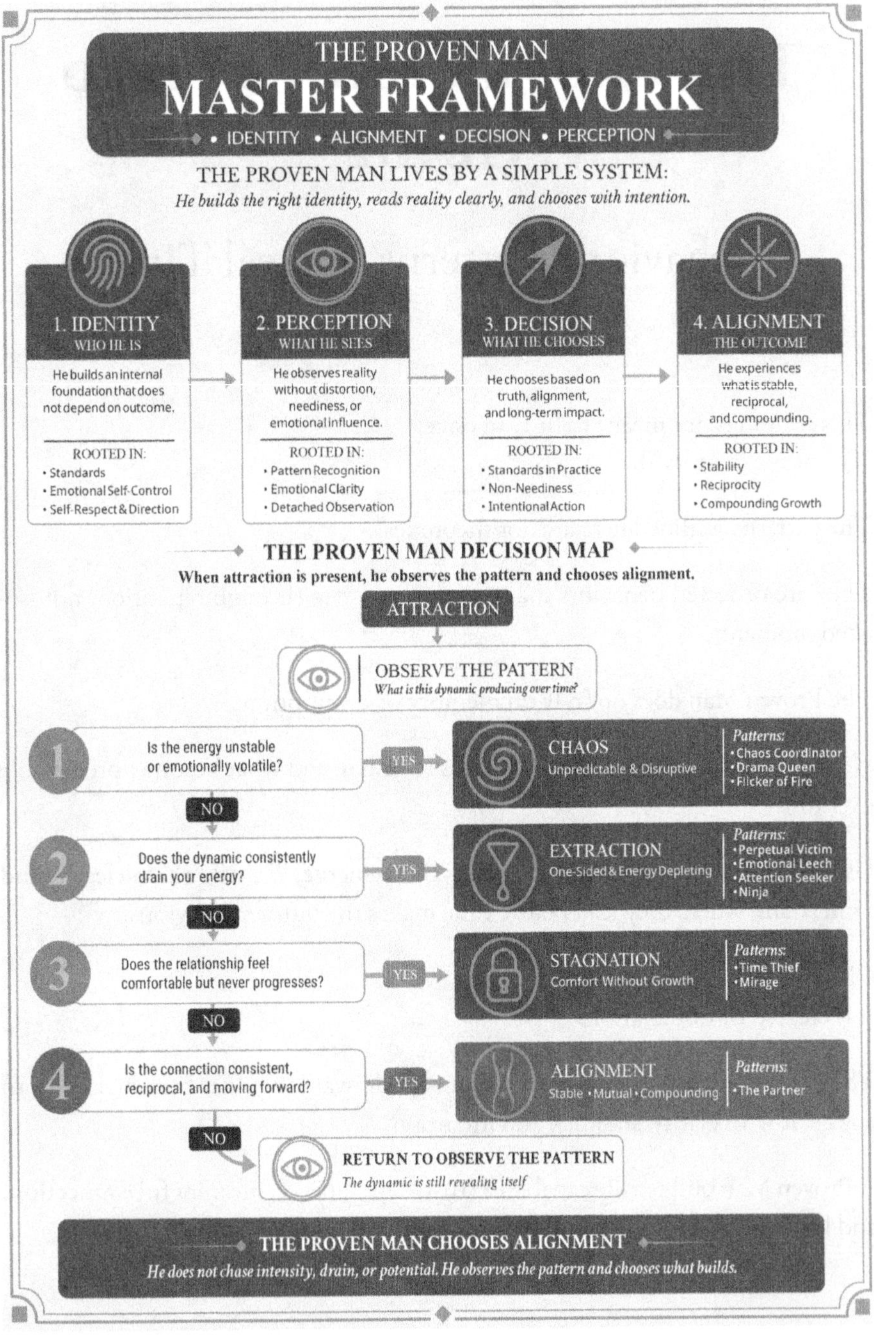
THE PROVEN MAN
MASTER FRAMEWORK
• IDENTITY • ALIGNMENT • DECISION • PERCEPTION
THE PROVEN MAN LIVES BY A SIMPLE SYSTEM:
He builds the right identity, reads reality clearly, and chooses with intention.
1. IDENTITY
WHO HE IS
He builds an internal foundation that does not depend on outcome.
ROOTED IN:
• Standards
• Emotional Self-Control
• Self-Respect & Direction
2. PERCEPTION
WHAT HE SEES
He observes reality without distortion, neediness, or emotional influence.
ROOTED IN:
• Pattern Recognition
• Emotional Clarity
• Detached Observation
3. DECISION
WHAT HE CHOOSES
He chooses based on truth, alignment, and long-term impact.
ROOTED IN:
• Standards in Practice
• Non-Neediness
• Intentional Action
4. ALIGNMENT
THE OUTCOME
He experiences what is stable, reciprocal, and compounding.
ROOTED IN:
• Stability
• Reciprocity
• Compounding Growth
THE PROVEN MAN DECISION MAP
When attraction is present, he observes the pattern and chooses alignment.
ATTRACTION
OBSERVE THE PATTERN
What is this dynamic producing over time?
1
Is the energy unstable or emotionally volatile?
YES
CHAOS
Unpredictable & Disruptive
Patterns:
• Chaos Coordinator
• Drama Queen
• Flicker of Fire
NO
2
Does the dynamic consistently drain your energy?
YES
EXTRACTION
One-Sided & Energy Depleting
Patterns:
• Perpetual Victim
• Emotional Leech
• Attention Seeker
• Ninja
NO
3
Does the relationship feel comfortable but never progresses?
YES
STAGNATION
Comfort Without Growth
Patterns:
• Time Thief
• Mirage
NO
4
Is the connection consistent, reciprocal, and moving forward?
YES
ALIGNMENT
Stable • Mutual • Compounding
Patterns:
• The Partner
NO
RETURN TO OBSERVE THE PATTERN
The dynamic is still revealing itself
THE PROVEN MAN CHOOSES ALIGNMENT
He does not chase intensity, drain, or potential. He observes the pattern and chooses what builds.

Relationship Archetypes Overview

Recognizing Archetypes Through Patterns

Patterns—not moments—reveal the direction of a relationship.

While every individual is unique, certain patterns appear repeatedly. These patterns form recognizable archetypes.

An archetype is not a rigid label or a complete description of a person. It represents a dominant pattern of behavior that influences communication, emotional investment, and responses under pressure.

Recognizing these patterns allows the Proven Man to interpret behavior with clarity. Rather than reacting to isolated moments, he observes how consistent tendencies shape direction over time.

The archetypes outlined here represent four broad behavioral patterns that commonly appear in relationships.

Each archetype reflects a recurring behavioral tendency, and not a fixed identity. The goal is not judgment, but recognition of direction over time.

The Princess
The Princess archetype is drawn to comfort, stability, and security. She often seeks reassurance and emotional support and may rely on external structure to maintain balance.

At her best, she brings warmth, connection, and a desire for stability. When imbalanced, she avoids responsibility or expects others to carry what she resists.

The Performer
The Performer archetype thrives on attention, excitement, and social energy. She is often charismatic, expressive, and highly engaging.

At her best, she creates energy, attraction, and momentum. When imbalanced, her need for validation leads to inconsistency, distraction, and emotional volatility.

The Parasite
The Parasite archetype relies heavily on the emotional or practical support of others. She often forms connections through vulnerability or shared struggle, drawing others into the role of caretaker.

At her best, she is open, expressive, and emotionally available. When imbalanced, the relationship becomes one-sided, with energy flowing primarily in her direction.

The Partner
The Partner archetype values mutual investment, emotional stability, and shared direction. She approaches relationships with independence while contributing to long-term alignment.

At her best, she creates balance, reciprocity, and forward movement. This archetype represents the dynamic most capable of sustaining alignment.

Recognizing Archetypes in Real Life

Archetypes rarely appear in isolation. Most individuals display a mixture of traits that shift depending on circumstances, maturity, and personal growth.

For this reason, the Proven Man does not label individuals rigidly. He observes patterns over time. The goal is not to categorize people, but to understand how recurring behaviors influence direction.

When patterns become clear, the dynamic becomes clear.

Pattern Recognition Map

Recognizing Relationship Patterns

Recognizing Patterns Across Interactions

Patterns—not moments—reveal the direction of a relationship.

Attraction, communication, emotional stability, and long-term alignment are not determined by single interactions. They emerge through repeated signals over time.

The Proven Man does not react to individual situations. He observes patterns as they develop. Instead of interpreting each moment emotionally, he watches how behavior unfolds across multiple interactions.

Clarity is not something he chases. It is something he recognizes.

Several core elements support that process.

Relationship Archetypes
Certain behavioral patterns appear repeatedly in relationships. These archetypes influence communication, emotional investment, and responses under pressure.

Recognizing them early allows direction to be seen before deeper investment occurs.

The Four Relationship Outcomes
Every relationship moves toward one of four outcomes.

Chaos
Instability driven by emotional volatility.

Extraction
One-sided investment where energy flows primarily in one direction.

Stagnation
Comfort without growth or forward movement.

Alignment
Mutual investment, stability, and shared direction.

Recognizing the direction of a relationship allows decisions to be made with clarity.

The Seven Core Interaction Moments

Within every interaction, certain moments reveal how a dynamic is developing. These moments provide insight into emotional stability, communication, reciprocity, and long-term alignment.

Observed over time, they form patterns that reveal the true direction of a connection.

The Proven Man Perspective

The Proven Man does not react to isolated events. He observes patterns.

He does not chase clarity. He allows behavior to reveal it.

Because of this, he recognizes alignment before others do.

The Seven Core Interaction Moments

The Moments Where Relationship Dynamics Reveal Themselves

The Seven Core Interaction Moments

Relationships rarely unfold randomly. Most interactions move through a small number of recognizable moments—points where behavior begins to reveal direction, alignment, and long-term potential.

Many people react to these moments without noticing them. They interpret individual events emotionally, responding to what feels significant rather than observing what behavior consistently produces over time.

The Proven Man approaches these moments differently. Instead of reacting impulsively, he observes how behavior unfolds across repeated interactions. Over time, these moments form patterns that clarify direction.

1. The First Signal
The moment when interest first appears. Curiosity, engagement, or attraction becomes visible.

Many interpret this moment as certainty. In reality, it marks only the beginning.

The Proven Man recognizes early signals as information, not conclusions.

2. The Uncertainty Moment
At some point, an interaction becomes less clear. Responses slow, enthusiasm shifts, or direction becomes uncertain.

This is where most begin to seek reassurance or force clarity.

The Proven Man does not pursue certainty. He allows behavior to reveal it.

3. The Tension Moment

Tension appears in every real interaction. A disagreement surfaces, a perspective differs, or discomfort emerges.

These moments expose how both individuals respond to pressure, difference, and emotional depth.

Tension does not weaken connection. It reveals character.

4. The Investment Moment

As interactions deepen, effort becomes visible. Time is invested, attention becomes focused, and emotional openness may increase.

This is where intention becomes measurable.

The Proven Man observes whether effort is naturally reciprocated.

5. The Alignment Test

Over time, deeper signals of compatibility emerge. Values, priorities, communication style, and emotional stability become clear.

Words may suggest alignment. Behavior confirms it.

The Proven Man trusts what is demonstrated, not what is promised.

6. The Instability Moment

In some interactions, attention fluctuates. Interest rises and fades, engagement appears and disappears, and consistency becomes uncertain.

This is where many begin to chase or attempt to regain control.

The Proven Man does not react to instability. He observes whether it becomes a pattern.

7. The Decision Moment

Eventually, direction becomes visible. Consistency either appears—or it does not.

Nothing new is created here. The pattern has already formed.

The Proven Man does not force resolution. He responds to what has been consistently shown.

Closing Perspective

These moments appear in nearly every relationship. They do not determine the outcome on their own. They reveal how a dynamic develops over time.

The Proven Man does not react to isolated moments. He observes the patterns that form between them.

Clarity is not created in a single moment. It is revealed through what repeats.

The Four Relationship Outcomes

The Four Directions Every Relationship Ultimately Moves Toward

The Four Relationship Outcomes

Relationships rarely remain static. Over time, the interaction between two people begins to move in a particular direction. That direction is shaped by behavior, emotional stability, communication, and the level of mutual investment within the relationship.

While every connection is unique, most relationships move toward one of four recognizable outcomes. These outcomes are not determined by isolated moments or temporary emotion. They emerge through patterns that develop across repeated interaction.

The Proven Man does not evaluate a relationship based on how it feels in a single moment. He observes what the dynamic consistently produces over time. By paying attention to these patterns, he recognizes direction before deeper investment occurs.

Chaos

Chaos is driven by emotional volatility and instability. Intensity may be high, but consistency is not. The relationship often swings between attraction and conflict, excitement and exhaustion.

Clarity is difficult to maintain because emotional reactions dominate the interaction. Over time, instability prevents the development of a stable foundation.

Extraction

Extraction occurs when investment flows primarily in one direction. One person consistently gives more time, emotional energy, or support than the other.

What may initially feel meaningful becomes draining. Without mutual contribution, the relationship revolves around sustaining one person rather than building something shared.

Stagnation

Stagnation appears when a relationship becomes comfortable but lacks growth or direction. Conflict may be minimal, yet progress is equally limited.

The connection continues through familiarity rather than shared momentum. Over time, the absence of growth erodes fulfillment.

Alignment

Alignment represents mutual investment, emotional stability, and shared direction. Both individuals contribute while maintaining independence and personal responsibility.

Communication remains open, effort is reciprocated, and the connection develops through consistent behavior rather than emotional pressure. This creates the conditions for a relationship that can grow over time.

Recognizing Relationship Direction

Most relationships do not begin clearly within one of these outcomes. They move gradually as patterns develop.

The Proven Man observes these patterns without forcing direction. He allows behavior over time to reveal what the relationship is becoming.

Clarity is not found in isolated moments. It is revealed through what consistently occurs.

THE PROVEN MAN

VARIANT DYNAMICS

PATTERNS REVEAL THEMSELVES THROUGH REPETITION.

Recognition Determines Direction.

CHAOS

HIGH INTENSITY, CONSTANT DISRUPTION.

CHAOS COORDINATOR

Creates conflict to stay in control.

- Instability becomes normal.
- Drama keeps the system moving.

OUTCOME: CHAOS

FLICKER OF FIRE

Starts strong, can't sustain sustain.

- Intensity spikes early.
- Withdrawal replaces commitment.
- The cycle repeats.

OUTCOME: CHAOS

DRAMA QUEEN

Escalates everything.

- Small issues become emotional explosions
- Attention accountability.

OUTCOME: CHAOS

EXTRACTION

ENERGY DRAINS. PROGRESS STALLS.

PERPETUAL VICTIM

Stays stuck and keeps you stuck.

- Problems are constant.
- Responsibility is avoided or redirected.

OUTCOME: EXTRACTION

EMOTIONAL LEECH

Takes without returning.

- Drains energy through one-sided connection.
- Support is expected, never reciprocated.

OUTCOME: EXTRACTION

NINJA (COVERT CONTROL)

Influences without transparency.

- Controls through silence, pilt, or ambiguity.
- You're never sure where you stand.

OUTCOME: EXTRACTION

ATTENTION SEEKER

Demands focus to feel significant.

- Validation is the primary driver.
- Behavior shifts to maintain visibility.

OUTCOME: EXTRACTION

STAGNATION

LOOKS FINE, GOES NOWHERE.

MIRAGE

Looks aligned but fails over time.

- Promises don't match behavior.
- Early potential fades under pressure.

OUTCOME: STAGNATION

TIME THIEF

Consumes time without progress.

- Conversations go in circles.
- Decisions are delayed. Momentum disappears.

OUTCOME: STAGNATION

ALIGNMENT

STABLE. RECIPROCAL. BUILT TO COMPOUND.

THE PARTNER

Alignment isn't luck. It's recognized and built.

- Energy is returned, not drained.
- Stability is created, not negotiated.
- Growth is mutual, not one-sided.
- Direction is shared, not assumed.

OUTCOME: ALIGNMENT

THE PROVEN MAN CHOOSES ALIGNMENT.

He does not chase intensity, drain, or potential.

He recognizes the pattern and chooses what builds.

Decision Map

A Framework For Making Clear Relationship Decisions

The decision map presented here provides a practical framework for evaluating relationship dynamics through the patterns they consistently produce over time.

The Proven Man does not rely on isolated moments, emotional intensity, or initial attraction when interpreting a relationship. Instead, he observes how behavior unfolds across repeated interactions. Patterns reveal whether a connection is stable, one-sided, stagnant, or aligned.

The decision map follows a straightforward process. Beginning with attraction, the Proven Man observes the dynamic and asks a series of clarifying questions about emotional stability, energy investment, and forward movement. Each step helps reveal which outcome the relationship is naturally moving toward.

When the pattern becomes clear, the direction of the relationship becomes clear as well.

The purpose of this map is not to force conclusions prematurely. If the pattern remains uncertain, the Proven Man simply continues observing. Over time, consistent behavior reveals the truth of the dynamic.

Used this way, the decision map serves as a practical reference for interpreting relationship patterns with clarity rather than reacting to individual moments.

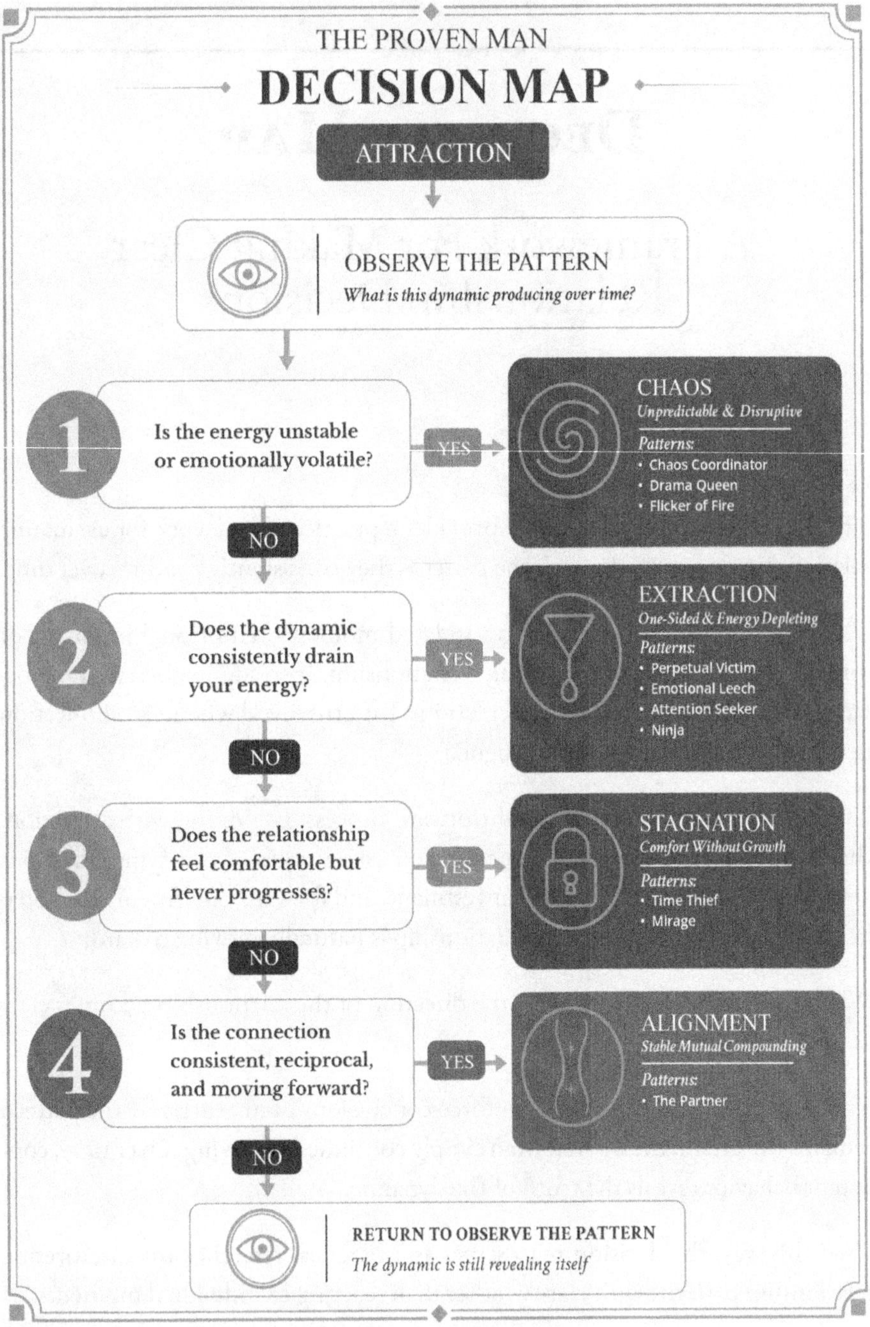
THE PROVEN MAN
DECISION MAP
ATTRACTION
OBSERVE THE PATTERN
What is this dynamic producing over time?
1
Is the energy unstable or emotionally volatile?
YES
CHAOS
Unpredictable & Disruptive
Patterns:
• Chaos Coordinator
• Drama Queen
• Flicker of Fire
NO
2
Does the dynamic consistently drain your energy?
YES
EXTRACTION
One-Sided & Energy Depleting
Patterns:
• Perpetual Victim
• Emotional Leech
• Attention Seeker
• Ninja
NO
3
Does the relationship feel comfortable but never progresses?
YES
STAGNATION
Comfort Without Growth
Patterns:
• Time Thief
• Mirage
NO
4
Is the connection consistent, reciprocal, and moving forward?
YES
ALIGNMENT
Stable Mutual Compounding
Patterns:
• The Partner
NO
RETURN TO OBSERVE THE PATTERN
The dynamic is still revealing itself

Acknowledgements

Acknowledgments

This work was developed through long periods of reflection, observation, and writing. Much of that process unfolded quietly, allowing the ideas in these pages to take shape with patience and clarity.

While the writing itself was largely independent, the experiences that shaped it were not. Every interaction, every challenge, and every lesson contributed to the understanding that became this framework.

To the reader—thank you for taking the time to explore these ideas. The principles in this book only become meaningful when they are lived. If these pages help you see more clearly, hold your standards more firmly, and choose your direction more deliberately, then the work has served its purpose.

Matthew Koeppen

ABOUT THE AUTHOR

About the Author

Matthew Koeppen is the creator of *The Proven Man*, a framework centered on clarity, standards, perception, and intentional decision-making.

The ideas in this book emerged during a period of major life transition that required deeper examination of identity, relationships, behavior, and personal direction. What began as a search for greater clarity and self-understanding eventually evolved into a structured philosophy focused on pattern recognition, alignment, discipline, and self-actualization.

Through that process, The Proven Man framework was developed as a practical system for evaluating patterns, making intentional decisions, and building a stable, purpose-driven life.

Today, his work focuses on helping men—and those becoming them—recognize patterns clearly, choose alignment over chaos, and build lives shaped by intention rather than impulse.

Made in the USA
Coppell, TX
13 June 2026

81368312R00204